Lesson Planning for Skills-Based Health Education

Meeting Secondary-Level National Standards

Sarah Benes, EdD

Holly Alperin, EdM

SHAPE America

SOCIETY OF HEALTH AND PHYSICAL EDUCATORS®

health. moves. minds.

HUMAN KINETICS

Library of Congress Cataloging-in-Publication Data

Names: Benes, Sarah, 1982- author. | Alperin, Holly, 1977- author.
Title: Lesson planning for skills-based health education / Sarah Benes, Holly
  Alperin.
Description: Champaign, IL : Human Kinetics, [2019] | Series: Shape america
  sets the standard | Includes bibliographical references.
Identifiers: LCCN 2018004318 (print) | LCCN 2017045475 (ebook) | ISBN
  9781492558057 (e-book) | ISBN 9781492558040 (print)
Subjects: LCSH: Health education--Curricula--United States. | Health
  education--Standards--United States. | Health education teachers--Training
  of--United States. | Lesson planning.
Classification: LCC LB1588.U6 (print) | LCC LB1588.U6 .B46 2019 (ebook) | DDC
  613.071--dc23
LC record available at https://lccn.loc.gov/2018004318

ISBN: 978-1-4925-5804-0 (print)

The web addresses cited in this text were current as of December 2017, unless otherwise noted.

Acquisitions Editor: Scott Wikgren; **Developmental Editor:** Jacqueline Eaton Blakley; **SHAPE America Editors:** Joe Halowich and Joe McGavin; **Managing Editors:** Derek Campbell, Anne E. Mrozek, and Anna Lan Seaman; **Copyeditor:** Janet Kiefer; **Permissions Manager:** Dalene Reeder; **Senior Graphic Designer:** Joe Buck; **Cover Designer:** Keri Evans; **Cover Design Associate:** Susan Rothermel Allen; **Photograph (cover):** © Human Kinetics; **Photographs (interior):** © Human Kinetics, unless otherwise noted; © Photodisc/Getty Images (p. 1), © Photodisc (p. 3), © gajatz - Fotolia.com (p. 21), © Christopher Futcher/Getty Images (p. 101), © PhotoCreate - Fotolia.com (p. 145), © 2001 Brand X Pictures (p. 231); **Photo Asset Manager:** Laura Fitch; **Photo Production Manager:** Jason Allen; **Senior Art Manager:** Kelly Hendren; **Illustrations:** © Human Kinetics, unless otherwise noted; **Printer:** Sheridan Books

SHAPE America – Society of Health and Physical Educators
1900 Association Drive
Reston, VA 20191
800-213-7193
www.shapeamerica.org

Printed in the United States of America   10 9 8 7 6

The paper in this book is certified under a sustainable forestry program.

Human Kinetics
1607 N. Market Street
Champaign, IL 61820
USA

United States and International
Website: **US.HumanKinetics.com**
Email: info@hkusa.com
Phone: 1-800-747-4457

Canada
Website: **Canada.HumanKinetics.com**
Email: info@hkcanada.com

E7175

Tell us what you think!
Human Kinetics would love to hear what we
can do to improve the customer experience.
Use this QR code to take our brief survey.

Contents

Preface

This book is written for health educators teaching at the secondary level who are looking for ideas to use in their classrooms as they implement a skills-based approach to health education. We know that improving the quality of health education programs can lead to increases in health literacy and improve student outcomes. Giving students opportunities to apply the National Health Education Standards skills in authentic, real-world situations helps them develop proficiency in these skills, which in turn will help improve outcomes. We must ensure that students have ample time and instruction to learn about, understand, practice, and receive feedback on each skill being assessed. This book provides a unit plan, lesson plans, activities, and assessments for each skill of the National Health Education Standards that will help health educators maximize the effectiveness of their time with students.

A key role of schools is to provide curriculum and instruction that challenges all students, provides students opportunities to meet high standards, and helps all students feel safe and supported in their journey. Teachers must create a classroom environment that is engaging, thought provoking, and relevant. This text is written to assist health educators at the secondary level in developing a course of study that addresses these areas.

Through collaboration with health educators in the field, this text provides meaningful and engaging health education tools to implement skills-based instruction in the middle or high school classroom. This book supports health teachers in their quest to increase students' health literacy through skill development and the acquisition of functional information and provides examples of classroom-tested, skills-based health education learning activities, lessons, units, and assessments that you can use with limited modification or personalize to meet the needs of your students.

The chapters contained here will assist in implementing a skills-based approach whether you are beginning the transition from a traditional, content-based health education curriculum toward a skills-based approach or you have been teaching skills for years. All educators can use this text to build a new curriculum, gain ideas, and revise existing curricula. The new health educator can take the units and plan a curriculum that addresses all the skills, a veteran educator can pick activities to supplement his or her existing curriculum, and all health educators in between can find what they need to implement a skills-based approach to health education.

Recognizing that every school, student, and educator is different, this text targets secondary-level programs and is organized by each skill of the National Health Education Standards. To ensure adequate coverage of the National Standards at both the middle school and high school grade spans, we encourage conversation within your district about when each skill is taught and which topics are most appropriate for meeting the needs of your students. A well-developed scope and sequence helps provide a framework that includes the skills within and across grade spans and avoids redundancy. This text expands on the underpinnings of developing a skills-based program discussed in *The Essentials of Teaching Health Education: Curriculum, Instruction, and Assessment*, which thoroughly explains the rationale and foundation for transitioning from a content-based health education program to a skills-based approach. It also provides examples, tools, resources, and strategies to help as you begin putting a skills-based approach into practice. You might find that the *Essentials* text provides a good starting point as you begin developing your own curriculum or can support your current teaching practice.

However, this text provides two chapters dedicated to laying the foundation for a skills-based approach so that you can use this text as a standalone or in conjunction with the *Essentials* text. This resource provides practical application for the development of student learning experiences. With a focus on how a skills-based approach looks in the classroom, this text allows you to jump right into the planning. This text will set you on the path of embracing and implementing a skills-based approach in your health education classroom.

As a reader, you will find that this text is organized in a user-friendly format with significant input from practitioners in the field. Part I, Setting the Foundation for Skills-Based Health Education, is an introduction to the key aspects of planning, implementing, and assessing in a skills-based approach. Chapter 1, Skills-Based Health Education: An Overview provides an overview of the key aspects of skills-based health education. This chapter sets the foundation for the rest of the book and gives the reader the background necessary to understand how the items included in the book support a skills-based approach. Chapter 2, Designing Your Health Curriculum, includes a discussion of backward design, skill development and assessment, and how each should be used in the skills-based classroom. Chapters 1 and 2 are intended to provide an overview of core concepts; more in-depth information can be found in *The Essentials of Teaching Health Education*.

Part II, Skills in the Classroom, is organized by each of the seven skills of the National Health Education Standards: analyzing influences; accessing valid and reliable information, products, and services; interpersonal communication; decision making; goal setting; self-management; and advocacy. Each chapter is dedicated to one skill, and each chapter has the following sections:

- Skill overview
- Skill cues
- Unit outline
- Assessment
- Lesson plans and learning activities

Each chapter begins with an overview that will frame the key aspects of the skill, including the performance indicators from the National Health Education Standards and skill cues to use as students work through the skill development model (see part I). We also point out some things to consider when teaching and assessing each standard.

Next, the unit outline presents the objectives for the unit, which are addressed in the sample assessment provided *and* form the basis of lesson plans and activities. Because we want to make this text useful for secondary teachers both at the middle school and high school levels, the unit outline of each chapter includes skill-based unit objectives for middle school and for high school. Use whichever objectives align with the grade span you are teaching. We then include additional unit objectives for grades 6 through 12. Everything included in this part of the chapter aligns with a backward-design approach: The unit objectives are presented, an assessment that measures student progress toward those objectives is presented, and then the lessons that address the objectives follow. We recognize that you might wish to modify the objectives by increasing or decreasing the complexity to meet the needs of your students. If you make any changes in the assessment or the objectives, be sure to review the entire unit for consistency. This will help to ensure proper alignment in your revised curriculum.

Following the unit objectives is a sample assessment to help you evaluate students' ability to meet the objectives and demonstrate skill proficiency. As with unit objectives, the assessments might need modifications if unit objectives have been changed, to ensure alignment.

Finally, you will find lesson plans and learning activities. Learning activities are included after each corresponding lesson. Many of these activities also include worksheets, assessments, or other resources. These resources are available in the web resource and are identified with the icon shown in the margin here. Some chapters contain bonus activities not in the unit plan. All activities support skill development or the acquisition of functional information for the purpose of applying the skill in a real-world context. Each was carefully selected to ensure that time spent on the activity would further a student's ability to demonstrate skill proficiency and meet the standards for effective health education curriculum and instruction. Even though the lessons and activities are aligned with the unit objectives provided, you have flexibility in their use. You can use the lessons as a unit, take one or two lessons and integrate into your existing units, choose activities to integrate into your curriculum, or build off the ideas presented here to create your own new activities.

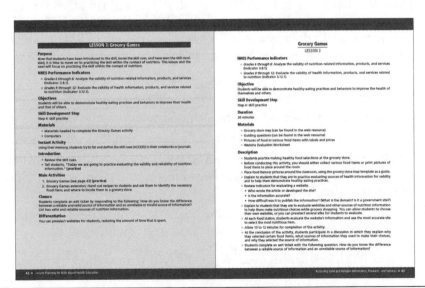

Lesson plans have a shaded background. They are followed by activities, which have a white background.

Many health educators in the field are doing amazing work in the classroom and teaching in a skills-based way. While we are not able to capture all the quality work going on, we value sharing activities from others in the field who have implemented ideas with students and then refined these ideas based on reflection and feedback. Therefore, a majority of the learning activities included in this text are submitted by current secondary-level health educators—including many SHAPE America Teacher of the Year honorees! These activities have been tried and tested in the real world and have been included with little modification.

Being able to include ideas from educators in the field was a central focus from the start of the development of this text. You will benefit from the expertise and experience of colleagues in the field.

Another benefit of this text is that everything is adaptable. Because no two schools (or classrooms) are alike, you might find that one style of lesson will work in your school but another needs to be adjusted. Perhaps you like the lesson design, but the topic isn't one that you plan on using or is not supported by your local data. Topics are interchangeable, and we encourage you to select the topics that align with your student-need data and are most relevant to your students. You can use as much (or as little) from the lessons as you need to make your curriculum work. Perhaps you don't think one of the activities we included will work but you have an idea for one that will. Use it! Or maybe you have some activities that you know will work because you have used them with success multiple times. Find ways to include them within this framework or modify them in a way that will help students become proficient in the skill.

eBook
available at
HumanKinetics.com

We put much thought into how to provide the most useful resource for educators. This is why the learning activities can be easily added into an existing lesson, lesson plans could be added to an existing unit, assessments can be added to existing units, and a completely laid-out unit plan shows how it all can come together in a unit that is ready to go into your skills-based curriculum. We also created this text to serve as a reference for you and your teaching colleagues to spark ideas, refresh your memory, start discussions, and, in general, support the vital work you are doing in the field. We hope that you will find this format useful, whether you are hoping to find units to use with little modification or looking to spark new ideas and address areas for revision in your existing curriculum.

Some of the features of this book are as follows:

- The activities and ideas presented in this text can be used in a variety of ways to meet the needs of a wide range of educators.

- A majority of activities are from health educators in the field.

- The book includes units, assessments, lessons, and learning activities.

- The book is organized by skill, and activities are aligned with the skill development model and address National Health Education Standards performance indicators.

- All learning activities, lessons, and units further skill development and use health topics as the context for developing and applying skills.

- The web resource includes modifiable documents to support lessons and learning activities, all in an effort to make implementation easier for you.

About SHAPE America

SHAPE America – Society of Health and Physical Educators is committed to ensuring that all children have the opportunity to lead healthy, physically active lives. As the nation's largest membership organization of health and physical education professionals, SHAPE America works with its 50 state affiliates and is a founding partner of national initiatives including the Presidential Youth Fitness Program, Active Schools and the Jump Rope For Heart and Hoops For Heart programs.

Since its founding in 1885, the organization has defined excellence in physical education, most recently creating *National Standards & Grade-Level Outcomes for K-12 Physical Education* (2014), National Standards for Initial Physical Education Teacher Education (2016), National Standards for Health Education Teacher Education (2017) and *National Standards for Sport Coaches* (2006). Also, SHAPE America participated as a member of the Joint Committee on National Health Education Standards, which published *National Health Education Standards, Second Edition: Achieving Excellence* (2007). Our programs, products and services provide the leadership, professional development and advocacy that support health and physical educators at every level, from preschool through university graduate programs.

The SHAPE America website, www.shapeamerica.org, holds a treasure trove of free resources for health and physical educators, adapted physical education teachers, teacher trainers and coaches, including activity calendars, curriculum resources, tools and templates, assessments and more. Visit www.shapeamerica.org and search for Teacher's Toolbox.

Every spring, SHAPE America hosts its National Convention & Expo, the premier national professional-development event for health and physical educators.

Advocacy is an essential element in the fulfillment of our mission. By speaking out for the school health and physical education professions, SHAPE America strives to make an impact on the national policy landscape.

Our Vision: A nation in which all children are prepared to lead healthy, physically active lives.

Our Mission: To advance professional practice and promote research related to health and physical education, physical activity, dance and sport.

Our Commitment: 50 Million Strong by 2029

50 Million Strong by 2029 is SHAPE America's commitment to put all children on the path to health and physical literacy through effective health and physical education programs. We believe that through effective teaching, health and physical educators can help students develop the ability and confidence to be physically active and make healthy choices. As educators, our guidance can also help foster their desire to maintain an active and healthy lifestyle in the years to come. To learn more visit www.shapeamerica.org/50Million.

Acknowledgments

There are many people who we need to thank for making this book happen! We first must give a huge thank-you to our families! We are grateful for the love and support of Rick, Lillian, Brynn, Todd, Taylor, and Jenna! The work we do is better because you support us and always cheer us on.

In particular with this book, we are forever grateful for the many educators who trusted us with their learning activities, lessons, and assessments! This book would not exist without the work of leaders in the field of skills-based health education. We are humbled to have the opportunity to share their work; we know that magic happens in health education classrooms every day, and we are thrilled to be able to share some of the magic with you.

To the teams at Human Kinetics and SHAPE America: Thank you for believing in our work and for your guidance in bringing our ideas to life. None of this would be possible without your efforts. In particular, we want to thank Scott Wikgren, Joe McGavin, Joe Halowich, and Jackie Blakley for keeping us on task, making us laugh, providing us with song lyrics, and taking our drafts and making them into an amazing, engaging resource for teachers.

Finally, we want to thank you, the reader! Thank you for being a lifelong learner who is willing to advance your practice in order to support the health and wellness of your students. Thank you for trusting us to help you on your journey. One of the best parts about writing this book is that we can support the vital work that you do with your students and provide some tools and strategies for your journey. We know how powerful health education can be, and we thank you for being a (skills-based) health education hero!

PART I

Setting the Foundation for Skills-Based Health Education

To help you understand and use the activities included in this book, part I provides a foundation for applying a skills-based approach during curriculum development. Here, we provide an overview of a skills-based approach to health education, including key components of the approach and considerations for implementation. In chapter 2, we review curriculum development using a backward-design approach and some basic principles of effective assessment.

By the end of this part, you will be able to

- discuss the importance of and align curriculum and instruction with the National Health Education Standards,
- describe and apply a skill development model and assess levels of skill performance,
- incorporate functional information into your curriculum and implement participatory methods, and
- apply a backward-design approach to developing your scope and sequence, unit plans, and lessons to reflect a skills-based framework.

Reading part I will prepare you for part II, in which we provide resources for your curriculum for each skill of the National Health Education Standards.

CHAPTER 1

Skills-Based Health Education: An Overview

A skills-based approach to health education prepares students for success by supporting the development of skills and acquisition of knowledge they need now—and will need in the future—to maintain or enhance their health. This chapter is intended to provide a background of key aspects of skills-based health education and lay a foundation for understanding the approach presented in this book. The information presented here aligns with material presented in *The Essentials of Teaching Health Education: Curriculum, Instruction, and Assessment* (Benes & Alperin, 2016) and provides concrete strategies for integrating skills-based teaching into your classroom.

Before we delve into the key aspects of a skills-based approach, let's define it. A skills-based approach is "a planned, sequential, comprehensive, and relevant curriculum that is implemented through participatory methods in order to help students develop skills, attitudes, and functional knowledge needed to lead health-enhancing lives" (Benes & Alperin, 2016, p. 24). The definition includes the key aspects of the approach that we will address in this chapter:

- Alignment with the National Health Education Standards
- Skills development and assessment
- Participatory methods
- Functional information

ALIGNMENT WITH THE NATIONAL HEALTH EDUCATION STANDARDS

At its core, a skills-based approach to health education is one that emphasizes the National Health Education Standards and shifts the focus away from giving students lots of new content and information to one that allows students to develop the competencies needed for leading a health-enhancing life. The skills of the National Health Education Standards include the following (Joint Committee on National Health Education Standards, 2007):

- Accessing valid and reliable information, products, and services
- Analyzing influences
- Interpersonal communication
- Decision making
- Self-management
- Goal setting
- Advocacy

We know from health behavior theory that knowledge alone will not change behaviors. *Knowing* is not, on its own, going to help us change behaviors or adopt new ones. Just think—how often do you engage in a behavior or behaviors that you know aren't the healthiest option? We all do sometimes! But we aren't doing it because we don't know better; it is usually because other factors are, in those moments, affecting and influencing our behaviors.

The reverse is true, also. While visiting a high school health education class during a student teaching practicum observation, one of the authors saw students working through the following scenario. Students were asked to identify the action they would take if they saw a friend passed out after drinking at a party. Their options were (a) do nothing, (b) give the friend coffee, (c) call 9-1-1, or (d) call their parents. Students all chose either option (a) or (b)—*even though* they knew that the right answer was to call 9-1-1. They knew what the right option was, but they admitted that they wouldn't choose that option in real life because they feared getting in trouble. Again, knowing what they *should* do was not the same as what they *would* do.

As health educators, we need to provide space for students to consider their realities and engage in thoughtful conversation about what supports and resources will help or encourage their ability to make healthy choices and what barriers might prevent them from making those choices. In this case, maybe students needed more confidence in their ability to advocate or more confidence in their ability to identify and weigh options in decision making, or maybe they needed more self-efficacy in communicating with parents or the police. No matter what it was that these students needed, it wasn't the knowledge about the healthier choice; they needed something else to implement the healthy decision in this situation. When we teach from a skills-based approach, we are keeping these other considerations at the forefront in order to help our students to overcome the barriers holding them back from making the health-enhancing choice.

In fact, both the Centers for Disease Control and Prevention (in its 2015 *Characteristics of Effective Health Education Curriculum*) and the World Health Organization (in its 2003 *Skills for Health* document) promote this approach. Also, research examining effective health education programs reveals that skill development is a key element. More support for this approach is found in literature discussing 21st century skill development. The skills taught in health education are transferable to all areas of students' lives (including other academic subjects).

Alignment with the National Health Education Standards means that the skills become the emphasis of the curriculum. They frame not only the written curriculum but its implementation and assessment as well. In a skills-based approach, your goal is to support the development of skills that will aid students in leading health-enhancing lives now and in the future. In practice, these skills become the units of instruction, and the traditional topic areas become the context through which students learn and develop the skills. While some information does need to be taught in the health classroom, the best use for this information is as a means for developing the skills and supporting the students in applying the information to their lives rather than being something taught for the sake of students' knowing about a topic. We encourage you to include functional information that aids students in determining the healthiest path and guides them toward how to be healthy as opposed to knowing multiple risk factors or negative outcomes of poor behavior. For example, instead of offering units on nutrition, drugs and alcohol, and mental health, you could offer units on analyzing influences, decision making, and advocacy that discuss topics such as how to analyze the influence of peers, culture, and family on dietary choices, or how to set a goal for managing one's time that reduces stress and helps students prioritize commitments. You still would be covering the same topics, but you would be delivering the information in such a way that students will apply it during skill practice and performance. This switch ensures not only that the skills are emphasized but also that the curriculum is designed such that it supports students' development of skill proficiency as a primary purpose of health education.

SKILL DEVELOPMENT AND ASSESSMENT

For students to have the confidence and competence to apply skills, we first must take the time to teach them about the skill, demonstrate how the skill looks in action, and provide opportunities for practice and feedback. The following skill development model provides a step-by-step approach to framing each skills-based unit (Benes & Alperin, 2016, p. 29):

1. Discuss the importance of the skill, its relevance, and its relationship to other learned skills.
2. Present steps for developing the skill.
3. Model the skill.
4. Practice the skill using real-life scenarios.
5. Provide feedback and reinforcement.

During step 1, we introduce students to the skill, provide a foundation for understanding the skill, and explain why the skill is relevant and meaningful for them. It's often helpful to use the stem "_____ is the ability to . . ." because a skill is something that you are able to *do*. Here is an example:

> Advocacy is the ability to stand up for what one believes and to influence others. When we advocate for healthy behaviors, we are encouraging others to replace unhealthy behaviors with healthier ones, such as not smoking or putting your phone out of reach while driving to prevent you from texting while driving.

Students will be motivated to learn the skill if they understand and buy into why the skill matters to them and why and how their ability to perform the skill effectively will benefit them.

> Advocacy is important for students your age because many kids look to their peers for support and as role models. When we advocate for safer cell phone use while driving, we are helping our peers to be healthier in their choices and are creating a safer community. Can you think of other reasons why advocacy is important to you and your peers?

Finally, during this step we explain the educational outcomes for the unit—what students will know and be able to do at the end of the unit.

> To do this, we will spend some time practicing being an advocate, and by the end of this unit, you will be able to
>
> ■ describe the importance of advocacy on improving our health,
> ■ consider peer and societal norms to design an advocacy campaign that encourages peers to adopt healthier behaviors, and
> ■ demonstrate how to influence others by sharing your health-enhancing message with your peers.

For more detail on developing objectives, see chapter 2.

During step 2, you present the steps of the skill or the skill cues. To support skill development, we need to break down the skill into its critical components and then create cues to help students remember the steps. Creating memorable cues can assist students during your course and beyond—especially if you use mnemonics or other strategies to help the skill cues stick with the students. For example, we use the mnemonic skill cue I CARE with advocacy (Benes & Alperin, 2016):

> **I**dentify a relevant and meaningful issue
>
> **C**reate a health-enhancing position or message about the issue that is supported by facts and evidence and is geared toward the audience
>
> **A**ct passionately and with conviction
>
> **R**elay your health-enhancing message to your audience
>
> **E**valuate the effectiveness of the advocacy effort

Step 3 is modeling the skill. For each skill, it is important for students to see the skill applied accurately and effectively. To do this, the skill needs to be modeled for or by students. During this step, you want to highlight the application of the skill cues so students can see the cues in action. There are many ways to model the skill—role-play, video clips, excerpts from books, or a guided example with the class. The most important things to remember are that your modeling of the skill is showing students how to apply the skill effectively and that the modeling provides an opportunity for them to identify the skill cues in action.

> To introduce you to an advocacy campaign, we will watch a short commercial that aims to persuade drivers to leave the phone in the back seat. Before watching the commercial, you will receive a worksheet with the skill cues listed. During the commercial, you should check off the criteria that the commercial does well. Following the viewing, we will discuss the key points that made the commercial effective.

Step 4 is practice. This step is critical for successful skill development. During this step, students receive opportunities to practice the skill in relevant and realistic situations. As the teacher, you are a guide on the side who provides feedback that will help students perform the skill successfully. Practice should be aligned with educational outcomes identified in step 1.

Whenever possible, providing opportunities for student input and choice during practice can help increase engagement and participation. Students feel more invested in the outcome of their work when it is personalized to them. Also, if you provide practice opportunities within one skill but with different health topics, it will facilitate positive transfer across a variety of situations and settings. We know that transfer is enhanced when learning takes place in multiple contexts. In the skills-based approach, this occurs when students have the opportunity to practice one skill (the focus of the learning) within multiple health topics (the topics are the different contexts). Practice is the step in which students not only can develop their ability to perform the skill effectively but also can increase their self-efficacy in using and applying the skill to see how the skill relates to their lives. To go back to our example,

> Let's put our knowledge of effective health advocacy to work. Your task is to work in small groups to create a one- to two-minute commercial advocating for a cause that it is important to you. Remember that you want to apply the skill cues here. You might want to refer to the checklist we used while watching the texting and driving commercial.

In step 5, you evaluate student performance using a summative assessment. The assessment and feedback should align with the educational outcomes presented in step 1 and should measure students' ability to demonstrate proficiency in the skill. *Reinforcement* refers to helping students see how they will use these skills in their lives. While feedback and reinforcement occur throughout the unit as students work toward understanding the skill, in the final step we want students to demonstrate their learning and to see how their learning carries over into their lives outside of the health classroom. In fact, over the course of your time with students, they will begin to see that every skill you cover in your health class is used nearly every day. The more we reinforce skill application in everyday life, the more our students will become confident and competent in their ability to use each skill to better their health.

> We now have the opportunity for everyone to share their advocacy projects and to learn more about causes that are important to people in this class. Each group will introduce its video by sharing the topic the group chose, why it chose the topic, and what makes this topic important for teens to learn about. As we watch the videos, be prepared to provide feedback based on the skill cues. Remember that feedback helps us all improve!

Having students complete authentic, performance-based summative assessments allows you to measure the level of students' skill performance. This form of assessment requires students to *demonstrate* the skill—this is the performance aspect of performance-based authentic assessment. In authentic assessments, students demonstrate the skills in relevant and meaningful contexts. Provide prompts or tasks that are similar to situations and scenarios that students are currently experiencing or might experience in the near future. To evaluate the assessment, design a rubric that includes the educational outcomes that you identified in step 1. Also, include a measure of student performance of skill cues and consider including criteria related to the health topics covered in the unit. Make sure that the criteria align with the educational outcomes introduced in step 1 and that your practice opportunities help students improve their ability to address the criteria successfully.

PARTICIPATORY METHODS

A skills-based approach is not just about aligning curriculum with the skills of the National Health Education Standards. It also means teaching through the use of participatory methods. Participatory teaching and learning involves modeling, observation, and social interaction (WHO, 2003). We need to implement our skills-based curriculum through interactive, student-centered strategies. Consider how you can decrease the amount of teacher-directed content and increase the amount of time that students are engaging actively in the content.

For participatory methods to be successful, you must create a positive and supportive learning environment. Starting the very first day that your students enter your classroom, establish and maintain a safe space for students to be active participants. You want students to ask questions, to work outside of their comfort zone, to be honest and open, and to share opinions and ideas. You also want to create a space where students feel safe, take responsibility for their learning, and think critically and challenge themselves and one another. While this isn't always easy, it is important that we encourage students to be engaged learners who take ownership of their learning, their experience in class, and their health.

FUNCTIONAL INFORMATION

The last critical component of a skills-based approach is the use and integration of functional information. As described earlier, we know that knowledge alone does not change behavior and we also know that we do need *some* knowledge to provide meaning to the behavior change we seek. What we need is *functional* information. Functional information is information that is relevant, usable, and applicable (Benes & Alperin, 2016). It is the *need-to-know* information about a health topic.

While we can't tell you what functional information is the *right* information in your school or district, we are confident that taking a closer look at student needs will help you determine the most appropriate topics to include in your curriculum. This is because many factors can influence which pieces of information are most appropriate for the students in your community. For example, what do your students need to learn, what health behaviors do you want to see improve, what risk factors are affecting your students, what community behaviors are on the rise, and what have your students already been taught? To determine this, we suggest that you start by looking at state and local standards and then at local needs-assessment data (e.g., teen birth rates, student reports of feeling unsafe at school, absentee data) to determine which areas are priorities in your school and community. If students are engaging in certain risky behaviors (drinking, smoking, texting while driving) or not engaging in positive behaviors in certain areas (e.g., physical activity, handwashing skills, standing up to bullying, using interpersonal communication skills)—those are the places to start. After determining the larger topic areas to cover, take time to drill down to determine what, specifically, it is about that topic that would benefit your students and help them to apply one of the health skills. For example, instead of saying that students need to learn about nutrition, consider what, specifically, your students need to learn about nutrition in order to make healthier choices. Is it understanding a nutrition facts label, how food affects performance, strategies for improving hydration, or how much sugar is in their beverages?

We suggest asking yourself these questions to help narrow down a larger topic into specific parts:

- When my students learn this information, how will they use it to benefit their health or the health of those around them?
- What will happen if my students are not presented with this information?
- Without this information, will students be able to apply this skill effectively in a real-life situation?

Based on your answers, you should have a good idea of which information to include or exclude from your curriculum. Always be sure, also, to cross-check the information that you are including with any applicable state or local standards to ensure alignment. This may mean removing some topics or information that have become standard in your curriculum but do not serve a strong purpose within a skills-focused program. It helps if you are willing to think critically about what information you are including in your curriculum and why that information is important to include. You likely will start to realize that not all information needs to be included or that you can pull higher-level themes out of the information that will be more relevant and useful to students. We recognize that reducing the number of topics and the amount of information you teach can be tough. This process requires reflection and prioritization, but remember that it is easier to add information if you have time than it is to take information out once you have started. Focusing on the need-to-know information will help support behavior change in students and will open up space in the curriculum that you can use to focus on skill development. At this point, you also should refer to Standard 1 of the National Health Education Standards, which is the "core concepts" standard. The performance indicators in this standard can help you craft your information-based objectives once you have decided on what functional information to include.

All these components—aligning with the National Health Education Standards, focusing on skill development and performance-based authentic assessment, using participatory methods, and including functional information—are keys to implementing a skills-based approach to health education. We hope that this overview provides a foundation for understanding and implementing the units, lessons, activities, and assessments included in this text. Remember: The journey isn't always easy, but it is worth it!

REFERENCES

Benes, S., & Alperin, H. (2016). *The essentials of teaching health education: Curriculum, instruction, and assessment.* Champaign, IL: Human Kinetics.

Centers for Disease Control and Prevention. (2015). Characteristics of effective health education curriculum. Accessed September 19, 2017, at https://www.cdc.gov/healthyschools/sher/characteristics/index.htm.

Joint Committee on National Health Education Standards. (2007). *National Health Education Standards* (2nd ed.). Atlanta, GA: American Cancer Society.

World Health Organization. (2003). *Skills for health.* Accessed September 19, 2017, from www.who.int/school_youth_health/media/en/sch_skills4health_03.pdf.

CHAPTER 2

Designing Your Health Curriculum

To ensure that your students develop the skills and knowledge needed to lead healthy lives, you must plan and implement an effective health education curriculum. This takes, among other things, planning for and consideration of developmental levels, student and community needs, and where your curriculum fits within the bigger picture of the district. (That is, have students had health education before your class? Will they have it after?) As discussed in chapter 1, a skills-based approach uses the skills of the National Health Education Standards as the foundation of the curriculum and integrates topic areas such as nutrition, alcohol and other drugs, and interpersonal relationships to help students develop the skills and acquire the knowledge necessary for maintaining or enhancing their health. This chapter provides strategies and tools for designing a skills-based health education curriculum.

Before we dive into specifics of curriculum design, let's take a moment to think about how well-designed learning experiences influence student outcomes. We will explore two scenarios that could play out in your classroom. In the first, you go into class having an idea of what you would like students to learn (although you have no specifically designed behavioral outcomes). You have thought about the information you want students to know and you design and teach your lessons in an engaging way to make sure they learn this new information. You create an assessment (near the end of the unit) to measure whether or not students can restate what they've just learned based on what you were able to cover in the lessons. Perhaps the assessment asks students to create a poster, make a presentation, or take a test. When students turn in their projects or their tests, you notice that they were able to include a lot of information on the topics discussed and their test scores reflect knowledge acquisition. Based on this information, you feel that students have retained information from the unit, and you hope that they will be able to use that information to make healthy choices.

Now we want you to consider a second scenario and notice the differences in both student output and transferability of learning. In this scenario, your curriculum and student learning experiences are predetermined. The learning experiences are created to support skill development while integrating the functional information and topics necessary for developing skills. You begin your unit by considering what *your* students need to know and be able to do. You consider the needs of your school, district, and community using data from a variety of resources—from state standards to school-based surveys. For example, suppose you have outlined your scope and sequence and are brainstorming topics to cover in the Analyzing Influences unit. While looking at Youth Risk Behavior Survey (YRBS) data, you notice an increase in alcohol use among high school students. Based on a local survey conducted by guidance counselors, you also know that students are experiencing high levels of stress and are using alcohol as a way to deal with their stress. Finally, you know from conversations with the parent–teacher organization that parents are concerned about the online activity of students. Using all of these data, you find it important to focus your unit on analyzing the influences of stress in students' lives by identifying stressors, including technology, and discussing healthy ways of managing stress without turning to alcohol or other unhealthy options. You use this information to develop your unit objectives.

Next, you create an assessment that will provide an opportunity for students to demonstrate their skill proficiency and the extent to which they have met the unit objectives. *After* creating the assessment, you design your lessons in such a way that students will acquire the knowledge and develop the ability to apply the skill in a health-enhancing way and demonstrate their learning through the assessment. All the while, you make sure that you are teaching in a way that is both engaging and meaningful to students. By the end of the unit, students are able to demonstrate to you how to apply the skill while also using the information taught to them. You now have greater levels of confidence in your students' ability to use the information learned and apply the skill developed in a health-enhancing way. You also feel confident that students will be able to analyze other influences in their lives that might lead to unhealthy behaviors.

These two scenarios have fundamental differences. In the first, students are able to tell you what they have learned and have built up a knowledge base of health-related information. While some of the information will resonate with students, behavior change theory suggests that they are unlikely to retain that information over the long term, nor will they necessarily use that information in their daily lives to make health-enhancing choices. Knowledge is a precondition for behavior change; it sets the stage, but on its own will not lead to change (Bandura, 2004). Initially, the information might become a topic of conversation and even spark interest in learning about something else, but the information alone does not ensure that students have the ability to apply that information in ways that support or maintain their health.

In contrast, in the second scenario, the unit is designed to give students opportunities to develop the skill and apply the information learned during the unit. Through this experience, the students must use health-related information to support their application of the skill, with the information itself secondary to skill development. The assessment designed before the lesson planning and implementation helps to ensure that learning activities included in the unit align with and contribute to students' ability to meet the unit objectives. Not only does this help guide your teaching, but also it helps to set clear expectations for students—they know where they will end up before they even start! Also, as students progress through the lessons, they build on their ability to apply the skill so as they approach the assessment they are prepared to demonstrate the skill and apply the information in a meaningful way. After completing the unit, students have the ability to perform the skill, apply the newly learned information, and transfer learning to their daily lives.

This chapter provides you with strategies and ideas to set up your health education classroom (and curriculum) in a way that more closely mirrors the second scenario. We believe that students who participate in meaningful, well-designed learning experiences that focus on skill development are more likely to leave their health classrooms prepared to handle the challenges they will experience in everyday life.

EIGHT STEPS OF CURRICULUM DESIGN

The design process that we describe here is an example of backward design in which you begin by identifying where you want students to end up and then work backward to develop lessons and learning activities. This method is an effective way of ensuring alignment in your curriculum and can help maximize the impact of your time with students.

A key component of a backward-designed curriculum is beginning with the end in mind. It might help to think of the process as an inverted triangle. The broad part of the triangle at the top is the big picture—the goals that you want your students to attain. This can be done at the course, school, or district level. For example, you might set a goal that students will be able to articulate the role of their health behaviors to overall health outcomes. Next, determine the objectives (the more specific "steps" that will help students to be able to address the goals) by writing them in terms of student outcomes. More measurable than curriculum goals, the objectives articulate specific student learning outcomes that will help students work toward the goals. For example, students will be able to describe how internal and external influences affect personal health choices.

To summarize the process, you begin by identifying goals that you want students to attain and then write the objectives that students will meet as a result of the unit, design an assessment to evaluate students' ability to demonstrate those objectives, write the lessons to prepare students, and write the activities intended to meet the objectives. We operate under the premise that having a well-developed curriculum is key to your success. To do this, we encourage the use of an eight-step process to help you design your curriculum. The following process is intended to help guide your planning and to align your planning with intended student outcomes.

Step 1: Get to Know the Students and the Community

Knowing the needs of your students and being familiar with the community in which they live will help you create a more relevant and meaningful curriculum. One of the questions we are often asked is, "How do we figure out what to include in our curriculum?" Our answer: get to know your students' needs. Knowing the unhealthy behaviors that are prevalent, issues facing your students, community norms and values, and the overall barriers students face will help you ensure not only that the topics are relevant for students but also that you can design a curriculum in which students can see themselves. For example, suppose you are redesigning your curriculum and you realize that you will need to eliminate some of the information that you usually teach but you aren't sure what to remove from the curriculum. You look at your YRBS or local health department data and notice that marijuana use is on the rise, alcohol use is decreasing, and other drug use is almost negligible. You decide that instead of teaching your usual alcohol and other drugs unit, you will focus only on marijuana, because this appears to be the more pressing need based on the fact that there is a rise in marijuana use and a decrease in or lack of other drug use. You mention to students these trends and explain that while the topic of focus is marijuana, the ability to refrain from engaging in risky behavior for any substance is the underlying message. As you are planning your curriculum, you use landmarks in the community in your scenarios so that students can relate to the situations described in the curriculum.

Step 2: Formulate Goals

Before developing your curriculum, it is key to decide the goals of your program at both the school and district level. If your district already has set goals for the health education program, review these existing goals or use this as an opportunity to advocate for the district to revisit and perhaps revise the goals in order to better meet the needs of your students. At the school or district level, consider answering the question: *What do we want our students to be able to do after they complete our health education program?* Or at the individual level: *What do I want my students to be able to do after completing my health education course?* Depending on the answers, you might decide that small program changes are needed, or perhaps a full program review is in order. All of this will depend on the current education climate and level of support for health education. Whether you create new goals or align your curriculum with existing goals, you need to consider the amount of time that you have with students, priority areas, and any other factors that might influence your ability to meet the goals.

Step 3: Develop Benchmark Assessments

Benchmark assessments are assessment measures that take a snapshot in time to determine student progress. These are included early in the curriculum development process and serve as measurement points for student growth and learning. While the goals created previously frame your whole program or are intended to span a longer amount of time, possibly even by the end of your K-12 program, step 3 helps to ensure that students are progressing appropriately throughout their K-12 experience. The intention is that measurements taken along a student's time in health education show growth and lead to expected outcomes by the time the student is in 12th grade (or at the end of your health education program) so that you can be confident that you will have met the goals set forth for what students should know and be able to do by the end of the program.

Establishing benchmark assessments at agreed-upon points along the way will provide valuable feedback that you can use to modify curriculum and instruction and understand student growth. The interval of benchmark assessments can vary based on your program design, but in general, assessments should be consistent and given at intervals that allow for the results to inform program improvement and support student success. For example, you might decide to administer a benchmark assessment at the end of each grade span into which the National Health Education Standards' performance indicators are grouped (e.g., pre-K through grade 2, and grades 3 through 5, 6 through 8, and 9 through 12). You also might decide to administer a benchmark assessment at the end of each grade in which health is taught if courses are not offered in consecutive grades. Regardless of their frequency, your benchmark assessments should align with the curriculum being taught and allow students to show growth toward program goals.

Step 4: Determine the Health Topics, Functional Information, and Skills

After determining the benchmark assessments that align with your program goals, you need to consider what skills, topics, and information to teach so that students are able to reach benchmark outcomes and meet program goals. To do this, it is important to consider the following factors:

■ Student and community needs
■ District goals and outcomes
■ State-level standards
■ National-level standards

By reviewing and understanding those four factors, you will have a better sense of the requirements for students at each grade level, along with identifying the topics most relevant to students in your health education program. While you inevitably will come up with far more information and skills that you would like to teach, now is the time to filter through to determine what makes the most sense for your students given the time you have together.

At this point, you will need to consider which skills to teach at each grade level, recognizing that it likely is impractical to teach each skill at every grade. Next, identify which topics fit best with each skill. For example, you might decide to teach accessing valid and reliable information, products and services, analyzing influences, and goal setting in sixth grade. In your school, students do not take health education in seventh grade. In the eighth-grade curriculum, the focus is on decision making, interpersonal communication, and advocacy. You feel that self-management will be addressed throughout the curriculum, so you don't include it as a separate unit. Having determined what skills you will teach in each grade, you need to decide the topics that fit best within each unit. For example, you find that healthy relationships has emerged as a key topic for students in both sixth and eighth grades. In sixth grade, you include healthy relationships as part of your analyzing influences unit, and in eighth grade, you include it as part of your interpersonal communication unit and build upon what students learned in sixth grade.

Step 5: Create a Scope and Sequence

Now that you have a better idea of the skills and topics that you want to include in your curriculum, the creation of a scope and sequence becomes the map showing how all of the pieces fit together at each grade level. Also, the scope and sequence details how students will progress in their learning, serves as a framework for ensuring that students are able to meet benchmark assessment goals, and provides a sequence of learning that is intended to prevent overlap or gaps in the curriculum. When creating district-level scope and sequence, be sure to include administrators or other health educators in the process to ensure that the final product aligns with district goals and that everyone is on the same page as to what will be taught and when.

In a skills-based approach, we encourage you to create a scope and sequence that uses the skills of the National Health Education Standards as the units, then integrates the topics and information within each of the units. This emphasizes skill development and aligns the topics and information easily underneath. Remember, the goal is skill development using topics and information as the context for how students apply the skills in a real-world setting. It is for this reason that the unit name matters. Saying that we have an Advocating for Environmental Health unit reinforces the skill more so than an Environmental Health unit that includes advocacy, which places the emphasis on the topic over the skill.

Step 6: Develop Unit Plan Objectives and Outcomes

Once you've developed a scope and sequence, putting your road map for student learning in place, you can plan your units for each grade. While the scope and sequence identifies what to teach in each grade level, the unit plans map out how each of the skills and all of the topics work within a particular class.

At this stage, you will identify the unit objectives. Objectives should be based on identified student needs and written for each unit within each grade level. These written student outcomes should be specific to the skill and topics included within the unit. Objectives answer the question, *What will students know and be able to do as a result of this unit?* Use the following guide to help you write the unit objectives.

■ *Choose performance indicators from the National Health Education Standards:* The performance indicators listed under each National Standard specify what students must be able to do to demonstrate proficiency in the skill named in the standard. Choose the indicators that you want to work toward in your unit. For example, suppose that while planning your middle school Analyzing Influences unit, you realize that curriculum demands will prevent you from covering all 10 indicators listed under Standard 2 for middle school students. So, you choose to focus on the indicators regarding the influence of media on health behaviors (indicator 2.8.5) and the influence of technology on personal and family health (indicator 2.8.6) and how they might influence the likelihood of engaging in unhealthy behaviors (indicator 2.8.9).

■ *Determine coverage of indicators:* Once you have chosen the indicators to include in your unit, determine whether you will cover each performance indicator as written or will modify it based on the needs of your students. You will need to consider the assessment being used to measure student outcomes and whether or not the assessment will measure the entire performance indicator or only part of it. For example, let's take a look at performance indicator 2.8.10 for the skill of analyzing influences—explain how school and public health policies can influence health promotion and disease prevention. Perhaps you would like to focus on school policies but are unable to take a deeper look into other public health policies. In this case, you would write an objective that captures what you will cover and that has clear intent.

■ *Use student-appropriate terms:* Keep in mind that some of the performance indicators are not written in terms that all students will understand. Take the time to explain to students the meaning of any terms that are unfamiliar or confusing.

■ *Write student outcomes:* Take all of the information gathered from the previous unit-writing steps and write the outcomes—what students will know and be able to do by the end of the unit. You will need to specify the skill and topic for each objective. For example, in keeping with analyzing influences, the final objective is: *By the end of this unit, students will be able to analyze the influence of media and technology on personal health behaviors.*

Note that this is a combination of two performance indicators, 2.8.5 and 2.8.6. You ended up with this objective by following our guide for writing objectives and making decisions about what to include and how to phrase the objective.

You may also wish to include topic information in your objectives. The objective still is skill-specific and open to a variety of topic areas such as personal health behaviors. Now, you might wish to write a secondary objective that spells out more deliberately the topic information you intend for students to know from this unit. Here are two examples:

■ By the end of this unit, students will be able to describe how media and technology influence individual perception of body image. Here, *body image* is the topic.

■ By the end of this unit, students will be able to *explain how school policies on media and technology* can support their mental health. Here, *mental health* is the topic.

Step 7: Develop Unit Assessments

At this stage, you will review your unit objectives and develop assessment measures that require students to demonstrate learning and skill proficiency related to the intended outcomes. This is best achieved through the use of performance-based assessment items. That is, assessment prompts that require students to demonstrate applying the skill in a real-world example. Throughout this text we will provide examples of performance-based assessments for each of the skills. Keep in mind that when we allow students to demonstrate their learning in meaningful ways, we equip them for future success. Unlike asking students to recite facts or remember statistics, using assessments that measure a student's ability to apply a skill offers a better demonstration of what the student is able to do and provides valuable information on how the student can improve.

Step 8: Create Lesson Plans

Once you have detailed the unit outcomes, plans, and assessments, now is the time to write your detailed lesson plans. This book will provide you with many examples of lessons and activities that demonstrate a skills-based approach in action. While unit plans form the foundation, it is through the lessons and activities that the magic happens.

When planning your lessons, keep these key points in mind.

■ *Keep lesson activities focused on outcomes:* While it might be tempting to add activities that are fun for students, make sure that all activities serve a meaningful purpose. While we might want to use creative ways to get our students' attention, we must be sure to use the limited time we have with students wisely by planning engaging activities that also help students meet the objectives we have identified.

■ *Remember your audience:* As with planning your scope and sequence, it is important to keep in mind who is sitting in your classroom. Each student comes to class with a history and a unique set of experiences that he or she is dealing with. Keeping this in mind is key to creating a classroom environment that is safe for all students and allows each student to be successful.

■ *Focus on participatory methods:* You want to engage students as much as possible. When you use participatory methods, you provide the opportunity for students to be active participants in their own learning, to think critically, solve problems, and take ownership of their learning experience.

USING THIS TEXT

The steps for developing a curriculum detailed in this chapter are intended to help you through a process that results in a curriculum that is relevant and meaningful for your students. This can be implemented at the district level, the school level, and even the course level. We recognize that there will be variations in the ability to apply these steps and in the ability to design a curriculum specifically for your students. We hope that no matter how much experience you have in curriculum development, how much flexibility you have to create your own curriculum, and how comfortable you are with skills-based health education, this chapter provides you with a baseline for thinking about how you can implement a backward-design approach to create a purposeful, aligned curriculum that meets the needs of your students.

REFERENCE

Bandura, A. (2004). Health promotion by social cognitive means. *Health Education and Behavior, 31*(2), 143-164.

PART II

Skills in the Classroom

The number-one question we hear from health educators in the field is "Where can I find lessons, activities, and resources to help me transition to a skills-based approach?" Part II of this text is designed to deliver those resources, no matter where you are in the process. In this part of the book, you will find seven chapters, each one dedicated to a skill of the National Health Education Standards and offering rich teaching resources. Skills explored include accessing valid and reliable information, products, and services; analyzing influences; interpersonal communication; decision making; goal setting; self-management; and advocacy.

Designed for a range of audiences with varying needs to maximize their use, these chapters contain reminders for you to modify any of the resources presented in part II to meet your teaching and student needs. All material presented aligns with part I of the book, and we encourage you to consider the principles of skills-based health education as you read through the chapters and consider making any changes to the materials provided here.

By the end of this part, you will be able to

- discuss key considerations when teaching the skills of the National Health Education Standards,

- use the performance indicators from the National Standards to develop unit plans,

- implement performance-based assessments for monitoring skill development, and

- implement effective lessons and learning activities that support skill development.

Our aim in part II is to provide you with the materials and inspiration you need to design effective skills-based units.

CHAPTER 3

Accessing Valid and Reliable Information, Products, and Services

This chapter focuses on the skill of accessing valid and reliable information, products, and services, which is Standard 3 of the National Health Education Standards (NHES). Within this chapter, you will see examples of the skill in action. You can use the sample assessments, lesson plans, and learning activities in your classroom to guide students as they develop this skill.

The materials presented here are designed to support each step of the skill-development model (see chapter 1) and are presented and organized to reflect a backward-design approach (see chapter 2). We begin with the end in mind by looking at the big picture of what the skill is and what students should be able to do once they develop the skill, as specified in the performance indicators under Standard 3. We also include sample skill cues for teaching the skill. The rest of the chapter includes assessments, lesson plans, and learning activities that you can implement in your classroom as is or with modifications to meet the needs of your program and your students. We have included both sets of NHES performance indicators (grades 6-8 and grades 9-12) in the unit overview and in each lesson as appropriate. Take the materials here and make them your own in order to meet the needs of your students and to address the objectives adequately. Our goal is to provide a usable framework that also is easily modifiable.

To provide a context for teaching your students how to access valid and reliable information, products, and services, we use the topic of nutrition. While we use nutrition in this example, many other health topics could be relevant to and appropriate for teaching this skill to your students. We encourage you to use any other health topics that fit into your overall scope and sequence and address your curriculum and student needs.

SKILL OVERVIEW

To develop the skill of being able to access valid and reliable information, products, and services, students must take a thoughtful look at the information they are using to determine health-behavior choices, at the products that can affect their health, and at the services that they might seek out to maintain or enhance their health. Each of these functions of the skill is relevant to students because they must make choices that affect their health on a daily basis. We often make these choices based on the information, products, and services that we are able to find and access, perhaps without giving much thought to their validity and reliability.

By learning and practicing this skill, we provide students the opportunity to review information, a product, or service thoughtfully and critically and determine whether or not it is the best fit for their particular need. This skill also provides students with the tools to determine the extent to which they can be assured that the information, product, or service is valid and reliable. This skill is more than finding the appropriate information, product, or service related to a specific health topic. It also requires students to evaluate what they have found and to determine whether the source is most appropriate to fit their needs. By adding this additional layer, we help students to be critical thinkers and informed consumers who can more easily navigate a media- and information-saturated world.

Table 3.1 shows the performance indicators under Standard 3, which outline what students should be able to do while developing this skill, within each grade span in grades 6 through 8 and 9 through 12.

SKILL CUES

While the ability to access valid and reliable information, products, and services is a complex skill, it is a fairly straightforward skill to teach as the criteria for determining validity and reliability for all aspects are similar and can be transferred. Skill cues can help students remember the parts of the skill. When students learn and are able to apply the skill cues within a given context, their ability to apply the skill in a real-world capacity increases. Remember that you can use these as they are or modify them to meet the needs of your students.

TABLE 3.1   Performance Indicators for Standard 3 of the NHES (Grades 6-12)

	6-8		9-12
3.8.1	Analyze the validity of health information, products, and services.	3.12.1	Evaluate the validity of health information, products, and services.
3.8.2	Access valid health information from home, school, and the community.	3.12.2	Use resources from home, school, and the community that provide valid health information.
3.8.3	Determine the accessibility of products that enhance health.	3.12.3	Determine the accessibility of products and services that enhance health.
3.8.4	Describe situations that may require professional health services.	3.12.4	Determine when professional health services may be required.
3.8.5	Locate valid and reliable health products and services.	3.12.5	Access valid and reliable health products and services.

Reprinted, with permission, from the American Cancer Society. *National Health Education Standards: Achieving Excellence*, Second Edition (Atlanta, GA: American Cancer Society, 2007), 24-36, cancer.org/bookstore

Figure 3.1 shows some sample skill cues for accessing valid and reliable information, products, and services that may be used for grades 6 through 12.

Access

Skill Cues ■ Grades 6-12

STANDARD 3	Students will demonstrate the ability to access valid information, products, and services to enhance health.

ACCESS

- Is it **a**ccurate?

- Is it **c**redible?

- Is it **c**urrent?

- Is it **e**asy to use and access?

- What **s**ituations is it best used in?

- Are claims or information **s**upported?

 HUMAN KINETICS

From S. Benes and H. Alperin, 2019, *Lesson planning for skills-based health education* (Champaign, IL: Human Kinetics). Reprinted, by permission, from S. Benes and H. Alperin, 2016, *The essentials of teaching health education* (Champaign, IL: Human Kinetics).

FIGURE 3.1 Skill cues for accessing valid and reliable information, products, and services.

UNIT OUTLINE

This section includes an outline of the unit for Standard 3; table 3.2 shows this outline, including lesson titles, lesson objectives, the step(s) of the skill development model that are addressed in each lesson, and the titles of the main learning activities in each lesson.

Students begin by being able to identify valid and reliable sources of information, products, and services and progress to applying their learning to a nutrition topic of their choice. Standard 1 is not included in this unit as none of its performance indicators align with the content in this unit. If you modify the unit, you might be able to add Standard 1 performance indicators.

All of the performance indicators for Standard 3 grades 6 through 12 are covered in this unit and form the basis for the unit objectives. Additional unit objectives that are not directly related to the National Health Education Standards performance indicators but are addressed through the unit also are listed. As a note, it is important to review unit objectives and lesson outcomes prior to teaching in your classroom. Because we use the topic of nutrition here, you would need to modify the objectives if you select a different topic for your students.

Unit Objectives, Grades 6 Through 8

By the end of this unit, students will be able to

- analyze the validity of nutrition-related information, products, and services related to a variety of health-related topics (indicator 3.8.1);
- access valid health information about nutrition from home, school, and the community (indicator 3.8.2);
- determine the accessibility of nutrition-related products that enhance health (indicator 3.8.3);
- describe situations that may require professional health services (indicator 3.8.4); and
- locate valid and reliable nutrition-related products and services (indicator 3.8.5).

Unit Objectives, Grades 9 Through 12

By the end of this unit, students will be able to

- evaluate the validity of health information, products, and services related to nutrition (indicator 3.12.1);
- use resources from home, school, and the community that provide valid health information about nutrition (indicator 3.12.2);
- determine the accessibility of products and services that enhance health (indicator 3.12.3);
- determine when professional health services may be required (indicator 3.12.4); and
- access valid and reliable nutrition-related products and services (indicator 3.12.5).

TABLE 3.2   Standard 3 Unit Outline

Lesson title	Lesson objectives (indicators in parentheses) *By the end of this lesson, students will be able to:*	Step of the skill development model addressed in the lesson	Main learning activities
Lesson 1: To Trust or Not to Trust	• Define the skill of being able to access valid and reliable information, products, and services • Discuss the relevance of being able to access valid and reliable information, products, and services to health outcomes	Skill introduction (step 1)	• Two Truths and a Lie (p. 32) • To Trust or Not to Trust (p. 33)
Lesson 2: ACCESSing Valid and Reliable Information, Products, and Services	• List the steps for determining website validity and reliability • Analyze the validity of nutrition-related information, products, and services (3.8.1) *or* • Evaluate the validity of health information, products, and services related to nutrition (3.12.1)	Steps of the skill and modeling (steps 2 and 3)	Accessing Valid Health Information on the Internet (p. 36)
Lesson 3: Grocery Games	• Demonstrate healthy eating practices and behaviors to improve the health of themselves and others • Analyze the validity of nutrition-related information, products, and services (3.8.1) *or* • Evaluate the validity of health information, products, and services related to nutrition (3.12.1)	Skill practice (step 4)	Grocery Games (p. 43)
Lesson 4: Is It Healthy?	• Identify unhealthy foods to avoid and research healthier alternatives • Research ingredients used in processed food and the effects of these ingredients on the human body • Choose food options that support lifelong health • Analyze the validity of health information, products, and services related to a variety of health-related topics (3.8.1) • Access valid health information about nutrition from home, school, and the community (3.8.2) *or* • Evaluate the validity of health information, products, and services related to a variety of health-related topics (3.12.1) • Use resources from home, school, and the community that provide valid health information about nutrition (3.12.2)	Skill practice (step 4)	What Is in Our Food? (p. 47)
Lessons 5 and 6: Podcasts	• Apply and demonstrate their knowledge and understanding of a nutrition-related topic of their choice • Analyze the validity of nutrition-related information, products, and services (3.8.1) • Access valid health information about nutrition from home, school, and the community (3.8.2) *or* • Evaluate the validity of health information, products, and services related to nutrition (3.12.1) • Use resources from home, school, and the community that provide valid health information about nutrition (3.12.2)	Skill practice (step 4)	Health Podcasts (p. 51)

(continued)

Table 3.2 *(continued)*

Lesson title	Lesson objectives (indicators in parentheses) *By the end of this lesson, students will be able to:*	Step of the skill development model addressed in the lesson	Main learning activities
Lessons 7 and 8: Who and What Are in My Neighborhood?	• Analyze the validity of nutrition-related health information, products, and services related to a variety of health-related topics (3.8.1) • Access valid health information about a variety of nutrition topics from home, school, and the community (3.8.2) • Determine the accessibility of nutrition-related products that enhance health (3.8.3) • Describe situations that may require professional health services (3.8.4) • Locate valid and reliable nutrition-related health products and services (3.8.5) *or* • Evaluate the validity of health information, products, and services (3.12.1) • Use resources from home, school, and the community that provide valid health information (3.12.2) • Determine the accessibility of products and services that enhance health (3.12.3) • Determine when professional health services may be required (3.12.4) • Access valid and reliable health products and services (3.12.5)	Skill practice (step 4)	Who and What Are in My Neighborhood? (p. 55)
Lesson 9: Wrap-Up and Assessment	• Analyze the validity of nutrition-related health information, products, and services related to a variety of health-related topics (3.8.1) • Access valid health information about a variety of nutrition topics from home, school, and the community (3.8.2) • Determine the accessibility of nutrition-related products that enhance health (3.8.3) • Describe situations that may require professional health services (3.8.4) • Locate valid and reliable nutrition-related health products and services (3.8.5) *or* • Evaluate the validity of health information, products, and services (3.12.1) • Use resources from home, school, and the community that provide valid health information (3.12.2) • Determine the accessibility of products and services that enhance health (3.12.3) • Determine when professional health services may be required (3.12.4) • Access valid and reliable health products and services (3.12.5)	Assessment (step 5)	

Performance indicators are from: Joint Committee on National Health Education Standards. (2007). *National Health Education Standards: Achieving Excellence* (2nd ed.). Atlanta, GA: American Cancer Society.

Additional Unit Objectives, Grades 6 Through 12

By the end of this unit, students will be able to

■ define the skill of being able to access valid and reliable information, products, and services;

■ discuss the relevance of being able to access valid and reliable information, products, and services to health outcomes;

■ list the steps for determining website validity and reliability;

■ analyze a website and determine whether it is a valid source of health information about a variety of health topics;

■ demonstrate healthy eating practices and behaviors to improve the health of themselves and others;

■ identify unhealthy foods to avoid and research healthier alternatives;

■ research ingredients used in processed food and the effects of these ingredients on the human body;

■ choose food options that support lifelong health; and

■ apply and demonstrate their knowledge and understanding of a nutrition-related topic of their choice.

ASSESSMENT

Here is a sample assessment that will evaluate the extent to which students can meet the objectives identified for this unit. In this assessment, students are required to research one information source, product, and service resource related to a topic within nutrition.

Objectives

Through this assessment, students will demonstrate their ability to

■ evaluate the validity of health information, products, and services (indicator 3.12.1);

■ use resources from home, school, and the community that provide valid health information (3.12.2);

■ determine the accessibility of products and services that enhance health (3.12.3);

■ determine when professional health services may be required (3.12.4); and

■ access valid and reliable health products and services (3.12.5).

Description

This assessment is the final practice for students to show that they have achieved proficiency in the skill. In this assessment, students are required to research one information, product, and service resource related to their topic. Share the Standard 3 Assessment Worksheet with your students through Google in view-only mode. This requires them to make a copy, rename the document under their name, and add their content, including uniform resource locators (URLs), before submitting it to you. This also provides you with easy access to their web resources from the document itself rather than having to type in each website address individually.

Modifications

This assessment is based on information and activities contained in this chapter and, as with the lessons, should be modified to address changes to the objectives or as necessary for your students. Modifications to the assessment may include:

■ *Assessing additional objectives:* This assessment is focused on evaluating whether students are able to access and evaluate health information, products, and services; however, the assessment also could include a measure of the health topic knowledge.

■ *Assessing different skill cues:* This assessment is based on the ACCESS skill cues presented in figure 3.1. If you modify the skill cues for your students, be sure to modify them here as well.

Implementation Tips

■ Access the assessment worksheet on the web resource, make any necessary modifications, and distribute it to students electronically. Students will need to rename the document using their name and add their content, including URLs, before submitting it for evaluation. Asking students to submit their completed forms electronically will allow you to link directly to resource URLs rather than having to type in each web address individually.

■ Allow yourself ample time to evaluate the assessments so that students can receive meaningful feedback from you related to their skill performance. Depending on the size of your class, you might wish to break this into smaller chunks by having students submit the information part of the assignment first, the product part next, and the service part last. This would allow students to apply your feedback from their first submissions to their later submissions and will spread out the amount of time you need to spend on feedback (three times with less feedback needed versus one time with more feedback needed).

■ During student practice, students might need support in navigating the validity of their resources as they apply the ACCESS model. Students might struggle when they put their time and effort into researching something only to learn that it doesn't apply or that they shouldn't use it.

Assessment and worksheet modified from a submission from Amy Prior, middle school health teacher in South Carolina.

Standard 3 Assessment Worksheet: Accessing Valid and Reliable Information, Products, and Services

Your ability to access valid and reliable information, products, and services is a key element in determining whether the information, product, or service you are using (or wish to use) is appropriate for your needs. Through this assignment, you will research and find three valid and reliable nutrition resources that you can use to help you as you work toward your goal.

Use the following chart to prove the validity and reliability of your resources. For the product and service resources, you must be able to access them locally either by physically going to a facility, having a product shipped to your home, or buying it from a local store.

Are My Sources Valid and Reliable?

	Information resource	Product resource	Service resource
What is the name of your resource?			
What is the URL of your resource (if appropriate)?			
Why is this a good resource for you and your goal?			
Please explain in detail how you would use this resource to help you achieve your goal?			
Is the resource accurate? (Please explain in detail.)			
Is the resource credible? (Please explain in detail citing the resource for example.)			
Is the resource current? (Please explain in detail citing the resource for example.)			
Is the resource easy to use and access? (Please explain in detail citing the resource for example.)			
In what situations is the resource best used? (Please explain in detail citing the resource for example.)			
Are claims or information about the resource supported? (Please explain in detail citing the resource for example.)			
Justify why this resource is valid and reliable. (Please explain in detail citing the resource for example.)			
What barriers would you encounter in using this resource to help you work toward reaching your goal? Please explain in detail.			
List one way in which you could overcome the barriers that you listed in the previous row. Please explain in detail.			

LESSON PLANS

The lesson plans that follow are the ones detailed in the unit outline earlier in the chapter. They are designed to help students advance toward achieving unit objectives and prepare them to demonstrate the skill (evaluated in the assessment) successfully. The lessons assume a 50-minute class period. For lessons that require more time, consider planning multiple class periods to ensure adequate time for instruction and activities. Consider this prior to implementation.

Lesson plans include suggested activities, and those activities follow the lesson plans. Lesson plans and activities can be used together or independently to meet the needs of your classes.

Throughout the lesson plans, you will see the steps of the skill development model in **boldface type** after activities that address each skill development step.

Purpose

This lesson introduces students to the skill of being able to access valid and reliable information, products, and services. This lesson familiarizes students with the skill cues for the skill and has them become more familiar with the requirements and steps for applying this skill.

NHES Performance Indicators

None addressed in this introductory lesson. See the following lesson objectives.

Objectives

Students will be able to

- define the skill of being able to access valid and reliable information, products, and services and
- discuss the relevance of being able to access valid and reliable information, products, and services.

Skill Development Step

Step 1: definition, relevance, and educational outcomes

Materials

- Individual paper and pencils (or personal notepads) for instant activity
- Materials needed for the Two Truths and a Lie and To Trust or Not to Trust activities

Instant Activity

After students take their seats, they write their responses to the prompt: "If you are worried about your health, where can you go and what can you do to get help? List all of the places where you can find information, products, and services for addressing a health problem. (Be creative!)"

Introduction

- Introduce the new unit—Accessing Valid and Reliable Information, Products, and Services.
- Provide a definition of the skill. Being able to access valid and reliable information, products, and services is the ability to evaluate and use sources of health-related information, health products, and health services that you can trust. **(definition)**

Main Activities

1. Two Truths and a Lie (page 32)
2. To Trust or Not to Trust (page 33)

Closure

- *Debrief:* Ask students, what did we learn from these activities today? Why does it matter whether we can find valid and reliable information, products, and services? **(relevance)**
- *Tell students:* By the end of this unit, you will be able to determine when it is appropriate to access certain services and products to support or improve your health; be able to evaluate health-related information, products, and services; and have the ability to properly access information, products, and services related to a health issue or behavior of your choice. **(educational outcomes)**

Differentiation

- Activities could be scaffolded with worksheets.
- Posters or other visuals can be included with the definition.

Two Truths and a Lie
LESSON 1

NHES Performance Indicators
None addressed

Objectives
Students will be able to

- identify valid and reliable information, products, and services and
- identify misinformation about certain topic areas and products.

Skill Development Step
Step 1: introduction

Duration
10 to 15 minutes (or longer)

Materials

- Examples of online sources, products, and services
- The statements (explained in the Preparation section that follows) for each topic area or product

Description

Preparation

- Create statements (two that are true and one that is a lie or a myth, or is misinformation) about multiple topic areas or products that you want to cover with students.
- Keep your sources of information for students to see during the activity.

Activity

- Show students all three statements for each topic area or product.
- Ask students to identify the lie. They also should be able to explain why they think it is a lie.
- Once students have identified the lie correctly, show them all three resources that match the statements.
- Have students try to identify which resource the lie came from.
- Discuss the validity and reliability of each resource. You do not need to get too involved in this discussion, as this is just an introduction activity.

Debrief

- Ask students about any observations they might have about the differences (or similarities) between the true and misleading information.
- Ask students about why they should be able to find valid and reliable information.
- Ask students about any characteristics of valid and reliable versus invalid and unreliable resources.

Tips and Extensions
None

Modifications

- You could do this in a small group with a worksheet or in small groups as a game, in which students record their answers and win points for each correct answer.
- Ask students to record and submit one piece of misinformation or a myth they often hear about the topic. Use the student-driven myths in the activity.

To Trust or Not to Trust
LESSON 1

NHES Performance Indicators

None addressed

Objective

Discuss the relevance of being able to access valid and reliable information, products, and services to health outcomes.

Skill Development Step

Step 1: introduction

Duration

10 to 15 minutes (or longer)

Materials

Examples of online resources, products, and services. Try to use examples related to nutrition to stay consistent with the health topic of the unit.

Description

Preparation

- Prepare lists (even better, show the actual examples) of valid and reliable *and* not valid and not reliable online information sources, products, and services.
- Create Trust or Do Not Trust posters or papers to hang on either side of the room.

Activity

- Students move to one side of the room or another depending on whether they think the online information source, product, or service is valid and reliable.
- Show the example, and students move to the side of the room that corresponds with whether they trust it or not.
- After each, discuss why it is or is not a valid and reliable source.
- This could serve as an opportunity for introducing the steps of accessing valid and reliable information, products, and services.

Tips and Extensions

Have students work in small groups to explore some of the valid and reliable online information sources to see if they can identify characteristics of valid and reliable online sources of information.

Modifications

- Have students work in small groups. Each time you show a resource, students write whether you should trust or not trust it on a whiteboard.
- Make the activity like a game. Number each resource, and students, working alone or in small groups, identify whether or not each should be trusted, recording answers on a piece of paper. Then review the answers and see how students did. If you like, you can keep score. Each correct answer is worth a point. The winner is the student or group with the highest score (or select a winner randomly from students who received the highest score, if appropriate).

LESSON 2: ACCESSing Valid and Reliable Information, Products, and Services

Purpose
The previous lesson introduced students to the skill definition for being able to access valid and reliable information, products, and services. The activities helped students realize the importance and relevance of the skill. In this lesson, students will consider a health topic of interest in order to learn more about it while considering the steps of the skill.

NHES Performance Indicators
- *Grades 6 through 8:* Analyze the validity of nutrition-related information, products, and services (indicator 3.8.1).
- *Grades 9 through 12:* Evaluate the validity of health information, products, and services related to nutrition (indicator 3.12.1).

Objective
Students will be able to list the steps for determining the validity and reliability of a website.

Skill Development Steps
- Step 1: relevance (review from lesson 1)
- Step 2: steps of the skill
- Step 3: modeling

Materials
- Skill cues posters
- Materials needed to complete the Accessing Valid Health Information on the Internet activity

Instant Activity
After students take their seats, they write their responses to the prompt: "What are the characteristics you would look for to determine whether information, a product, or a service is valid and reliable?"

Introduction
- *Ask students:* Who can tell me, based on what we did last time, why middle or high school students should care about finding valid and reliable information, products, and services? **(relevance)**
- *Tell students:* Today we will discuss the characteristics that you should look for to determine whether you can trust an information source, product, or service.

Main Activities
1. Introduce the skill cues ACCESS. **(skill cues)** You might want to consider creating a worksheet, guided notes, or other resource so that students can have these notes in a folder or binder to refer to.
   - Accuracy
   - Credibility
   - Currency
   - Ease of use
   - Situations best used in
   - Support is provided for claims and information
2. Have students complete the Accessing Valid Health Information on the Internet activity (see page 36). **(modeling)**

Closure

Ticket to leave—submit the URL of the website that you chose to learn more about your topic of interest. You must include an ACCESS evaluation with the website.

Differentiation

- Have students work in pairs or in small groups.
- Provide guided notes or predetermine websites for students to evaluate.

Resources

- A.D.A.M., www.adam.com
- Trust It or Trash It?, www.trustortrash.org
- Search term *health information*

Accessing Valid Health Information on the Internet
LESSON 2

NHES Performance Indicators

- *Grades 6 through 8:* Analyze the validity of nutrition-related information, products, and services (indicator 3.8.1).
- *Grades 9 through 12:* Evaluate the validity of health information, products, and services related to nutrition (indicator 3.12.1).

Objective

Students will be able to list the steps for determining website validity and reliability.

Skill Development Step

Step 3: modeling

Duration

20 to 30 minutes

Materials

- List of sample topics for students to research
- Laptops, tablet computers, or desktop computers
- Provide students with the Website Evaluation Record worksheet (hard copy or electronic copy via Google Forms).
- Provide students with links to the Website Evaluation Checklist via Google Forms.

Description

1. Conduct this activity after you have introduced National Health Education Standard 3 and the skill cues. Begin by modeling the use of the Website Evaluation Checklist and making connections to the ACCESS skill cues by evaluating a website together as a class.
2. Students choose a nutrition-related topic they would like to research. Provide a list of suggested topics from which students may choose, or they can use an idea of their own.
3. Students use laptops, tablet computers, or desktop computers to research the validity of three websites—two chosen by the teacher and one chosen by the student and related to their topic of interest—using the Website Evaluation Checklist. Have students fill out a separate form for each website evaluated.
4. Summarize the findings from the Website Evaluation Checklist for each website on the Website Evaluation Record.
5. The purpose of the activity is not to complete the research first but to help students choose a website through a series of evaluation steps.

Tips and Extensions

- Practicing the process of using the evaluation tool helps students experience having an "aha!" moment while they look at each site. Have students open both the evaluation tool and the website they are viewing.
- Provide students with a worksheet (as an attachment) that enables them to fill in each yes or no answer. These will be added to the final presentation of the project.

Modification

For students needing accommodation, provide access to Trust It or Trash It?, a website that helps students with a simpler form of evaluating. For English language learners, select a shorter list of evaluation statements for them to complete.

Resources

- *Skills-Based Health Education* by Mary Connolly
- Health on the Net
- A.D.A.M.
- Trust It or Trash It?
- Search term *health information*

Submitted by Claudia T. Brown, former high school health teacher in Massachusetts.

Website Evaluation Record

Name: _____ Date: _____

Instructions: Please use this sheet to takes notes on web evaluation only. Eventually, these notes will help you complete a reflection on how valid each website is with regard to your topic.

Centers for Disease Control and Prevention

Positive (+)	Negative (–)

Wikipedia

Positive (+)	Negative (–)

Student Choice

Positive (+)	Negative (–)

Website Evaluation Checklist

Name: _____ Date: _____

The purpose of the site is stated clearly.
Yes
No
Not applicable

The information does not appear to be an infomercial.
Yes
No
Not applicable

There is no bias.
Yes
No
Not applicable

If the site is opinionated, the author discusses all sides of the issue, respecting each point of view.
Yes
No
Not applicable

All aspects of the subject are covered sufficiently.
Yes
No
Not applicable

External links fully cover the subject.
Yes
No
Not applicable

The site has been updated in the past six months.
Yes
No
Not applicable

The information on my topic is accurate.
Yes
No
Not applicable

Sources are documented clearly.
Yes
No
Not applicable

The website states that it conforms to Health on the Net or A.D.A.M.

Yes

No

Not applicable

The site is sponsored by or is associated with an institution or organization.

Yes

No

Not applicable

Individually created sites have the author's credentials stated clearly (education background, profes-sional experience, etc.).

Yes

No

Not applicable

Contact information for the author or webmaster is included.

Yes

No

Not applicable

It is evident whom the author is addressing (youth, minority, general audience, etc.).

Yes

No

Not applicable

The level of detail is appropriate for the audience.

Yes

No

Not applicable

The reading level is appropriate for the audience.

Yes

No

Not applicable

Technical terms are appropriate for the audience.

Yes

No

Not applicable

Internal links increase the usefulness of the site.

Yes

No

Not applicable

Information is retrievable within a reasonable amount of time.

Yes

No

Not applicable

(continued)

Website Evaluation Checklist   *(continued)*

A search instrument is required to make this site functional.
Yes
No
Not applicable

A search instrument is provided.
Yes
No
Not applicable

The site is organized logically, making it easy to find information.
Yes
No
Not applicable

If software is needed to use the page, download links are included (e.g., Adobe Acrobat Reader).
Yes
No
Not applicable

External links are relevant and suitable for this site.
Yes
No
Not applicable

External links function properly.
Yes
No
Not applicable

External links are current and reflect changes that occur in the field.
Yes
No
Not applicable

External links are appropriate for the audience.
Yes
No
Not applicable

External links connect to reliable information from dependable sources.
Yes
No
Not applicable

The pages include external links to appropriate organizations.
Yes
No
Not applicable

Educational graphics and art add to the helpfulness of this site.

Yes

No

Not applicable

Decorative graphics do not slow downloading significantly.

Yes

No

Not applicable

A text-only option exists for text-only web browsers.

Yes

No

Not applicable

The usefulness of the site is not affected by the text-only option.

Yes

No

Not applicable

Options (large print, audio) exist for people with disabilities.

Yes

No

Not applicable

If the audio and video components of the site cannot be accessed, the information on the site is still complete.

Yes

No

Not applicable

Submitted by Claudia T. Brown, former high school health teacher in Massachusetts. Reprinted, by permission, from M. Connolly, 2012, *Skills-based health education* (Jones & Bartlett Learning).

LESSON 3: Grocery Games

Purpose

Now that students have been introduced to the skill, know the skill cues, and have seen the skill modeled, it is time to move on to practicing the skill within the context of nutrition. This lesson and the next will focus on practicing the skill within the context of nutrition.

NHES Performance Indicators

- *Grades 6 through 8:* Analyze the validity of nutrition-related information, products, and services (indicator 3.8.1).
- *Grades 9 through 12:* Evaluate the validity of health information, products, and services related to nutrition (indicator 3.12.1).

Objectives

Students will be able to demonstrate healthy eating practices and behaviors to improve their health and that of others.

Skill Development Step

Step 4: skill practice

Materials

- Materials needed to complete the Grocery Games activity
- Computers

Instant Activity

Using their memory, students try to list and define the skill cues (ACCESS) in their notebooks or journals.

Introduction

- Review the skill cues.
- Tell students, "Today we are going to practice evaluating the validity and reliability of nutrition information." **(practice)**

Main Activities

1. Grocery Games (see page 43) **(practice)**
2. Grocery Games extension: Hand out recipes to students and ask them to identify the necessary food items and where to locate them in a grocery store.

Closure

Students complete an exit ticket by responding to the following: How do you know the difference between a reliable and valid source of information and an unreliable or invalid source of information? List two valid and reliable sources of nutrition information.

Differentiation

You can preselect websites for students, reducing the amount of time that is spent.

Grocery Games

LESSON 3

NHES Performance Indicators

- *Grades 6 through 8:* Analyze the validity of nutrition-related information, products, and services (indicator 3.8.1).
- *Grades 9 through 12:* Evaluate the validity of health information, products, and services related to nutrition (indicator 3.12.1).

Objective

Students will be able to demonstrate healthy eating practices and behaviors to improve the health of themselves and others.

Skill Development Step

Step 4: skill practice

Duration

20 minutes

Materials

- Grocery store map (can be found in the web resource)
- Guiding questions (can be found in the web resource)
- Pictures of food or various food items with labels and prices
- Website Evaluation Worksheet

Description

- Students practice making healthy food selections at the grocery store.
- Before conducting this activity, you should either collect various food items or print pictures of food items to place around the room.
- Place food items or pictures around the classroom, using the grocery store map template as a guide.
- Explain to students that they are to practice evaluating sources of health information for validity and to help them demonstrate healthy eating practices.
- Review indicators for evaluating a website.
  - Who wrote the article or developed the site?
  - Is the information accurate?
  - How difficult was it to publish the information? (What is the domain? Is it a government site?)
- Explain to students that they are to evaluate websites and other sources of nutrition information to help them make nutritious choices while grocery shopping. You can allow students to choose their own websites, or you can preselect several sites for students to evaluate.
- At each food station, students evaluate the website's information and use the most accurate site to select the most nutritious item.
- Allow 10 to 12 minutes for completion of the activity.
- At the conclusion of the activity, students participate in a discussion in which they explain why they selected certain food items, what sources of information they used to make their choices, and why they selected the source of information.
- Students complete an exit ticket with the following question: How do you know the difference between a reliable source of information and an unreliable source of information?

Tips and Extensions

■ After students complete this activity in the classroom, take them to a grocery store, where they are to use their nutrition information to plan meals or snacks.

■ Assign students a recipe and ask them to use this process to select recipe ingredients.

Modification

You can preselect websites for students, reducing the amount of time.

Submitted by Erin Lumpkins, Health Education Specialist, District of Columbia Public Schools.

Website Evaluation Worksheet

Use this sheet to evaluate the quality of an Internet source. Add the points in each category to determine whether the source is credible.

	Site 1	Site 2	Site 3
Author's credentials I can't tell who the author is. 0 points The author is listed. 1 point Based on the information I found, the author or organization is qualified to write about this topic. 3 points This was written by a government agency or national news organization. 3 points	Score _____	Score _____	Score _____
Accuracy of the information I can't tell when the article was written. 0 points The article was written by a person or organization that has a conflict of interest. 0 points The date is listed, and the article is current enough to be relevant. 1 point The article presented looks professional and is grammatically correct. 1 point The information is unbiased and presents more than one side of an issue. 1 point The article lists other sources of information. 1 point The article has clear references for statistics and facts. 3 points	Score _____	Score _____	Score _____
Type of website .com, .5 points .biz, 0 points .net, 0 points .us, 0 points .org, .5 points .co, 0 points .edu, 2 points .gov, 3 points .mil, 3 points	Score _____	Score _____	Score _____
	Total _____	Total _____	Total _____

Should I use this article?

11 or more points: *This a great source for valid and reliable information!*

6 to 10 points: *Use this information along with other sources of information.*

0 to 5 points: *This is not a good source for valid and reliable information.*

Purpose

This lesson provides an opportunity to continue practicing the skill of accessing valid and reliable information about nutrition.

NHES Performance Indicators

Grades 6 Through 8

- Analyze the validity of health information, products, and services related to a variety of health-related topics (indicator 3.8.1).
- Access valid health information about nutrition from home, school, and the community (indicator 3.8.2).

Grades 9 Through 12

- Evaluate the validity of health information, products, and services related to a variety of health-related topics (indicator 3.12.1).
- Use resources from home, school, and the community that provide valid health information about nutrition (indicator 3.12.2).

Objectives

Students will be able to

- identify unhealthy foods to avoid while researching healthier alternatives;
- research ingredients used in processed food and the effects of these ingredients on the human body; and
- choose food that supports lifelong health.

Skill Development Step

Step 4: skill practice

Materials

Materials needed to complete the What Is in Our Food? activity

Instant Activity

After students take their seats, they write their responses to the prompt: "Turn to a partner and name three snacks items you eat regularly from at least two different areas of the grocery store. Rate each snack item from 1 to 10 in terms of how healthy the snack item is, with a rank of 1 being the healthiest and 10 being the least healthy."

Introduction

- Explain the objectives for the class.
- Introduce the concept of moderation and help students understand that while all foods can have a place in a healthy diet, some foods are better choices for eating on a regular basis.
- Discuss the importance of eating foods that are closer to a natural state and the role of preservatives in food.

Main Activities

What Is in Our Food? (see page 47) **(practice)**

Closure

Exit ticket—Write down two foods that you eat as snacks and identify a healthier alternative for each.

(continued)

Differentiation

- Print sheets with various foods commonly seen as snack items in your school. Give students the ratings list and have them compare and contrast foods.
- Consider visiting local stores, bodegas, or shops that students might frequent to select items that are common choices.

Resources

- *Fed Up* movie and educational materials, www.fedupmovie.com
- Valid and reliable web resources for environmental health, food policies, food regulation, and the like (for example, www.EWG.org)

What Is in Our Food?

LESSON 4

NHES Performance Indicators

Grades 6 Through 8

- Analyze the validity of nutrition-related information, products, and services (indicator 3.8.1).
- Access valid health information about nutrition from home, school, and the community (indicator 3.8.2).

Grades 9 Through 12

- Evaluate the validity of health information, products, and services related to nutrition (indicator 3.12.1).
- Use resources from home, school, and the community that provide valid health information about nutrition (indicator 3.12.2).

Objectives

Students will be able to

- identify unhealthy foods to avoid and research healthier alternatives;
- research ingredients used in processed food and the effects of these ingredients on the human body; and
- choose foods that support lifelong health.

Skill Development Step

Step 4: skill practice

Duration

100 to 110 minutes

Materials

- Computer or tablet for each student, pair, or group
- Internet access

Description

1. This activity is intended for students who have a background in basic nutrition information such as the United States Department of Agriculture's (USDA) Dietary Guidelines for Americans, obesity, reading food labels, and calories in versus calories out; and who have created personal nutrition menus. It is an extension into understanding further how sugar consumption has contributed to unhealthy diets and the rise in obesity rates.

2. Students use the Environmental Working Group's (EWG) website, www.ewg.org, to research snacks that they eat, choose one snack and find its EWG health rating, and research a healthier snack using the EWG guide. Students have to find another valid and reliable resource to support their evaluation of the snack they chose.

3. When students complete their EWG food assessment, they research their beauty products using the same tools from EWG and will have to find another valid and reliable resource to confirm findings.

4. When students are done with this assessment, have a class discussion on student findings and reactions, what they will do to change their lifestyles, how they will communicate this to their family, and ways to stay healthy when choosing foods and products.

Tips and Extensions

- If you are unfamiliar with the topics included in this lesson, we recommend the Fed Up Nutrition Education Kit for additional information.
- You can conduct this learning activity as part of a larger unit using the Fed-Up Nutrition Education Kit.

Modifications

- Use technology (word processing software or interactive apps) to write reflection questions.
- Students work in small groups to reflect on the movie.
- Students work with partners to complete the EWG research project.

Resources

- *Fed Up* movie and educational materials, www.fedupmovie.com
- Valid and reliable web resources for environmental health, food policies, food regulation, and the like (for example, www.EWG.org)

Modified from a submission from Danielle Petrucci, middle school health teacher in Massachusetts.

Purpose

These lessons provide opportunities for students to continue practicing the skill of accessing valid and reliable information related to a nutrition topic of their choice. This one lesson plan covers two class periods, and we anticipate that the corresponding activity will take multiple class sessions to complete.

NHES Performance Indicators

Grades 6 Through 8

- Analyze the validity of nutrition-related information, products, and services (indicator 3.8.1).
- Access valid health information about nutrition from home, school, and the community (indicator 3.8.2).

Grades 9 Through 12

- Evaluate the validity of health information, products, and services related to nutrition (indicator 3.12.1).
- Use resources from home, school, and the community that provide valid health information about nutrition (indicator 3.12.2).

Objective

Students will be able to apply and demonstrate their knowledge and understanding of a nutrition-related topic of their choice.

Skill Development Step

Step 4: skill practice

Materials

- Sample podcasts
- Materials needed for the Podcasts activity

Instant Activity

After students take their seats, they write their responses to the prompt: "Based on what you have learned so far about accessing valid and reliable information, products, and services, what do you think are three topics that students your age do not have the appropriate information about? Why?"

Introduction

- Introduce podcasts as a way that many people now get information about health (and other) topics they want to learn more about.
- Show an example of a podcast. (Consider using a SHAPE America podcast to show how you stay current and receive professional development.)

Main Activity

Health Podcasts (see page 51) **(practice)**

Closure

Discuss the experience of developing a podcast and why students chose the topic of importance to their group. For a writing exercise, students could list three new and useful things they have learned about their topic as a result of this project.

Differentiation

- Provide scripts or other guides to help students, if necessary.
- Students could choose a different medium (but still use technology) to present the information.

(continued)

Homework

Students complete their podcast work (depending on time and structure).

Resources

Educational blogs and websites such as Tools2Engage for tips on using podcasts

Health Podcasts

NHES Performance Indicators

Grades 6 Through 8

- Analyze the validity of nutrition-related information, products, and services (indicator 3.8.1).
- Access valid health information about nutrition from home, school, and the community (indicator 3.8.2).

Grades 9 Through 12

- Evaluate the validity of health information, products, and services related to nutrition (indicator 3.12.1).
- Use resources from home, school, and the community that provide valid health information about nutrition (indicator 3.12.2).

Objective

Students will be able to apply and demonstrate their knowledge and understanding of a nutrition-related topic of their choice.

Skill Development Step

Step 4: skill practice

Duration

100 to 110 minutes

Materials

- Something to capture audio (such as smartphones, headphones with a built-in microphone, or a tablet or desktop computer).
- App to create the podcast (suggestions include Garageband and Audacity)

Description

Podcasts have become easy to create, and this activity could result in a podcast that you create from students' audio submissions or that students create themselves, depending on their age and ability with the software and hardware. This activity replaces traditional pen and paper extended writing activities, although we recommend writing a script prior to recording. You may ask for the script to be submitted as part of the activity.

Modeling (if Appropriate)

Have students listen to a podcast that you created that models expectations for the assignment and provides a model for how to justify the validity and reliability of resources (you can mention the resources in the podcast or list them separately). After students listen, have them identify how the skill cues were represented in the podcast and how the example met expectations for the assignment. You can create podcasts that align with any health topic(s) that are being covered in the unit. The podcasts could also be used as a method for presenting the necessary health information for the unit.

Practice

After teaching the health topic, create a series of prompts that will elicit deep responses. An easy way to do this would be to take the National Health Education Standards performance indicators (particularly for Standard 1, but any would work) and use them as prompts. In groups of no more than four, students create an audio recording in response to the initial prompt. For example, an eighth-grade class is looking at National Health Education Standard 5, Decision Making. You give them this prompt: "Write and record a script in which you tell your peers how they can identify which health-related situations require a thoughtful decision-making process. Explain the steps of the process in your recording."

Tips and Extensions

- Use student phones and headphones with a built-in microphone to get the best quality audio. If students know that this podcast might be shared, they will work hard to ensure that what they turn in is of the highest quality.

- Share the podcast with other classes or on social media (with permission). Students could review the podcasts. The individual recordings could be used as a public service announcement. You can embed the podcasts into e-books to share with future students, essentially creating a "flipped classroom" (a term used in the education world to refer to classrooms where students engage in learning, usually online, outside of class and come to class ready to engage in activities that extend what was learned online). Students can listen to a podcast in advance of a lesson and come to the lesson with questions.

- You can use this as a formative or summative assessment, and you can use the end product for further extension work.

Modification

Students could choose to record long responses or just say a sentence or two, as long as they have contributed to the group effort and script writing.

Resources

Educational blogs and websites such as Tools2Engage for tips on using podcasts

Modified from a submission from Andy Milne, high school health teacher in Illinois.

Purpose

The previous lessons asked students to record a podcast that identified valuable sources of information about a nutrition-related topic that is important to them. In this lesson, students will continue to use the topic they selected to research for identifying information and identifying products or services that will help students maintain or improve their health.

NHES Performance Indicators

Grades 6 Through 8

- Analyze the validity of nutrition-related information, products, and services (indicator 3.8.1).
- Access valid health information about nutrition from home, school, and the community (indicator 3.8.2).
- Determine the accessibility of nutrition-related products that enhance health (indicator 3.8.3).
- Describe situations that may require professional health services for assistance with nutrition-related health issues (Indicator 3.8.4).
- Locate valid and reliable nutrition-related products and services (indicator 3.8.5).

Grades 9 Through 12

- Evaluate the validity of health information, products, and services related to nutrition (indicator 3.12.1).
- Use resources from home, school, and the community that provide valid health information about nutrition (indicator 3.12.2).
- Determine the accessibility of nutrition-related products and services that enhance health (indicator 3.12.3).
- Determine when professional health services may be required for assistance with nutrition-related health issues or support (indicator 3.12.4).
- Access valid and reliable nutrition-related products and services (indicator 3.12.5).

Objectives

Students will be able to

- apply and demonstrate their ability to locate products and resources to maintain or improve their health and
- access and evaluate valid and reliable products and services related to their health topic.

Skill Development Steps

- Step 1: relevance (review)
- Step 4: skill practice

Materials

Materials needed for the Who and What Are in My Neighborhood? activity

Instant Activity

Students will return to their small group and prepare their work station to research products and services about their health topic.

Introduction

Refer to how information is important to help guide our decisions, but information alone won't change our behavior. Explain how we also need to be able to locate the products and services to support our efforts. **(relevance)**

(continued)

Main Activities

1. Who and What Are in My Neighborhood? activity (see page 55) **(practice)**
2. Groups present their maps to the class, explaining the validity and reliability of products and services and any tips to help their peers access these resources.

Closure

Students individually write down one new service that they are willing to use to address a health-related concern and why that new service or product is valuable to them and their health. (Ideally, each student would write about a concern that he or she is facing currently, although it could be something that the student is concerned about encountering in the future.)

Differentiation

Provide a list of local services that students could access and provide them with one or two to research.

Homework

Students complete the assignment in a group (depending on time and structure).

Resources

List of local community resources

Who and What Are in My Neighborhood?

LESSONS 7 AND 8

NHES Performance Indicators

Grades 6 Through 8

- Analyze the validity of nutrition-related information, products, and services (indicator 3.8.1).
- Access valid health information about nutrition from home, school, and the community (indicator 3.8.2).
- Determine the accessibility of nutrition-related products that enhance health (indicator 3.8.3).
- Describe situations that may require professional health services for assistance with nutrition-related health issues or support (indicator 3.8.4).
- Locate valid and reliable nutrition-related products and services (indicator 3.8.5).

Grades 9 Through 12

- Evaluate the validity of health information, products, and services related to nutrition (indicator 3.12.1).
- Use resources from home, school, and the community that provide valid health information about nutrition (indicator 3.12.2).
- Determine the accessibility of nutrition-related products and services that enhance health (indicator 3.12.3).
- Determine when professional health services may be required for assistance with nutrition-related health issues or support (indicator 3.12.4).
- Access valid and reliable nutrition-related products and services (indicator 3.12.5).

Objectives

This activity addresses no additional lesson objectives.

Skill Development Step

Step 4: skill practice

Duration

100 to 110 minutes

Materials

Computers or other electronic devices

Description

Part I

- Place students into small groups.
- Provide students with a health topic or issue (or have students choose an area they want to look into based on previous activities).
- Students work to locate at least three products and services that might be useful in addressing this health topic.
- Students choose one resource and complete the following:
  - Create a list of four to six questions that they (or their peers) might have about the resource or service (or what they might want to know in general).
  - Students call the resource and try to get answers to the questions.

Part II

Students create a map that shows the locations of services that they determine are valid and reliable, provide directions and transportation options to each, and give a justification for why it is valid and reliable. Students may create the maps by hand or by using a computer mapping site.

Tips and Extensions

- Provide students with a list of examples of the types of places to consider. Examples could be health clinics, food stores, or pharmacies.
- Have members of the community resources come and speak to students.

Modification

Depending on technology capacity, students can complete the activity by computer or by hand.

Resources

Research your local health department to see whether it has a list of local clinics or health service providers at low or no cost.

Purpose

This lesson provides class time to work on the final assessment or an opportunity to review key learning from the unit.

NHES Performance Indicators

Grades 6 Through 8

- Analyze the validity of nutrition-related health information, products, and services related to a variety of health-related topics (indicator 3.8.1).
- Access valid health information about a variety of nutrition topics from home, school, and the community (indicator 3.8.2).
- Determine the accessibility of nutrition-related products that enhance health (indicator 3.8.3).
- Describe situations that may require professional health services (indicator 3.8.4).
- Locate valid and reliable nutrition-related health products and services (indicator 3.8.5).

Grades 9 Through 12

- Evaluate the validity of health information, products, and services (indicator 3.12.1).
- Use resources from home, school, and the community that provide valid health information (indicator 3.12.2).
- Determine the accessibility of products and services that enhance health (indicator 3.12.3).
- Determine when professional health services may be required (indicator 3.12.4).
- Access valid and reliable health products and services (indicator 3.12.5).

Objectives

This activity addresses no additional lesson objectives aside from the NHES performance indicators.

Skill Development Step

Step 5: evaluation and feedback

Materials

- List of local community resources
- Access to phone, tablet, or computer for research

Instant Activity

After students take their seats, they write their responses to the prompt: "As a result of learning this skill, what two important aspects will you remember when accessing health-related information?"

Introduction

Welcome students to class and answer any questions they have about the skill.

Main Activities

Hand out the assessment prompt and instruct students to complete the assessment during their time in class.

Closure

Have students return the completed assignment and share one piece of key learning with the class.

(continued)

Differentiation

Allow students to work in pairs or small groups for each category and then share their learning with the group.

Homework

Students complete their assignment with a group (depending on time and structure).

BONUS ACTIVITY

This activity is not included in the unit plan but could be added into this unit or used as a supplemental activity for your accessing valid and reliable information, products, and services unit.

Being a Health Reporter

NHES Performance Indicators

Grades 6 Through 8

- Analyze the validity of health information, products, and services (indicator 3.8.1).
- Access valid health information from home, school, and the community (indicator 3.8.2).

Grades 9 Through 12

- Evaluate the validity of health information, products, and services (indicator 3.12.1).
- Use resources from home, school, and the community that provide valid health information (indicator 3.12.2).

Objective

Students will be able to apply and demonstrate their knowledge and understanding of the selected health topic.

Skill Development Step

Step 4: skill practice

Duration

45 to 60 minutes

Materials

Worksheet: Two-page document in advance with six text boxes containing the initial questions. This is shared digitally, with students typing into the box, saving, and returning the document online.

Description

- Provide students with a series of questions written in the style of an email or tweet from a peer. Questions should relate to a particular health topic area (you could also use this with other NHES skills—see example that follows). Students must access valid and reliable resources in order to answer the questions in the form of a magazine or newspaper article, and they respond in their roles as health-literate journalists.
- Responses must be detailed and use health-literate language. The response must include the valid and reliable resources that were used to research the article. Students also should submit an evaluation of the resources used to justify their validity and reliability. Award 2 points for each question and require two good pieces of information to earn those points. Also, award points for their justifications.
- Students may write in any style but some of the best responses come from those students who get into character and write like a journalist.

Example: Eighth-grade class looking at National Health Education Standard 5, Decision Making.
   Q1—@confusedteen tweets: "When should I make a decision on my own, and when should I seek advice? #confused"

This question is related to the performance indicator 5.8.3: Distinguish when individual or collaborative decision making is appropriate.

Include as many questions as you wish that allow students to show what they know. (We suggest using six questions and encouraging full sentences and extended answers, when appropriate.)

Tips and Extensions

- Seeing examples of good work from previous classes allows students to understand what is being asked of them from this task. Informing students that the best responses might be displayed, printed in a magazine article, or shared on social media (with permission) usually raises the standard of the finished product.

- After returning the graded material, have students get together in groups and rewrite the perfect answers for each question based on teacher feedback. This could be used as a script for a public service announcement or podcast recording.

- You can use this as a formative or summative assessment. You can use the end product for further extension work.

Modifications

- Allow rewrites.
- Ensure that the language used in the questions accommodates the reading levels of all students.

Modified from a submission from Andy Milne, high school health teacher in Illinois.

CHAPTER 4

Understanding and Analyzing Influences on One's Health Behaviors

This chapter examines the skill of analyzing influences, Standard 2 of the National Health Education Standards. In this chapter, you will find examples of ways to help your students develop the skill of analyzing influences. The assessments, lesson plans, and learning activities in this chapter are ready to use. We also have included skill cues that you could use when teaching the skill. Everything that you need to help students develop the skill of analyzing influences can be found here.

The materials presented here are designed to support each step of the skill development model (see chapter 1) and reflect a backward-design approach (see chapter 2). The first items presented are the unit objectives. The unit objectives are the end—what you want your students to be able to do once they have developed the skills. When examining Standard 2, you will notice that the following influences are highlighted: family, peers, culture, media, and technology. In this chapter, we have focused our unit on the influence of media. You can easily modify most of these activities to fit into other influences as well. After the unit objectives, we provide an overview of the unit, a sample assessment, lesson plans, and then learning activities. Modify materials as necessary to meet the needs of your students.

This unit does not go in depth into any specific health information or topics, but it touches on many different behaviors that adolescents might encounter. The materials presented here provide opportunities for students to explore a variety of influences and uses school- and community-level data to ensure relevance. If appropriate, add health topics and functional information to your unit as needed. Just be sure to keep the focus on the skill.

SKILL OVERVIEW

We all make health-related decisions on a regular basis, but we don't always take the time to consider what factors might influence those choices. In fact, all of our decisions are influenced in some way, whether it is the people around us, our own attitudes, or the environment we are in (just to name a few). Being able to analyze internal and external influence helps our students to consider what factors are influences, the messages received from the influences, and the impact the influences might have on health-related decisions.

There are many examples of possible influences on our decisions. One influence can be something about ourselves—an internal drive to be healthier, to do the right thing, or to make the world a better place. It also could be our desire to fit in, look cool, or impress others. Maybe the influence is external, from a parent who expects his or her child to reach certain expectations, from friends who exert peer pressure, or from some forms of media that portray an often unrealistic image of success, beauty, and health. However, culture, technology, environment, socioeconomic status, and a whole host of other factors also can influence our health decisions. It would be impossible for us to cover all of these possible influences in our health classes. The good news is that you don't have to because once students have learned the skill of analyzing influences, they can apply the process to any influence! For example, once students are able to analyze the influence of media, they can use that same ability to analyze the influence of peers, family, or the environment. This is similar to a student's learning to throw a ball. Once the student can do that, he or she can apply that skill in multiple sports and activities.

Being able to analyze both internal and external influences is a skill that helps our students think more critically about their health decisions and forms a foundation for learning other skills, because being able to analyze potential (or actual) influences effectively in situations is key, whether you are setting a goal, advocating for improved health, or communicating with others. Being able to identify and examine influences on behaviors and decisions will help students make more informed, thoughtful, and, we hope, effective health-enhancing decisions that lead to healthier practices throughout life.

In comparison with other skills of the National Health Education Standards, analyzing influences has the most performance indicators at the secondary level, and rightly so. Consider that family, peers, culture, school and community norms, social and other media, technology, health policy, or personal beliefs and practices may influence adolescents. The National Health Education Standards work to capture all of these aspects within the skill through the performance indicators. However, within your curriculum, it will be important to determine which aspects of the skill are covered at various grade levels. While it is true that the process for analyzing influences is similar for each type of influence, there are certain considerations that are important to discuss and have your students contemplate. For example, when considering cultural influences, you might wish to highlight culture as a broader concept that can encompass things such as race, ethnicity, peer group, gender, social class, and the like. This broader concept of culture takes time to delve into, and having students determine appropriate artifacts representing cultures they belong to and how the culture plays a role in their health choices is a way for students to share insights and build understanding.

When talking about personal values and beliefs, you also might wish to discuss how family, peer, and friend relationships both influence and are influenced by our choices. Having students consider what they value and in turn where those values come from can be a powerful and eye-opening experience for students. Then, if you were to take the conversation to a larger community, national, or global level, your students might engage in conversations about how the policies leaders create can help or hinder the health of the population. Perhaps you choose to broaden the discussion and introduce students to the dimensions of wellness and have students identify various influences across different dimensions. This allows them to select from a variety of influences while keeping it relevant to their personal health. While these are all valuable and important lessons to teach students, most health teachers need to streamline the conversation based on available time and intended outcomes for students at a given grade level.

Another key component of this skill is that throughout the entire process, students are asked to think critically by describing, explaining, and analyzing various influences. While media is the context used in the following example, it will be important for you to help students understand that media influences do not stand alone. Media can be a powerful source of influence (or no specific influence for that matter), but it cannot operate independent of other factors in our lives. Students must consider what the media message is around a particular topic *and* how media can act as an influence. For example, when looking at print advertisements, you should discuss both the way print ads are used to influence behavior and the messages that are being sent when cartoon characters are used to sell products with high amounts of sugar or low nutritional value to children. Students might have a hard time being able to recognize the influence of media because some forms of media often use subtle messages and are an influence that, with the unprecedented access to technology that students have at such young ages, often is just a part of their day-to-day lives. At the same time, the multidimensional nature of media provides ample opportunities for engaging students in relevant and meaningful ways.

When assessing this standard, keep in mind that students must demonstrate their ability to identify influences, discuss whether the influence is positive or negative, describe messages they receive from these influences, understand the impact the influence might have on them, and ultimately, determine whether the influence is one to embrace to support their health or to mitigate to prevent harm to themselves or others. You can do this through a variety of performance tasks and self-reflections. The process however, may be difficult for students. The difficulty arises when students struggle with either identifying influences (because they have not previously thought in this way) or when they begin to recognize people or settings have a negative effect on their health, and it becomes an internal struggle to understand these feelings. A struggle can also arise during the process of reflection and increasing self-awareness. Reflection, in general, can be difficult, and some students will be more thoughtful and more comfortable than others. This is compounded when students are asked to reflect on themselves and their personal behaviors. We encourage you to be supportive and allow your students to work through the process in a meaningful way. When students are given the flexibility to explore on a personal level, the results can be very powerful.

Table 4.1 shows the performance indicators from the National Health Education Standards that outline what students should be able to do within each grade span in grades 6 through 8 and 9 through 12.

TABLE 4.1   Performance Indicators for Standard 2 of the NHES (Grades 6-12)

	6-8		9-12
2.8.1	Examine how the family influences the health of adolescents.	2.12.1	Analyze how the family influences the health of individuals.
2.8.2	Describe the influence of culture on health beliefs, practices, and behaviors.	2.12.2	Analyze how the culture supports and challenges health beliefs, practices, and behaviors.
2.8.3	Describe how peers influence healthy and unhealthy behaviors.	2.12.3	Analyze how peers influence healthy and unhealthy behaviors.
2.8.4	Analyze how the school and community can affect personal health practices and behaviors.	2.12.4	Evaluate how the school and community can affect personal health practice and behaviors.
2.8.5	Analyze how messages from media influence health behaviors.	2.12.5	Evaluate the effect of media on personal and family health.
2.8.6	Analyze the influence of technology on personal and family health.	2.12.6	Evaluate the impact of technology on personal, family, and community health.
2.8.7	Explain how the perceptions of norms influence healthy and unhealthy behaviors.	2.12.7	Analyze how the perceptions of norms influence healthy and unhealthy behaviors.
2.8.8	Explain the influence of personal values and beliefs on individual health practices and behaviors.	2.12.8	Analyze the influence of personal values and beliefs on individual health practices and behaviors.
2.8.9	Describe how some health risk behaviors can influence the likelihood of engaging in unhealthy behaviors.	2.12.9	Analyze how some health risk behaviors can influence the likelihood of engaging in unhealthy behaviors.
2.8.10	Explain how school and public health policies can influence health promotion and disease prevention.	2.12.10	Analyze how public health policies and government regulations can influence health promotion and disease prevention.

Reprinted, with permission, from the American Cancer Society. *National Health Education Standards: Achieving Excellence,* Second Edition (Atlanta, GA: American Cancer Society, 2007), 24-36, cancer.org/bookstore

SKILL CUES

Skill cues are used during step 2 of the skill development model to highlight the critical elements of the skill—in this case, analyzing influences. The sample skill cues included here are intended for grades 6 through 12 (figure 4.1) and to support your students on their journey. We encourage modifications at the local level to meet the needs of your students. There is no wrong way to create skill cues. Just keep in mind that you want the skill cues to represent the critical aspects of the skill, be memorable for students, and serve as reminders of the steps they need to implement when using the skill.

Analyzing Influences

STANDARD 2

Students will analyze the influence of family, peers, culture, media, technology, and other factors on health behaviors.

Identify the influence.

Analyze the influence.

- How do I know it is influencing me?
- What messages am I receiving from this influence?
- Is this a positive or a negative influence?
- How much is this influencing my thoughts, values, beliefs, or actions?

Examine factors and impact.

- How are other factors interacting with this influence?
- How might these factors affect my thoughts, values, beliefs, and behavior choices?

Consider an action plan.

- Do I need to do anything about this influence?
- What is the best plan of action for handling this influence in my life?

 **HUMAN KINETICS**

From S. Benes and H. Alperin, 2019, *Lesson planning for skills-based health education* (Champaign, IL: Human Kinetics). Reprinted, by permission, from S. Benes and H. Alperin, 2016, *The essentials of teaching health education* (Champaign, IL: Human Kinetics)

FIGURE 4.1   Skill cues for the skill of analyzing influences.

UNIT OUTLINE

This section includes an outline of the unit for Standard 2; table 4.2 shows this outline, including lesson titles, lesson objectives, the step(s) of the skill development model that are addressed in each lesson, and the titles of the main learning activities in each lesson.

The materials included here are appropriate, with certain modifications, for students in grades 6 through 12. Unit objectives are included for both grades 6 through 8 and 9 through 12. Rather than focus on any specific health topics, this unit focuses on examining multiple influences on health that are particularly relevant for adolescents, including personal values and beliefs, perceptions of norms, media, as well as social media and technology. You will notice that there are areas where you are asked to use data from your school and community to identify behaviors that students are (or are not) engaging in. This would be a place to include functional information if you wanted to add to the unit. You might also focus on specific health topics in lessons 5 to 7. We have left it open ended intentionally so that you can explore the many behaviors subject to influence (rather than focusing only on behaviors within a specific topic area). It is also important to note that some performance indicators from Standard 2 are not covered in this unit. Review your scope and sequence to ensure adequate coverage of Standard 2 within your health program(s).

In the final assessment for this skill, students are asked to reflect on their social media use and how the time they spend on social media influences their health choices. By tracking the time they spend on social media and creating a written reflection, students will be able to consider the influence that social media might be having on their lives.

Unit Objectives, Grades 6 Through 8

By the end of this unit, students will be able to

- analyze how messages from some forms of media influence health behaviors (indicator 2.8.5);
- analyze the influence of technology on personal and family health (indicator 2.8.6);
- explain how the perceptions of norms influence healthy and unhealthy behaviors (indicator 2.8.7); and
- explain the influence of personal values and beliefs on individual health practices and behaviors (indicator 2.8.8).

Unit Objectives, Grades 9 Through 12

By the end of this unit, students will be able to

- evaluate the effect of media on personal and family health (indicator 2.12.5);
- evaluate the impact of technology on personal, family, and community health (indicator 2.12.6);
- analyze how the perceptions of norms influence healthy and unhealthy behaviors (indicator 2.12.7); and
- analyze the influence of personal values and beliefs on individual health practices and behaviors (indicator 2.12.8).

Additional Unit Objectives, Grades 6 Through 12

By the end of this unit, students will be able to

- describe how influences affect health behaviors;
- list influences on their own behavior;
- define the skill of analyzing influences;

■ analyze the influences on two health behaviors;

■ identify personal values and beliefs;

■ analyze situations to determine how factors, including personal values, might be influencing behaviors;

■ apply the skill cues in real-life situations;

■ analyze media messages related to drunk and distracted driving;

■ analyze various forms of media and their impact on thoughts, beliefs, and behaviors;

■ describe how social media and access to technology influence health and health behaviors; and

■ analyze the influence of social media and technology on their own health.

TABLE 4.2   Standard 2 Unit Outline

Lesson title	Lesson objectives (indicators in parentheses) By the end of this lesson, students will be able to:	Step of the skill development model addressed in the lesson	Main learning activities
Lesson 1: Influences, Influences, All Around	• Describe how influences affect health behaviors • List influences on their own behavior • Define the skill of analyzing influences	Skill introduction and steps of the skill (steps 1 and 2)	• Influences Snowball (p. 74) • Impact of Influences (p. 75)
Lesson 2: Web of Influences	• Analyze the influences on two health behaviors	Modeling and skill practice (steps 3 and 4)	Web of Influence (p. 77)
Lesson 3: What Would You Do?	• Identify personal values and beliefs • Analyze situations to determine how factors, including personal values, might be influencing behaviors (2.12.8 or 2.8.8) • Apply the skill cues in real-life situations	Skill practice (step 4)	• What Are My Values and Beliefs? (p. 81) • What Would You Do? (p. 83)
Lesson 4: Perceptions, Norms, and Behaviors	• Explain how the perception of health problems shapes personal beliefs and behaviors • Analyze the influence of perceptions and norms on behaviors and beliefs (2.12.7 or 2.8.7)	Skill practice (step 4)	Perception Versus Reality (p. 87)
Lesson 5: Exploring the Impact of Media	• Analyze media messages related to drunk and distracted driving	Skill practice (step 4)	Media as a Positive Influence (p. 89)
Lessons 6 and 7: Media: The Good, the Bad, and the Ugly	• Analyze various forms of media and their impact on thoughts, beliefs, and behaviors (2.8.5 or 2.12.5)	Skill practice (step 4)	• Lesson 6: Analyzing Print Media (p. 93) • Lesson 7: Analyzing Music (p. 94)
Lesson 8: Social Media and Technology	• Describe how social media and access to technology influence health and health behaviors • Analyze the influence of social media and technology on their own health (2.8.6 or 2.12.6)	Skill practice and feedback and reinforcement (steps 4 and 5)	Examining Social Media (p. 97)

Performance indicators are from: Joint Committee on National Health Education Standards. (2007). *National Health Education Standards: Achieving Excellence* (2nd ed.). Atlanta, GA: American Cancer Society.

ASSESSMENT

Here is a sample assessment that will evaluate the extent to which students can meet the objectives identified for this unit. In this assessment, students are required to write a reflection discussing the amount of time they spend on social media and how spending that time on social media influences their health behaviors.

Objectives

Through this assessment, students will be able to

- evaluate the effect of social media on personal and family health (indicator 2.12.5);
- evaluate the impact of technology on personal, family, and community health (indicator 2.12.6);
- analyze how the perceptions of norms influence healthy and unhealthy behaviors (indicator 2.12.7); and
- analyze the influence of personal values and beliefs on individual health practices and behaviors (indicator 2.12.8).

Description

The assessment for this unit is a written reflection. Given that students spend a large amount of time on social media, it is important for students to quantify the amount of time they actually spend on social media and then consider how the time spent on social media means that there is less time spent on other behaviors. For example, being on social media could mean that students are getting less sleep, engaging in less physical activity, or avoiding interpersonal interactions.

The assessment is added to the last lesson (including directions and rubric) of the unit and serves as a homework assignment. Ultimately, the intention is for self-reflection. If you think that students will not complete the reflection on their own time, you could devote additional class time to allow students to complete it. You might consider setting aside a time to share personal reflections or have students turn in the assignment through standard procedures.

Social Media Reflection Assessment

This assignment asks students to reflect on their social media use and how this affects their health behaviors. Throughout this lesson, they have discussed social media usage with their peers. This assignment is based on personal experience and will require students to analyze their own use of social media and ask them to develop strategies to ensure that their social media use does not influence their health negatively. The assignment must meet the following criteria:

1. For the next two days, have students keep a log of how often they check a social media site, which site they visit, and how long they stay on each site.

2. After the tracking for those two days is completed, have students take a 24-hour break from *all* social media.

Once students have completed both the log and the 24 hours off social media, they are to write a paper that reflects on their experiences with both. The paper should be one to two pages in length and answer the following questions completely.

1. Analyze your social media use. How often did you visit various sites? Which sites did you visit? How long (in total) did you spend on social media each day?

2. How does your use of social media influence how you behave? Compare this to your day off of social media. Was it hard to stay off of social media? What were your feelings? What kinds of things did you do instead?

3. Is your social media use a positive or negative influence? Do you think your social media use helps to make you more or less healthy? Please explain.

4. Considering your current social media use, discuss whether you should spend less time on social media. If so, list strategies you will take to avoid using social media as often and outcomes that you think you might experience. If not, explain how your use of social media is supporting your health and wellness.

Score the assignment according to the following rubric.

Rubric for Social Media Reflection Assessment

Criteria	4	3	2	1
Social media log	The log is thoroughly completed for two days.	The log is mostly completed for two days.	The log is somewhat completed for two days.	The log is poorly completed for two days.
Analysis of social media use	The question is answered in a complete and thorough manner.	The question is answered in a mostly complete manner.	The question is answered in a somewhat complete manner.	The question is poorly answered.
How does social media use influence behavior?	The question is answered in a complete and thorough manner.	The question is answered in a mostly complete manner.	The question is answered in a somewhat complete manner.	The question is poorly answered.
Is social media a positive or negative influence?	The question is answered in a complete and thorough manner.	The question is answered in a mostly complete manner.	The question is answered in a somewhat complete manner.	The question is poorly answered.
Strategies for reducing social media use	The topic is discussed in a complete and thorough manner.	The topic is discussed in a mostly complete manner.	The topic is discussed in a somewhat complete manner.	The topic is poorly discussed.

(continued)

Sample Student Log

Name: _____

Date	Name of site	Time visited	Length of time on site

LESSON PLANS

The lesson plans included here are the ones outlined in the unit outline earlier in the chapter and that will advance students toward achieving unit objectives and being able to successfully demonstrate the skill (evaluated in the assessment). The included lessons assume a 50-minute class period. Consider this prior to implementation.

Lesson plans include suggested activities, and those activities follow the lesson plans. Lesson plans and activities can be used together or independently to meet the needs of your classes.

Throughout the lesson plans, you will see the steps of the skill development model in **boldface type** after activities that address each skill development step.

Purpose

Before beginning the unit, it is important that students understand the relevance of the skill, have a clear definition of the skill and unit outcomes, and are aware of the critical elements of the skill (skill cues). This lesson introduces the skill and sets the stage for the rest of the unit.

NHES Performance Indicators

None addressed

Objectives

Students will be able to

- describe how influences affect health behaviors,
- list influences on their own behavior, and
- define the skill of analyzing influences.

Skill Development Steps

- Step 1: introduction
- Step 2: steps of the skill

Materials

- Visual of the skill cues (e.g., figure 4.1, or you could make your own)
- Materials needed for the Influences Snowball and the Impact of Influences activities

Instant Activity

After students take their seats, they write their responses to the prompt: "What are the top five influences on your health? Why did you choose these five influences?"

Introduction

Tell students that this is the beginning of the analyzing influences unit. Review the lesson objectives. Let students know that you will be exploring a variety of influences on our health and health behaviors. Today will focus on introducing the skill and skill cues.

Main Activities

1. Influences Snowball (page 74)
2. Impact of Influences (page 75) **(relevance)**
3. After the activities, ask students if they can provide a definition for analyzing influences. You may want to provide them with this prompt: "Analyzing influences is the ability to . . ." Once students have shared a few ideas, create a class definition for analyzing influences. This will be the definition used throughout the unit. **(definition)**
4. Using a poster or other visual, review the skill cues with students. Introduce the key terms and ideas. You may want to use one of the influences that were generated in the Influences Snowball activity and make reference to their ideas from the Impact of Influences worksheet. For example, during the identify the influence skill cue, refer to the list you created. In the analyze the influence skill cue, use the examples created to discuss whether the influence was a positive or negative influence on the behavior. Connecting the skill cues to concrete examples can be helpful. **(skill cues)**

Closure

Review the skill cues with students and let them know that in the next lesson we will expand on today's instant activity and explore influences on their personal health.

Differentiation

- Add visuals to worksheets to help students remember the steps.
- Implement any modifications as necessary to meet the needs of students.
- The Influences Snowball activity could be done using classroom polling technology such as Poll Everywhere so that the influences could be shown right on the screen.
- Students could complete the Impact of Influences worksheet on a desktop computer or tablet.

Influences Snowball

LESSON 1

NHES Performance Indicators
None addressed

Objective
Students will be able to identify a variety of influences on health behaviors.

Skill Development Step
Step 1: introduction (relevance)

Duration
10 minutes

Materials
White paper for the influences

Description

1. Ask students for a health-enhancing behavior that students their age might be engaging in. Write the behavior in the middle of a circle on the board. Ask students to write one influence they think might affect a high schooler's (or middle schooler's) decision to engage, or not engage, in the health behavior on the board. After writing the influence, students are to crumple up the papers like snowballs and throw them into a bucket.

2. Repeat the activity with a second behavior, but this one should be a risky health behavior. Be sure to use a second bucket to keep the two sets of influences separate.

3. Ask the students to grab a "snowball" from the first bucket. Have students share the influences written on their papers. Write up each unique influence on the board around the health behavior. If an influence is repeated, place a check mark beside it.

4. Repeat with the risky behavior influences.

5. Have students share their observations about what is on the board. Are there similar influences for the health-enhancing and risky behaviors? What does that tell us? Are there differences? Which do you think are the strongest influences? Why do you think certain influences have more check marks than others?

Tips and Extensions
None

Modifications
You could do this with sticky notes instead of snowballs. Students could then post their sticky notes around the behavior.

Impact of Influences

LESSON 1

NHES Performance Indicators
None addressed

Objectives
Students will be able to describe how influences affect health behaviors.

Skill Development Step
Step 1: introduction (relevance)

Duration
15 minutes (more if discussion is added)

Materials
Copies of the Impact of Influences worksheet for all students

Description
In this activity, students will have a chance to reflect on the ways that different influences might impact healthy and unhealthy behaviors. Students should complete the Impact of Influences worksheet individually. After students have completed the worksheet (or time is up), discuss some of the key questions.

Tips and Extensions
- Students ask their parents, guardians, or older siblings the same questions for homework.
- Use the worksheet as a preassessment. Students can complete the worksheet again later in this unit to see how or if their answers changed.

Modifications
- Complete the activity in pairs or small groups rather than individually.
- Add movement through a gallery walk. Have students walk around in small groups writing their answers to each question. This would have the added benefit of students being able to see other students' ideas.

Modified from a submission by Kathleen McCullough, middle school health teacher in Massachusetts.

Impact of Influences

Name: _____

Our next unit will require us to examine the many influences in our lives that shape our behaviors, values, and lifestyles. To begin, answer the following questions honestly and in complete sentences.

1. How would peers and peer pressure influence a healthy or unhealthy behavior?

2. How would personal values and beliefs influence a healthy or unhealthy behavior?

3. How would technology influence healthy or unhealthy behavior?

4. How would life events influence healthy or unhealthy behavior?

5. How might influences change during our lifetime?

6. What influences do our families have on our lives?

Purpose

In the previous lesson, students were introduced to the skill and skill cues. Now the students need to have the skill modeled so that they have an example of the skill being applied effectively. In this lesson, the teacher leads the students through an example using the same format that the students will have to use. After the teacher has modeled the skill and answered any questions, the students will have a chance to work independently to practice.

NHES Performance Indicators

No performance indicators are covered in this introductory lesson. See the lesson objectives that follow.

Objectives

Students will be able to analyze influences on two of their health behaviors.

Skill Development Steps

- Step 3: modeling
- Step 4: skill practice

Materials

Materials needed for Web of Influence activity

Instant Activity

After students take their seats, ask them to write down the skill cues for analyzing influences from the previous class. Encourage students to write down any terms, questions, or concepts that they remember, even if they can't remember the skill cues exactly. This process can help with retention of material when students are encouraged to recall what they remember even if it isn't completely correct.

Introduction

Tell students that today they will analyze influences on their own health behaviors after reviewing the skill cues and going over an example together. Review the lesson objective and the skill cues.

Main Activities

1. Using the same model that the students will be using (see the Web of Influence worksheet) go through an example together. Be sure to highlight the skill cues as they are being applied in the example. Elaborate on ideas and engage students in the discussion. The goal is to show them how to conduct a thoughtful analysis of influences on a behavior. Areas that might be more difficult and you might want to plan to spend more time on are the messages aspect of the activity, because sometimes the message isn't always direct and it can be difficult for students to think about how a message could be relayed and received. **(modeling)**
2. Web of Influence (page 77) **(practice)**

Closure

Ask students to share their experiences with the activity. You might ask them what they found difficult, what was easy, and what they learned. Remind students that self-reflection can be difficult, and increasing awareness of influences on behavior can help us to be healthier and more in charge of our decisions.

Differentiation

- Implement any modifications as necessary to meet the needs of students.
- Provide students with scenarios for completing the Web of Influence activity if they are not ready for self-reflection yet. Eventually, it is important that students are able to reflect on their own situations, although it might be easier for them to start by looking at someone else and then moving to themselves.

Web of Influence

LESSON 2

NHES Performance Indicators
None addressed

Objective
Students will be able to analyze the influences on two health behaviors.

Skill Development Step
Step 4: skill practice

Duration
20 to 30 minutes

Materials
Copies of the Web of Influence worksheet

Description
In this activity, students will have a chance to explore personal influences on two health behaviors. Using the Web of Influence worksheet, have students examine two health behaviors. You can choose to facilitate the activity in a few ways. You could have students choose any two health behaviors. You could have them choose a healthy and an unhealthy behavior that they engage in. You also could have them choose behaviors from different dimensions of wellness if you have covered this.

During the activity, walk around and provide feedback for students. Aspects of this activity, particularly the messages and strength of the influence, can be challenging for students.

Tips and Extensions
- Include a discussion at the end of this activity to have students share their experience with the activity.
- Add a discussion debrief to have students share influences and other aspects of the activity to showcase similarities and differences among the class.

Modification
You might need to scaffold aspects of this activity or skip some steps.

Resource
Benes, S., & Alperin, H. (2016). *The essentials of teaching health education: Curriculum, instruction, and assessment.* Champaign, IL: Human Kinetics.

Web of Influence

Name: _____

This activity offers an opportunity for you to think about what (or who) influences you and how you are influenced. Complete this activity using the following steps:

1. Draw a circle in the center of a landscape-oriented page.

2. In the circle, write a health-related behavior that you engage in (or that you do not engage in—i.e., not smoking) within one of the 10 dimensions of wellness.

3. In smaller circles around the circle, write all the people or things that influence your behavior (the influences can be positive or negative). Try to come up with three to five influences.

4. Identify, by including a "+" or "−" sign (or you could use colors or other variations), whether the influences are positive or negative. Keep in mind that an influence might be positive *and* negative depending on the situation.

5. Draw lines from the behavior to the influence. Use a system of your choice to indicate the strongest influences on the behavior *most* of the time (different colors, types of lines, symbols).

6. After you have drawn all the lines, write a message that you receive from your strongest influences about this behavior. For example, the message from parents is "always made sure I brushed my teeth every morning and night." Keep in mind that the message may not always be easy to recognize and might not be something that is told directly to you.

7. Looking at the web you have created, make any other connections that you think exist between influences. For example, is there a connection between the influence of media and your peers? Represent these connections between the influences with lines.

Repeat steps 1 through 6 but use a different behavior as instructed by your teacher.

After completing this activity, write a short statement about how reflecting on personal influences has helped you learn more about yourself (or not, if you don't feel that it did).

Reprinted, by permission, from S. Benes and H. Alperin, 2016, *The essentials of teaching health education* (Champaign, IL: Human Kinetics).

Purpose

In the previous lesson, students had the chance to begin to identify influences on their health behaviors. In most cases, these influences and also the influences they identified in lesson 1 would relate more to external influences. Before continuing further into the unit, it is important that students take time to reflect on internal influences. Specifically, students will reflect on their personal values and how personal values interact with other influences and how they affect health behaviors.

NHES Performance Indicators

- *Grades 6 through 8:* Explain the influence of personal values and beliefs on individual health practices and behaviors (indicator 2.8.8).
- *Grades 9 through 12:* Analyze the influence of personal values and beliefs on individual health practices and behaviors (indicator 2.12.8).

Objectives

Students will be able to

- identify personal values and beliefs;
- analyze situations to determine how factors, including personal values, might influence behaviors; and
- apply the skill cues in real-life situations.

Skill Development Step

Step 4: skill practice

Materials

Materials needed for the What Are My Values and Beliefs? and What Would You Do? activities

Instant Activity

After students take their seats, they write their responses to the prompt: "List three people or items that are very important to you. Think of people or items that make your world better because they are in it."

Introduction

Tell students that in the previous few lessons, they have explored primarily external influences on health behaviors, and now they will explore internal influences that can affect the decisions that they make. Review the lesson objectives. Let students know that after reflecting on their own values and beliefs, they will use real-world examples to discuss how personal beliefs and values can influence behavior.

Main Activities

1. What Are My Values and Beliefs? (page 81) **(practice)**
2. Transition: Now that students have identified some of their personal values and beliefs, have the class explore some situations and analyze how values and beliefs, as well as external influences, can influence their behavior.
3. What Would You Do? (page 83) **(practice)**

Closure

Remind students that influences on behavior, both internal and external, can play a significant role on our behaviors (use some examples from the What Would You Do? activity). Let them know that you will be continuing to discuss these influences in the next lesson, but that the class will also be looking at how perceptions can influence our beliefs and our behaviors.

(continued)

LESSON 3: What Would You Do? *(continued)*

Differentiation

- Implement any modifications as necessary to meet the needs of students.
- You may need to supply a list of values for students to choose from (or at least to use as a support for brainstorming).
- Students may need additional prompting to identify their beliefs.

Resources

What Would You Do? television show from ABC.

What Are My Values and Beliefs?
LESSON 3

NHES Performance Indicators

- *Grades 6 through 8:* Explain the influence of personal values and beliefs on individual health practices and behaviors (indicator 2.8.8).
- *Grades 9 through 12:* Analyze the influence of personal values and beliefs on individual health practices and behaviors (indicator 2.12.8).

Objectives

Students will be able to identify personal values and beliefs that influence their health behaviors.

Skill Development Step

Step 4: skill practice

Duration

20 minutes

Materials

- Copies of the My Values and Beliefs worksheet for all students.
- Computer for the "This I Believe" curriculum if you include this modification.
- List of values or sample belief statements.

Description

Have students complete the My Values and Beliefs worksheet. This activity will help students identify their values and beliefs and how those might influence their health. Reflecting on values and beliefs can be difficult for students. You may need to scaffold this with examples and lists of values for students to choose from or use as examples.

Provide students with time to complete this activity individually. Once students have completed the My Values and Beliefs worksheet, you might want to debrief as a class or have students share a value and beliefs.

Tips and Extensions

- Have students complete "This I Believe" essays (see http://thisibelieve.org)
- You could include more from the "This I Believe" curriculum and website in your unit and spend more time on this aspect of the analyzing influences unit.
- Have students ask parents, guardians, or other trusted adults about their values and beliefs.

Modification

Scaffold as necessary for your students.

Resources

http://thisibelieve.org

My Values and Beliefs

Name: _____

For this activity, you will think about your *values* and your *beliefs*. A value is something that you think is important in life. A belief is an opinion you have about something or someone that you understand to be true. Then you will think about how these values and beliefs might influence your health and health behaviors.

My Values

List your top five values and explain how you think these values can influence your health and health behaviors.

My values	Impact on my health

My Beliefs

For this part of the activity, you will think about beliefs that you have about yourself, health, the world, and so on. It can be difficult to think about what you believe, but it can be a powerful influence on your behaviors. Try to think of at least two beliefs that you hold that might influence your health and health behaviors. Use the sentence stems to help:

I believe _____

_____

_____ .

I think this could affect my health or health behaviors because _____

_____

_____ .

I believe _____

_____

_____ .

I think this could affect my health or health behaviors because _____

_____

_____ .

What Would You Do?

LESSON 3

NHES Performance Indicators

- *Grades 6 through 8:* Explain the influence of personal values and beliefs on individual health practices and behaviors (indicator 2.8.8).
- *Grades 9 through 12:* Analyze the influence of personal values and beliefs on individual health practices and behaviors (indicator 2.12.8).

Objective

Students will be able to analyze situations to determine how factors, including personal values, might be influencing behaviors.

Skill Development Step

Step 4: skill practice

Duration

25 minutes

Materials

- Desktop or tablet computer and projector to show the clips
- Copies of the What Would You Do? worksheet for each student

Description

Preparation

Choose clips that are relevant for your students from the *What Would You Do?* show on ABC. There are sample clips suggested in the What Would You Do? worksheet, but you do not need to use these if you think that others will be more appropriate for your students. You can also find clips or short videos from other shows. Remember that any clips you use with this activity should involve some sort of ethical dilemma that the students have to analyze.

Activity

- Watch each video clip and have students record their ideas individually on the What Would You Do? worksheet.
- After watching the video clips, have a whole-group discussion or small-group discussions about their answers on the worksheet.
- Be sure to facilitate a discussion about the impact of personal values and beliefs *and* how external factors might make us act against our values (or consider acting against our values).

Tips and Extensions

- Include closed captions when watching the videos.
- Students could write their own What Would You Do? scenario or even make their own videos based on situations but with a twist. After the What Would You Do? scenario, they could make a What You Should Do! video showing a healthy resolution to the situation.

Modification

This could be done in small groups with tablet computers at stations.

Modified from a submission by Kathleen McCullough, middle school health teacher in Massachusetts.

What Would You Do?

Name: _____

Directions: After watching the video clip closely, thoughtfully answer the following questions.

Clip 1: Underage girls try to buy e-cigarettes

What would you do in this situation if you were a bystander? Why?
What values or influences in your life affect your decision?

Clip 2: Students peer pressure friend to abuse Adderall

What would you do in this situation if you were a bystander? Why?
What values or influences in your life affect your decision?

Clip 3: Self-entitled kid throws a tantrum

What would you do in this situation if you were a bystander? Why?
What values or influences in your life affect your decision?

Clip 4: Single mother can't afford food

What would you do in this situation if you were a bystander? Why?
What values or influences in your life affect your decision?

Purpose

Students, especially adolescents, can act on a belief that everyone is doing it, even if this is not true. Therefore, it is extremely important to spend time showing students the data about what behaviors students are or are not actually engaging in. This lesson focuses on using community-specific data (or as close as you can get) to show students what is happening in their school or community.

NHES Performance Indicators

- *Grades 6 through 8:* Explain how the perceptions of norms influence healthy and unhealthy behaviors (indicator 2.8.7).
- *Grades 9 through 12:* Analyze how the perceptions of norms influence healthy and unhealthy behaviors (indicator 2.12.7).

Objectives

Students will be able to

- explain how the perception of health problems shapes personal beliefs and behaviors and
- analyze the influence of perceptions and norms on behaviors and beliefs.

Skill Development Step

Step 4: skill practice

Materials

Materials needed for the Perception Versus Reality activity

Instant Activity

After students take their seats, they write their responses to the prompt: "If everyone else is doing it, should you?"

Introduction

Tell students that today they are going to look at how perceptions of norms can influence their behaviors. If necessary, define these terms for students at this point in the lesson. Review the lesson objectives.

Main Activities

Preparation

You will need to gather data to include in the Perception Versus Reality activity. You should use data that are as relevant to the students as possible. School data are ideal because they help students see themselves, but if school-level data are not available, the use of community-, state-, or even national-level data will also work. If community- or school-level data are unavailable, this might be a good time to begin discussions with administrators about ways to collect data from students.

Activity

Perception Versus Reality (page 87) **(practice)**

Closure

Ask students to reflect back on the question in the instant activity. Is their answer any different now than it was at the start of the lesson? Ask students what their key takeaways are from the lesson. Let students know that in the next few lessons, the class will be looking at the influence of media on perceptions of norms as well as beliefs and behaviors.

(continued)

Differentiation

- Implement any modifications as necessary to meet the needs of students. **(practice and feedback and reinforcement)**
- Add more movement by making this a four corners activity. Present students with four different percentages for the norms, with each norm assigned to a corner of the room, and have students move to the corresponding corner of the room for each percentage they think is correct.

Resources

- Local data
- Youth Risk Behavior Surveillance System data, www.cdc.gov/healthyyouth/data/yrbs/

Perception Versus Reality

LESSON 4

NHES Performance Indicators

- *Grades 6 through 8:* Explain how the perceptions of norms influence healthy and unhealthy behaviors (indicator 2.8.7).
- *Grades 9 through 12:* Analyze how the perceptions of norms influence healthy and unhealthy behaviors (indicator 2.12.7).

Objectives

Students will be able to

- explain how the perception of health problems shapes personal beliefs and behaviors and
- analyze the influence of perceptions and norms on behaviors and beliefs.

Skill Development Step

Step 4: skill practice

Duration

20 to 30 minutes

Materials

Slide show (sample slide show included in the web resource)

Description

Preparation

Create a slide show in which students need to estimate percentages of health behaviors, and then show them the actual numbers. Ideally, use school-level data. However, if those data are not available, use the closest level that you can (city, state, regional, or national). Choose behaviors that you want to cover in this unit based on the most prevalent risk behaviors in the school or risk behaviors that are increasing. There is flexibility in the data you include, although the selection should be intentional and based on your population.

Activity

- In a large-group formation, go through the slides soliciting student input on percentages before showing the actual percentages. Keep track of how often they are within 10% (or whatever range you want to give them).
- Discuss the question on the final slide and add additional discussion questions as desired. You could also include a discussion about the impact of the risky behaviors that you included in the presentation.

Tips and Extensions

Have students record their answers individually. They can correct themselves so that they can calibrate their own perceptions.

Modifications

Complete the activity in small teams rather than large groups. Have each team hold up their guesses on a white board or piece of paper. The closest team gets a point.

Resources

CDC Youth Risk Behavior Data (www.cdc.gov/healthyyouth/data/yrbs/)

Modified from a submission by Anya Eckhardt, high school health teacher in Massachusetts.

LESSON 5: Exploring the Impact of Media

Purpose

Media can exert powerful influence. We often focus on the negative impact of some forms of media, but media also can provide positive influences. In this lesson, you will use examples of media advertisements that influence teens not to drink and drive and to avoid distracted driving. This lesson is a precursor to the next two lessons, which will examine the negative influence of some forms of media. Having students explore both the positive and negative influences of some forms of media can show them how complex influences can be and how they can apply the skill cues to a variety of media influences.

NHES Performance Indicators

- *Grades 6 through 8:* Analyze how messages from media influence health behaviors (indicator 2.8.5).
- *Grades 9 through 12:* Evaluate the effect of media on personal and family health (indicator 2.12.5).

Objective

Students will be able to analyze media messages related to drunk and distracted driving.

Skill Development Step

Step 4: skill practice

Materials

- Access to online videos
- Materials needed for Media as a Positive Influence activity

Instant Activity

After students take their seats, they write their responses to the prompt: "In what ways can some forms of media be a positive influence on health behaviors?"

Introduction

Recap previous learning in the unit: Remind students that they have looked at the influence of values and beliefs on health behaviors, explored the impact of perceptions of norms on behaviors, and looked at influences in their own lives. Tell students that today, they will start a series of lessons on the influence of media on their behaviors. In this lesson, they will be exploring the positive impact media can have on behaviors, attitudes, and beliefs. Review the lesson objectives.

Main Activities

1. Before beginning, ask some students to share ways they've identified in which media can be a positive influence on behaviors. Make any connections from their answers to the main activity.
2. Media as a Positive Influence (page 89) **(practice)**

Closure

Refer to the instant activity and then ask students to share some of their overall reactions to the activities and the videos that were viewed during the lesson. Encourage students to reflect on how media can influence us to engage in healthier behaviors.

Differentiation

Implement any modifications as necessary to meet the needs of students.

Resources

- Examples of positive media usage (e.g., *Choices* magazine, *Scholastic News,* and social media campaigns)
- Tobacco prevention in Massachusetts, http://the84.org/

Media as a Positive Influence

LESSON 5

NHES Performance Indicators

- *Grades 6 through 8:* Analyze how messages from media influence health behaviors (indicator 2.8.5).
- *Grades 9 through 12:* Evaluate the effect of media on personal and family health (indicator 2.12.5).

Objective

Students will be able to analyze media messages related to drunk and distracted driving.

Skill Development Step

Step 4: skill practice

Duration

30 to 40 minutes

Materials

- Video clips
- Tablet or desktop computer for the videos
- Copies of the Media as a Positive Influence worksheet for each student

Description

This activity uses video clips related to drunk and distracted driving to show students one way in which some forms of media can be a positive external influence. Students will watch videos and then complete the Media as a Positive Influence worksheet.

Here are the suggested clips and suggested times for the clips. Review the videos ahead of time and decide if these are a good fit for your students. Include any videos or clips from videos that you feel would be most relevant or engaging for students. Just make sure the clips are supporting a health-enhancing message and then adjust the questions on the worksheet as needed.

- *Questions 1 through 4: Every 15 Minutes: Kenilworth 2016* (you can find this online by searching key words); stop after 43 seconds
- *Questions 5 and 6: Eleanor Roosevelt High School Every 15 Minutes 2016* (you can find this online by searching key words); play up through 9:13; have students watch 5:30 to 6:58 for question 5
- *Questions 7 through 9:* Distracted driving (search online for Alexxyss's story, by Oregon State Police, or find other videos that would work for your students, but be sure to adjust the worksheet as necessary)

Tips and Extensions

Have students create their own healthy behavior videos that try to *influence* their peers to engage in healthy behaviors.

Modifications

Find other videos that you feel would resonate with your students.

Modified from a submission by William Graham, high school health teacher in Massachusetts.

Media as a Positive Influence

Name: _____

Kenilworth High School

1. Identify the major influence in the video.

2. List both:
   - External influences (people, culture, media and technology, law, policy and regulation, life circumstances)
   - Internal influences (values, beliefs, and attitudes the characters might have)

3. Analyze how the influence has an impact on behaviors.

4. Name three things the boy does to overcome the influence.

   - _____
   - _____
   - _____

Eleanor Roosevelt High School

Internal influences: Temperament, personality, cognitive ability, sense of humor, fears, drive to succeed, and other personal needs are part of our internal being.

   - An outgoing person might have a more risk-taking personality and have a harder time refusing something.
   - A shy, introverted person might have a harder time expressing his or her needs or opinions openly.

5. Which character is which in this video?

6. Based on the personalities for both girls, give two examples for how each girl could have changed the outcomes. Write a dialogue (what could you say to the girls?)

Driving Commercial

7. How much is this influencing my thoughts, values, beliefs, or actions? (Why or why not?)

8. Consider whether I need to do anything about this influence. What is the best plan for handling this influence in my life when it happens? (Name three things I could do to prevent this from happening.)

9. This (video) is an external influence, but what internal influence is it trying to elicit in me (name two)?

Purpose

These lessons will explore some forms of media as a negative influence. Students need to become critical consumers of all forms of media. The goal of this lesson is to increase students' awareness of the subtle and not so subtle messages conveyed in much of the popular media. Lesson 6 looks at advertisements in print media and lesson 7 looks at music lyrics and videos.

NHES Performance Indicators

- *Grades 6 through 8:* Analyze how messages from media influence health behaviors (indicator 2.8.5).
- *Grades 9 through 12:* Evaluate the effect of media on personal and family health (indicator 2.12.5).

Objective

Students will be able to analyze various forms of media and their impact on thoughts, beliefs, and behaviors.

Skill Development Step

Step 4: skill practice

Materials

Materials needed for the Analyzing Print Media and Analyzing Music activities

Instant Activities

- *Lesson 6:* After students take their seats, they write their responses to the prompt: "What is the most recent advertisement you have seen? Where did you see it (online, magazine, TV)? Why do you remember it? Did the ad send positive or negative messages?"
- *Lesson 7:* After students take their seats, they write their responses to the prompt: "Think of your favorite song. Why do you like the song? Do you know the lyrics? Have you ever thought about what the lyrics are actually saying? Why or why not?"

Introduction

- *Lesson 6:* Tell students that, while the previous lesson examined media as a positive influence, some forms of media often provide a negative influence, especially when it comes to health behaviors. Let students know that the next two lessons will examine the influence of two forms of media. Today's lesson will look at print media and the next lesson will look at music. Review the lesson objectives. **(practice)**
- **Lesson 7:** In the previous lesson, we applied the skill cues in order to analyze the influence of print media. Today we will apply the skill cues to look at the influence of music. Review the lesson objectives. **(practice)**

Main Activities

- *Lesson 6:* Analyzing Print Media (page 93)
- *Lesson 7:* Analyzing Music (page 94)

Closure

- *Lesson 6:* Ask students what they learned from the activity today. Encourage students to be more thoughtful when they see ads in magazines or online. Remind students that even ads they see on TV will have similar features to print advertising and should be considered critically as well.
- *Lesson 7:* Encourage students to be more thoughtful in their music listening. Being more aware of messages in lyrics and music videos may lead to a change in music choice, but even if it doesn't, just being more aware of and stopping to think about the messages being sent in the music students are listening to is making them more aware of the influence, which means they can do something about it.

(continued)

Differentiation

Implement any modifications as necessary to meet the needs of students.

Homework

Between lessons 6 and 7, you could have students print out and bring in lyrics to a favorite song to use for the activity in lesson 7.

Resources

- Common Sense Media, www.commonsensemedia.org
- Media Smarts, http://mediasmarts.ca/

Analyzing Print Media

LESSONS 6 AND 7

NHES Performance Indicators

- *Grades 6 through 8:* Analyze how messages from media influence health behaviors (indicator 2.8.5).
- *Grades 9 through 12:* Evaluate the effect of media on personal and family health (indicator 2.12.5).

Objective

Students will be able to analyze various forms of media and their impact on thoughts, beliefs, and behaviors.

Skill Development Step

Step 4: skill practice

Duration

30 to 40 minutes

Materials

- Sample advertisements (enough for small groups)
- Multiple copies of a worksheet for the advertisement analysis

Description

Preparation

Find print advertisements that will be relevant and compelling for students to examine. Consider looking at magazines that students might be reading, billboards, and popular advertisements. Have enough ads for students to work in small groups for the activity. Create a worksheet for students. You can include your own questions based on what you have covered in your unit and that align with the skill cues used in the unit. A resource that might be useful is www.mediaed.org/handouts/DeconstructingAnAlcoholAd.pdf. You could use this PDF file or modify as necessary. You are encouraged to include ads related to multiple topic areas in addition to alcohol. Modify the questions to meet the needs to fit with any content area.

Activity

1. Place students into small groups. Each group receives one print advertisement. Working together, they complete the worksheet.
2. Have students rotate from one advertisement to another to analyze at least two advertisements.
3. If time allows, discuss students' analyses and their reactions to the activity.

Tips and Extensions

Instead of giving students advertisements, have students bring in examples of advertisements they see around them. They could print an ad off the computer, take a picture of a billboard, or cut out an ad from a magazine or newspaper.

Modifications

You also can conduct this lesson by having students work alone or in pairs. Ensure that advertisements are relevant to students and that they depict people and products they are likely to encounter in their surroundings.

Analyzing Music
LESSONS 6 AND 7

NHES Performance Indicators

- *Grades 6 through 8:* Analyze how messages from media influence health behaviors (indicator 2.8.5).
- *Grades 9 through 12:* Evaluate the effect of media on personal and family health (indicator 2.12.5).

Objective

Students will be able to analyze various forms of media and their impact on thoughts, beliefs, and behaviors.

Skill Development Step

Step 4: skill practice

Duration

30 to 40 minutes

Materials

- Copies of song lyrics
- Official music videos

Description

Preparation
Make copies of lyrics for two songs from the Billboard Hot 100 list. Bookmark links to official music videos (usually can be found through an online search).

Activity

1. Split students into two groups. Ideally, one group goes into the hallway or another room, and the second group remains in the classroom.
2. The group in the classroom watches the music video for song 1 *on mute*. As they watch, students record notes about the messages that the video is sending. Ask for examples to support their claims. At the same time, the group in the hallway analyzes the lyrics from song 1, looking for messages and writing down examples.
3. Then the groups switch. The group that analyzed the lyrics now watches the music video for song 2, *also on mute.* The group that watched song 1 now analyzes the lyrics for song 2.
4. Bring the groups together and list ideas for messages from the videos and lyrics. Discuss the findings. Questions you might ask include: Do the lyrics and the videos have the same messages? Why or why not? Are the messages being sent overall positive or negative? Why do you think that is? Do you usually pay attention to lyrics? Why or why not? What impact could the songs and videos have on adolescents?

Tips and Extensions

Be sure to listen to all music and review all lyrics ahead of time. While the intention is for students to see that songs often have lyrics and messages that go unnoticed, be sure that the songs selected do not violate school policy.

Modifications

If videos are unavailable, groups can read song lyrics and consider the influence of the words. While this is not quite the same as the approach discussed previously, this can be an eye-opener for students.

Resources

Search for the key words *sound relationships nutritional label* from the Boston Public Health Commission (www.bphc.org)

Purpose

Social media and access to technology are changing how we interact, how we receive information, and our health behaviors and practices. Many students have smartphones, tablets, computers, and more. Students are growing up in a digital world with instant and (sometimes) unmonitored access, and it has an impact. The goal of this lesson is to make students more aware of the ways that social media and technology can be harmful to their health. There are also great benefits to social media and technology, but we are increasingly seeing negative effects that are particularly relevant to students' health and well-being. This lesson will explore some of those issues.

Also, this lesson contains the final assessment for the unit. The assessment is a reflection. While you could add an additional lesson to allow students to complete the assessment in class, we have included it here as a homework assignment.

NHES Performance Indicators

Grades 6 Through 8

- Analyze how messages from media influence health behaviors (indicator 2.8.5).
- Analyze the influence of technology on personal and family health (indicator 2.8.6).

Grades 9 Through 12

- Evaluate the effect of media on personal and family health (indicator 2.12.5).
- Evaluate the impact of technology on personal and family health (indicator 2.12.6).

Objectives

Students will be able to

- describe how social media and access to technology influence health and health behaviors and
- analyze the influence of social media and technology on their own health.

Skill Development Steps

- Step 4: skill practice
- Step 5: feedback and reinforcement

Materials

Materials needed for the Examining Social Media activity

Instant Activity

After students take their seats, they write their responses to the prompt: "How would you feel if you had to give up your phone for 24 hours? Why would you feel this way?"

Introduction

Tell students that today's lesson will examine the influence of social media and technology on their health. Review the lesson objectives. Ask students to share their responses to the instant activity questions with a partner and then ask a few pairs of students to share their ideas.

Main Activities

Preparation

Gather evidence to share with students about the impact of technology and social media on health as part of the Examining Social Media activity. There is considerable information available about the negative effects, and the amount of information is growing. You can use data and evidence to help students understand the impact that technology and social media can have.

(continued)

Activity

Examining Social Media (page 97) **(practice, feedback and reinforcement)**

Closure

Encourage students to decrease their screen time and to examine their own personal technology and the impact it might be having on themselves and others.

Differentiation

Implement any modifications as necessary to meet the needs of your students.

Resources

- Social networking for children and teenagers, http://raisingchildren.net.au/articles/social_networking.html
- Kids Media Centre, http://kidsmediacentre.ca/
- Exploring the Relationship Between Media and Adolescent Health, www.rand.org/health/feature/media_influences.html

Examining Social Media

LESSON 8

NHES Performance Indicators

- *Grades 6 through 8:* Analyze the influence of technology on personal and family health (indicator 2.8.6).
- *Grades 9 through 12:* Evaluate the impact of technology on personal, family, and community health (indicator 2.12.6).

Objectives

Students will be able to

- describe how social media and access to technology influence health and health behaviors and
- analyze the influence of social media and technology on their own health.

Skill Development Step

Step 4: skill practice

Duration

30 to 40 minutes plus additional homework time

Description

This activity uses stations to have students examine the influence of social media and technology on their health and health behaviors. Set up three or four stations that are about 10 minutes each (depending on how much time you have). Modify the stations as appropriate for your students; here are some suggestions:

- Instagram and Snapchat
- Cell phone usage
- How do you communicate?
- Screen time

Here are suggested questions for students to discuss at each station. Have students record answers or just discuss. This activity will need to be modified for age and school policies.

- Instagram and Snapchat
  - Look at (or think about) your Instagram or Snapchat account. What kind of health behaviors are being posted? Are they positive or negative?
  - How often do you check your accounts? Why do you check this often?
  - What would happen if you stayed off of these accounts for a day? Two days?
  - Does your checking and posting to these accounts interfere with school? With family time?
- Cell phone usage
  - How often is your phone on or near you?
  - How often do you check or use your phone?
  - Does your cell phone usage interfere with school? With relationships?
  - Do you feel anxious when you can't check your phone? Why or why not?
  - Do you think that cell phones positively contribute to your health? Why or why not?
- How do you communicate?
  - How often do you text or use your phone to communicate?
  - How often do you communicate face to face with friends? With family?
  - How often do you worry about the tone or meaning of a text you send or receive?
  - Do you think it is more effective to communicate over the phone or in person? Why?

- Screen time
  - About how much time do you spend in front of a screen?
  - What are you doing most often in front of a screen?
  - How do you think your screen time might impact your health? Your peers' health?
  - Do you think teens spend too much time in front of a screen? Why or why not?
  - How do you think screens and media impact teen health?

Tips and Extensions

Social media use can become a hot button topic because many adolescents feel both connected and tied to their social media. Understanding the pull of being constantly connected is important for educators. While adults might feel that the connection to social media should not be as strong as it is, we must help our students to navigate in appropriate and meaningful ways, because social media isn't going away.

Modifications

The Social Media Reflection Assessment could take place during an additional class period or be spread out over a longer period for students to complete on their own. The intention is for students to complete it in a meaningful way.

Resources

- How using social media affects teenagers, https://childmind.org/article/how-using-social-media-affects-teenagers/
- Facebook, Instagram, and social, www.commonsensemedia.org/social-media/age/teens

Social Media Reflection Assessment

This assignment asks students to reflect on their social media use and how this affects their health behaviors. Throughout this lesson, they have discussed social media usage with their peers. This assignment is based on personal experience and will require students to analyze their own use of social media and ask them to develop strategies to ensure that their social media use does not influence their health negatively. The assignment must meet the following criteria:

1. For the next two days, have students keep a log of how often they check a social media site, which site they visit, and how long they stay on each site.

2. After the tracking for those two days is completed, have students take a 24-hour break from *all* social media.

Once students have completed both the log and the 24 hours off social media, they are to write a paper that reflects on their experiences with both. The paper should be one to two pages in length and answer the following questions completely.

1. Analyze your social media use. How often did you visit various sites? Which sites did you visit? How long (in total) did you spend on social media each day?

2. How does your use of social media influence how you behave? Compare this to your day off of social media. Was it hard to stay off of social media? What were your feelings? What kinds of things did you do instead?

3. Is your social media use a positive or negative influence? Do you think your social media use helps to make you more or less healthy? Please explain.

4. Considering your current social media use, discuss whether you should spend less time on social media. If so, list strategies you will take to avoid using social media as often and outcomes that you think you might experience. If not, explain how your use of social media is supporting your health and wellness.

Score the assignment according to the following rubric.

Rubric for Social Media Reflection Assessment

Criteria	4	3	2	1
Social media log	The log is thoroughly completed for two days.	The log is mostly completed for two days.	The log is somewhat completed for two days.	The log is poorly completed for two days.
Analysis of social media use	The question is answered in a complete and thorough manner.	The question is answered in a mostly complete manner.	The question is answered in a somewhat complete manner.	The question is poorly answered.
How does social media use influence behavior?	The question is answered in a complete and thorough manner.	The question is answered in a mostly complete manner.	The question is answered in a somewhat complete manner.	The question is poorly answered.
Is social media a positive or negative influence?	The question is answered in a complete and thorough manner.	The question is answered in a mostly complete manner.	The question is answered in a somewhat complete manner.	The question is poorly answered.
Strategies for reducing social media use	The topic is discussed in a complete and thorough manner.	The topic is discussed in a mostly complete manner.	The topic is discussed in a somewhat complete manner.	The topic is poorly discussed.

(continued)

Social Media Reflection Assessment *(continued)*

Sample Student Log

Name:_____

Date	Name of site	Time visited	Length of time on site

CHAPTER 5

Using Interpersonal Communication for Health and Wellness

This chapter explores the skill of interpersonal communication, which is Standard 4 of the National Health Education Standards. In this chapter, you will find many examples of the skill of interpersonal communication in action in the classroom. There are assessments, lesson plans, and learning activities—all the items you will need to develop the skill of interpersonal communication with your students.

Materials in this chapter reflect a backward-design approach (see chapter 2) and are designed to support each step of the skill development model (see chapter 1). Unit objectives are presented first, and then you will find a sample unit outline with an assessment to evaluate the learning objectives, lesson plans for the unit, and learning activities that can be used in the lesson plans, as well as an additional learning activity that wasn't included in the unit but might be useful in your classroom. Items in this chapter are designed for secondary students, grades 6 to 12. You might be able to use the ideas presented here with little to no modification; however, we encourage you to make any changes necessary to meet the needs of your students.

This chapter presents activities to support the development of interpersonal communication using the health topic of *relationships* as the context through which students will practice the skill. Even though relationships are used as the health topic in this example, there are other topics that could be used with interpersonal communication, including bullying, alcohol, tobacco, and other drugs, as well as sexuality education. Select and integrate a health topic (or multiple health topics) that will best serve your students. Make sure whatever topic you include is relevant and meaningful for your students and provides sufficient context to practice the skill. The easier it is for students to see themselves in a communication scenario, the more likely they will be to embrace the experience.

SKILL OVERVIEW

Interpersonal communication is the ability to communicate and receive messages effectively. Communication requires a sender, a receiver, and a message. Effective communication can be extremely challenging. You must consider how to deliver your message—the tone, the timing, the setting, audience or receiver, and the words you use. You must consider whether the message is being sent verbally (written or spoken) or nonverbally. Each of these factors has a direct impact on the ability of the sender to accurately relay the message and for the receiver to accurately interpret the message.

Think about the last time you had a frustrating experience with communication, perhaps with a student, a coworker, a family member, or a cashier. Why might it have gone wrong? Maybe you didn't send the message in the most effective way. Maybe the receiver wasn't open to your message or was just in a bad mood. Perhaps the other person misunderstood your intentions or thought the tone you used was too aggressive. Maybe the receiver didn't understand what you were trying to say because the language you used was unfamiliar to him or her. Think also of times that you feel as though you communicated clearly and effectively. What about the situation supported the effectiveness of the exchange? Many variables can affect the outcome of our communication—some we can control and some we cannot. Therefore, it is critical that we help students develop the skills they need for the aspects of communication that they do have some control over—conveying their message and listening.

Standard 4, at the secondary level, includes four types of interpersonal communication that students should be able to demonstrate: self-expression, refusal, negotiation, and conflict resolution. Each of these aspects of the skill should be addressed in the health education program. While you don't need to cover them all each year, when you map out a scope and sequence it is important that each type of communication gets covered appropriately before students complete their health education courses within the grade span. Also keep in mind that many characteristics of the four types of communication are transferable. For example, assertiveness is appropriate in all four types of communication. When students see that assertive communication is more effective when refusing unwanted sexual advances or when negotiating healthier food choices, they will begin to transfer the skill across a variety of contexts in the real world. Highlight the transferable aspects to support skill development and transfer outside of the classroom.

When assessing interpersonal communication skills, you might wonder whether students must demonstrate skills as individuals or as part of a group. If you look at the performance indicators of the National Standards, you will see the verb demonstrate. Therefore, if you want to ensure that you are addressing the standard and measuring each student's level of skill proficiency, all students will need to demonstrate self-expression, refusal, negotiation, and conflict resolution. Keep in mind that demonstrate in the context of this skill would be doing it—not just writing a script or a story. Communicating via the spoken word is important because much can be lost in communication in the written form, and we want to equip students for in-person interaction. When the work is done and presented as a group with only one or two students speaking, you are unable to measure the ability of all members of the group.

Another common question about assessment is: Does every student actually need to demonstrate each type of communication through speech? For example, does a student need to do a role-play, or will a written script be sufficient? Often this question arises because teachers have students who are uncomfortable speaking in front of the class or students who require modifications. For students with individualized education plans (IEPs), modifications are appropriate and necessary, although we encourage you to work toward safe and appropriate ways for these students to express their thoughts and feelings through speech. Some students on an IEP might need help coming up with the language, phrases to say, or more concrete examples to help them formulate their response. The extra practice, although difficult, is exactly what many need because there is no other venue for them to consider what to say in various situations and to practice in a safe environment. We suggest that your classroom be a safe place to work on skills such as communication, and that supporting students to work outside of their comfort zone is appropriate. This is especially important when you consider how much harder it can be to say no or to resolve a conflict in real-life situations than in your classroom. Students being uncomfortable is not a reason to avoid having them demonstrate appropriate use of the skill. Given that many students today avoid face-to-face interactions in favor of texting or instant messaging, we want to encourage and give them practice in ways that allow them to see and interpret facial expressions and voice inflection. Having students take the time to formulate a response and present it effectively carries a lot of weight in whether or not a student will be able to apply the skill later in a setting outside of the classroom. However, we also recognize that this isn't always going to work in your real-life classroom. The presentation of the skill may include role-plays in the classroom in front of peers, a performance in front of just you, a performance that is video recorded, or videos of just the student performing the skills. No matter what you decide for your classroom, do the best you can to provide a safe space for students to actually demonstrate their communication skills.

Table 5.1 shows the performance indicators from the National Health Education Standards, which outline what students should be able to do within each grade span in grades 6 through 8 and 9 through 12.

SKILL CUES

Skill cues are used during step 2 of the skill development model to highlight the critical elements of the skill; in this case, interpersonal communication. In figures 5.1 and 5.2 we have included sample skill cues for the aspects of interpersonal communication included in the unit that follows: effective communication (self-expression), refusal, and conflict resolution. These are just samples—you can use them as they are or make adjustments to meet the needs of your students. There is no wrong way to create skill cues. Just keep in mind that you want the skill cues to represent the critical aspects of the skill, be memorable for students, and serve as reminders of the steps they need to implement when using the skill.

TABLE 5.1 Performance Indicators for Standard 4 of the NHES (Grades 6-12)

	6-8		9-12
4.8.1	Apply effective verbal and nonverbal communication skills to enhance health.	4.12.1	Use skills for communicating effectively with family, peers, and others to enhance health.
4.8.2	Demonstrate refusal and negotiation skills that avoid or reduce health risks.	4.12.2	Demonstrate refusal, negotiation, and collaboration skills to enhance health and avoid or reduce health risks.
4.8.3	Demonstrate effective conflict management or resolution strategies.	4.12.3	Demonstrate strategies to prevent, manage, or resolve interpersonal conflicts without harming self or others.
4.8.4	Demonstrate how to ask for assistance to enhance the health of self and others.	4.12.4	Demonstrate how to ask for and offer assistance to enhance the health of self and others.

Communication

STANDARD 4	Students will demonstrate the ability to use interpersonal communication skills to enhance health and avoid or reduce health risks.

I TELL YOU

Identify feelings, thoughts, ideas

Tell feelings, thoughts, ideas

Express using "I" statements

Look at the person you are talking to

Listen to the response

Your body language is appropriate

Open mind

Use assertive communication style

CONFLICT RESOLUTION

CONFLICT

Calm attitude, manage stress

Open to opposing views

Never make assumptions about what the other person (party) is thinking or feeling

Focus on the action, not the person

Look for other options

I-statements

Compromise (negotiate a solution)

Teamwork (make the decision together)

REFUSAL

I SAY NO

I-statement

State a reason

Assertive voice

You are in control

The "**N**o" statement is clear and direct

Options (what else can you do: leave the situation, get help)

NEGOTIATION

SLIDE

State what you want or need

Listen and clarify

Identify with other perspectives

Determine common ground

Elicit agreement

  HUMAN KINETICS   From S. Benes and H. Alperin, 2019, *Lesson planning for skills-based health education* (Champaign, IL: Human Kinetics). Reprinted, by permission, from S. Benes and H. Alperin, 2016, *The essentials of teaching health education* (Champaign, IL: Human Kinetics).

FIGURE 5.1 Communication skill cues for grades 6 through 8.

Communication

STANDARD 4

Students will demonstrate the ability to use interpersonal communication skills to enhance health and avoid or reduce health risks.

I TELL YOU

I dentify feelings, thoughts, ideas

T ell feelings, thoughts, ideas

E xpress using "I" statements

L ook at the person (people) you are talking to

I isten to the response

Y our body language is appropriate

O pen mind

U se assertive communication style

REFUSAL
I SAY NO

I -statement

S tate a reason

A ssertive voice

Y ou are in control

The "**N** o" statement is clear and direct

O ptions (what else can you do: leave the situation, get help)

CONFLICT RESOLUTION
CONFLICTTS

C alm attitude, manage stress

O pen to opposing views

N ever make assumptions about what the other person (party) is thinking or feeling

F ocus on action, not the person

L ook for other options

I -statements

C ompromise (negotiate a solution)

T eamwork (make the decision together)

T iming (find a good time to communicate)

S etting (identify a good place to work through the issues)

NEGOTIATION
SLIDE

S tate what you want or need

L isten and clarify

I dentify with other perspectives

D etermine common ground

E licit agreement

 HUMAN KINETICS

From S. Benes and H. Alperin, 2019, *Lesson planning for skills-based health education* (Champaign, IL: Human Kinetics). Reprinted, by permission, from S. Benes and H. Alperin, 2016, *The essentials of teaching health education* (Champaign, IL: Human Kinetics).

FIGURE 5.2 Communication skill cues for grades 9 through 12.

UNIT OUTLINE

This section includes an outline of the unit for Standard 4; table 5.2 shows this outline, including lesson titles, lesson objectives, the step(s) of the skill development model that are addressed in each lesson, and the titles of the main learning activities in each lesson.

This unit uses the performance indicators of Standard 4, grades 6 to 12, to form the basis for the unit objectives. Throughout the unit, students will use the topic of healthy relationships to apply the skill. In our experience, the discussion of relationships is a good fit with the skill of interpersonal communication because you can easily integrate many different aspects of communication throughout a variety of relationships relevant to students' lives. Specifically, students will discuss various verbal and nonverbal communication strategies in order to effectively demonstrate refusal skills and conflict management approaches and to communicate in health-enhancing ways to a variety of individuals.

The objectives and materials included here are appropriate, with certain modifications, for students in grades 6 through 12. The additional objectives included would be suitable, with necessary modifications, for students in grades 6 through 12 as well. The materials here focus on effective communication (self-expression), refusal, and conflict resolution.

This unit contains all of the performance indicators for Standard 4, grades 6 through 12, with the exception of indicator 4.8.4, Demonstrate how to ask for assistance to enhance health of self and others, and indicator 4.12.4, Demonstrate how to ask for and offer assistance to enhance the health of self and others. This performance indicator is intentionally left out because the unit does not explicitly address the topic. In addition, negotiation is not included as part of this unit, and we encourage you to consider where negotiation would fit in your curriculum. When teaching a skill as large and complex as interpersonal communication, you might not be able to include all aspects of the skill (e.g., you might not be able to include negotiation) or objectives and have them covered by one unit. We often see that interpersonal communication units appear in multiple grades within the curriculum. This provides a rich opportunity that not only allows your students to practice the skill at a variety of different times but also allows you to vary the forms and components of communication. While possible to cover all aspects within one unit, the unit may become too big or cumbersome to manage and assess. Also, you might not feel that your students are ready to tackle the amount of material, and it will work better if it is broken up into smaller units. Be sure to modify the unit lessons and activities to fit within your curriculum and to meet the needs of your students.

The additional learning objectives presented with this unit reflect additional student outcomes. These objectives are related to the healthy relationships content in the unit. Note that some objectives show how they align with Standard 1 performance indicators from the National Health Education Standards. Our intention is to show how the Standard 1 performance indicators can be integrated into the health topics that are included in your units.

Other health topics could also easily integrate into this unit and still address the performance indicators from Standard 1.

Unit Objectives, Grades 6 Through 8

By the end of this unit, students will be able to

▪ apply effective verbal and nonverbal communication skills to enhance relationship health (indicator 4.8.1);

▪ demonstrate refusal skills that avoid or reduce health risks in relationship situations (indicator 4.8.2);

▪ demonstrate effective conflict management or resolution strategies within relationship situations (indicator 4.8.3);

▪ discuss the importance of healthy relationships on their social, emotional, intellectual, and physical health (indicators 1.8.1 and 1.8.2); and

▪ describe characteristics and benefits of healthy relationships, including healthy behaviors in a relationship (indicator 1.8.7).

Unit Objectives Grades 9 Through 12

By the end of this unit, students will be able to

▪ use skills for communicating effectively with family, peers, and others to enhance health (indicator 4.12.1);

▪ demonstrate refusal skills to enhance health and avoid or reduce health risks in relationship situations (indicator 4.12.2);

▪ demonstrate strategies to prevent, manage, or resolve interpersonal conflicts without harming self or others (indicator 4.12.3);

▪ discuss the importance of healthy relationships on their social, emotional, intellectual, and physical health (indicators 1.12.1 and 1.12.2); and

▪ discuss the possible implications of unhealthy relationships on personal health and wellness (indicators 1.12.5, 1.12.7, and 1.12.8).

Additional Unit Objectives, Grades 6 Through 12

By the end of this unit, students will be able to

▪ identify people in their lives they would like to communicate with and information they would like to share with those people;

▪ define the ability to effectively communicate;

▪ discuss the importance of effective communication in supporting healthy relationships;

▪ describe characteristics of effective communication;

▪ list the skill cues for effective communication, refusal, and conflict resolution;

▪ identify effective and ineffective communication in relationship scenarios; and

▪ observe and evaluate peers' communication skills, providing suggestions for improvement.

TABLE 5.2   Standard 4 Unit Outline

Lesson title	Lesson objectives (indicators in parentheses) *By the end of this lesson, students will be able to:*	Steps of the skill development model addressed in the lesson	Main learning activities
Lesson 1: I Wish I Could Talk To . . .	• Identify people in their lives they would like to communicate with and information they would like to share with those people • Define the ability to effectively communicate • Discuss the importance of effective communication in supporting healthy relationships	Skill introduction (step 1)	I Wish I Could Talk To . . . (p. 115)
Lesson 2: What Is Effective Interpersonal Communication?	• List the skill cues for effective communication, refusal, and conflict resolution • Describe characteristics of effective communication	Steps of the skill and modeling (steps 2 and 3)	What Is Effective Interpersonal Communication? (p. 119)
Lesson 3: Identifying Effective Communication	• Identify effective and ineffective communication in relationship scenarios • Describe characteristics and benefits of healthy relationships, including healthy behaviors in a relationship (1.8.7) *or* • Discuss the importance of healthy relationships on their social, emotional, intellectual, and physical health (1.12.1 and 1.12.2) • Discuss the possible implications of unhealthy relationships on personal health and wellness (1.12.5, 1.12.7, and 1.12.8)	Skill practice (step 4)	Do You See What I See? (p. 122)
Lesson 4: Fishing for Healthy Relationships	• Discuss the importance of healthy relationships on their social, emotional, intellectual, and physical health (1.8.1 and 1.8.2 *or* 1.12.1 and 1.12.2) • Describe characteristics and benefits of healthy relationships, including healthy behaviors in a relationship (1.8.7 *or* 1.12.1 and 1.12.7) • Discuss the possible implications of unhealthy relationships on personal health and wellness (1.12.5, 1.12.7, and 1.12.8) • Apply effective verbal and nonverbal communication skills in small groups to enhance relationship health (4.8.1) *or* • Use skills for communicating effectively with peers within small groups to prioritize characteristics of healthy relationships (4.12.1)	Health topic focus (no skill development in this lesson)	• Interpersonal Communication Quiz (p. 126) • Fishing for Healthy Relationships (p. 128)

Lesson title	Lesson objectives (indicators in parentheses) *By the end of this lesson, students will be able to:*	Steps of the skill development model addressed in the lesson	Main learning activities
Lesson 5: Real-Life Relationships	• Discuss the importance of healthy relationships on their social, emotional, intellectual, and physical health (1.8.1 and 1.8.2 *or* 1.12.1 and 1.12.2) • Describe characteristics and benefits of healthy relationships, including healthy behaviors in a relationship (1.8.7 *or* 1.12.1 and 1.12.7) • Discuss the role of effective communication in supporting healthy relationships (1.12.5 and 1.12.7)	Health topic focus (no skill development in this lesson)	Relationship Stations (p. 133)
Lesson 6: What's Your Story?	• Demonstrate effective communication, refusal, and conflict resolution skills (4.8.1, 4.8.2, and 4.8.3 *or* 4.12.1, 4.12.2, and 4.12.3)	Skill practice (step 4)	Skill Practice (p. 137)
Lessons 7, 8, 9 and 10: Let's Communicate Together!	• Demonstrate effective communication, refusal, and conflict resolution skills (4.8.1, 4.8.2, and 4.8.3 *or* 4.12.1, 4.12.2, and 4.12.3) • Observe and evaluate peers' communication	Skill practice (step 4) and feedback and reinforcement (step 5)	Relationship Role-Plays (p. 141)

Performance indicators are from: Joint Committee on National Health Education Standards. (2007). *National Health Education Standards: Achieving Excellence* (2nd ed.). Atlanta, GA: American Cancer Society.

ASSESSMENT

The Relationship Role-Play Assessment is a supplement to the activities that students will be completing in lessons 6 through 9. A full detailed description of these activities can be found in those lessons. The description here focuses on the assessment aspect only.

Objectives

Through this assessment, students will demonstrate their ability to

- communicate and collaborate with peers to solve a common relationship problem (addressing NHES performance indicators 4.8.1–4.8.3 or 4.12.1–4.12.3);
- observe and evaluate peers' communication skills, providing suggestions for improvement; and
- evaluate personal communication skills.

Description

This two-part assessment includes student role-plays and an evaluation of students' ability to communicate and work in teams. The role-play rubric includes criteria related to the content of relationships while maintaining a focus on students' ability to demonstrate the skill of interpersonal communication. The group work rubric should be used to evaluate students in class while they work on their role-playing. Use both aspects of the assessment to compile a final evaluation score for the unit. We have outlined a point distribution that weights the role-plays slightly more than the in-class assessment. Add the total points for the role-play to the points from the group work to determine a final score for the unit assessment.

Modifications

- When modifying the assessment to fit your particular needs, keep in mind that you might want to add additional criteria or aspects to the project.
- Reduce the number of role-plays each group is expected to complete to fit into allotted time.

Implementation Tips

- Obtain a parent's or guardian's permission prior to filming students.
- Refer to the skill cues prior to students starting the assignment, and clarify any questions related to how each cue is demonstrated.

Modified from a submission by Lindsay Armbruster, middle/high school health teacher in New York.

Relationship Role-Play Assessment

Name: _____

During the unit, you will be planning three role-plays that deal with situations related to family relationships, peer or friend relationships, and romantic partner relationships. In class, you will be asked to perform at least one role-play for your peers. For your grade, you must record all three role-plays that you will submit to me for evaluation.

Key Points:

- You must have *one* role-play that demonstrates effective communication (self-expression).

- You must have *one* role-play that demonstrates effective refusal skills.

- You must have *one* role-play that demonstrates effective conflict resolution.

- Your characters should demonstrate the skill cues we have been covering in the unit.

- Each person in your group needs to demonstrate each skill for the **assessment** (not for the role-play in front of the class).

- Come see me if you need help figuring out how to make sure each person can show the skill.

- Use the Relationship Role-Play rubric to make sure you cover all required components. Refer to the skill cues for explanation of each category. The rubric is useful when developing the scripts as well. Your group should be able to complete the assessment during class time.

(continued)

Relationship Role-Play Assessment *(continued)*

Relationship Role-Play Rubric

	4	3	2	1
Self-expression— Body language	Body language is appropriate, open or inviting, and supports effective communication.	Body language is appropriate, inviting, and mostly supports effective communication.	Body language is moderately inviting or appropriate for open communication to occur.	Did not demonstrate appropriate body language.
Self-expression— Assertiveness	Actions demonstrate assertiveness and express thoughts, feelings, or ideas in ways that support effective communication.	Actions demonstrate assertiveness and express thoughts, feelings, or ideas to support effective communication.	Actions do not demonstrate assertiveness or expressed thoughts, feelings, or ideas that loosely support effective communication.	Student is not assertive and does not express thoughts, feelings, or ideas appropriately.
Refusal—No statement	The student very clearly and assertively says *no* and states a reason.	The student says *no*, is assertive, and states a reason but is not convincing.	The student does not complete one or two of the criteria (does not say *no*, does not state a reason, or is not assertive) appropriately.	The student does not clearly say *no*, is not assertive, and does not state a reason (the student does not complete any of the criteria).
Refusal—Healthy resolution	Resolves the situation in a health-enhancing manner.	Resolves the situation, and the resolution is somewhat health-enhancing.	Resolves the situation in a risky or inappropriate manner.	Does not resolve the situation.
Conflict resolution—Attitude	Demonstrates effective stress management techniques, keeps an open mind, and is assertive during the conflict resolution.	Demonstrates stress-management techniques that are somewhat effective, demonstrates an open mind, and is assertive during the conflict resolution.	Addresses one or two of the criteria in ways that support conflict resolution.	Does not demonstrate an appropriate attitude during the role-play.
Conflict resolution—Solution	Compromises effectively and works with others to create a health-enhancing solution.	Compromise is weak though the student works together with others to create a health-enhancing solution.	Compromise is weak, does not work effectively with others, and the solution is not health enhancing.	Does not compromise, and the solution is not health enhancing.
Relationship content—Benefits of healthy relationships to health	Includes at least three accurate and appropriate benefits of healthy relationships.	Includes two accurate and appropriate benefits of healthy relationships.	States only one benefit or states more than one, but the benefits included are not accurate or appropriate.	Does not include any accurate or appropriate benefits.
Relationship content—Effects of healthy relationships	Includes at least three correct effects of healthy relationships.	Includes two correct effects of healthy relationships.	Includes two effects, but only one effect is accurate or appropriate.	Does not include any correct effects.
Total score (out of 32 points)				

Strengths:

Areas for Improvement:

Group Work Assessment Rubric

Name: _____

During group work, the student was observed:

	Yes (2 points)	No (0 points)
Contributing to the group positively		
Making eye contact		
Listening actively to others		
Working effectively with others		
Being assertive when expressing ideas		
Total (out of 10 points)		

Feedback:

LESSON PLANS

The lesson plans included here are the ones outlined in the unit outline earlier in the chapter and will advance students toward achieving unit objectives and being able to successfully demonstrate the skill (evaluated in the assessment). The included lessons assume a 50-minute class period. Consider this prior to implementation.

Lesson plans include suggested activities, and those activities follow the lesson plans. Lesson plans and activities can be used together or independently to meet the needs of your classes.

Throughout the lesson plans, you will see the steps of the skill development model in **boldface type** after activities that address each skill development step.

Purpose

A critical but often overlooked aspect of health is the role of effective communication in maintaining and enhancing health. The purpose of this lesson is to show students how important communication is and how often we actually use it in health-related and nonhealth-related situations.

NHES Performance Indicators

None addressed

Objectives

Students will be able to

- identify people in their lives they would like to communicate with and information they would like to share with those people;
- define the ability to effectively communicate; and
- discuss the importance of effective communication in supporting healthy relationships.

Skill Development Step

Step 1: introduction (definition, relevance, and educational outcomes)

Materials

- Materials for the I Wish I Could Talk To . . . activity
- Handouts for notes (if applicable)

Instant Activity

After students take their seats, they write their responses to the prompt: "How does communication affect health?"

Introduction

Let students know that today is the first day in the interpersonal communication unit. Explain what the students will be able to do at the end of the unit (unit objectives and assessment). **(educational outcomes)** Review the lesson objectives and then begin the first activity.

Main Activities

1. I Wish I Could Talk To . . . (see page 115)
2. Large-group discussion:
   - Ask students to share ideas about how communication can affect health (from their instant activity responses).
   - Conclude the discussion by agreeing on the relevance of communication to health. **(relevance)**
3. Review of a definition for interpersonal communication that will be used throughout the unit. **(definition)**

Closure

Preview the next lesson for students by explaining that next time they will be learning the steps to effective communication. At this time, you may also want to provide information about the assessment to students.

Differentiation

- Provide visuals and a handout with key information about the relevance and a definition of the skill.
- Provide guided notes to help students.

Homework

Before the next class, ask students to record at least two situations where they use interpersonal communication. They will bring their ideas to the next class.

I Wish I Could Talk To . . .

LESSON 1

NHES Performance Indicators

None addressed

Objective

Students will be able to identify people in their lives they would like to communicate with and information they would like to share with those people.

Skill Development Step

Step 1: introduction

Duration

10 minutes

Materials

- Sticky notes
- Poll Everywhere (if using the second modification)

Description

This activity serves as a way to get students thinking about the relevance of interpersonal communication and why it matters in their lives.

1. Students are given two sticky notes. On the first note, they answer this prompt: "I wish I could talk to . . ." On the second, they finish this phrase: "about . . ." It works best to leave this open ended; do not give students guidance about how they should answer. You may want to let students know that they will be sharing their ideas with others, albeit anonymously. See Modifications for an anonymous way to implement this activity.

2. Have students post their I-wish-I-could-talk-to . . . sticky note on the board. Once all sticky notes are on the board, invite students to come up and review all the sticky notes. Ask them to share observations about who is up on the board. You might prompt them with questions such as those that follow.

   - Do we want to talk to the same people?
   - What do you notice about the relationships your classmates may (or may not) have with the people on the board?
   - What are some conclusions we can draw from the sticky notes on the board about whom we want to talk to?
   - Was it easy or hard to come up with someone you wish you could talk to?

3. Next, have students get into small groups. In their groups, students should discuss the topics from their second sticky note. They should draw conclusions about what their classmates want to discuss and discuss whether or not they think these topics are applicable to high school students in their community and in general.

4. Bring the small groups back to the large group and ask groups to share and discuss the results.

Tips and Extensions

- Answers should be anonymous so that students feel more comfortable being honest in the activity.
- Type student answers in Wordle or other word cloud format—one for who and one for what, and share with the class to illustrate the importance of communication in relationships. Laminate the Wordles and use them to begin discussions in future classes.

Modifications

- For English language learners, translate or identify terms used in the activity to allow better understanding and comprehension.

- Use www.polleverywhere.com or another polling site to have students respond anonymously and in real time to each of the prompts. Poll Everywhere has a feature where the responses can be made into a word cloud.

Resources

- Poll Everywhere, www.polleverywhere.com
- Wordle, www.wordle.net

Modified from a submission by Claudia T. Brown, former high school health teacher in Massachusetts.

Purpose

In lesson 1, students were introduced to the definition and relevance of interpersonal communication. Now students will learn the skill cues for effective communication for general communication, refusal, and conflict resolution.

NHES Performance Indicators

None addressed

Objectives

Students will be able to

- list the skill cues for effective communication, refusal, and conflict resolution; and
- describe characteristics of effective communication.

Skill Development Step

Step 2: steps of the skill (skill cues)

Materials

- Handouts for skill cue review
- Materials needed for the What is Effective Interpersonal Communication? activity
- Relationship Role-Play Assessment materials

Instant Activity

Students enter the classroom and take a short quiz. The information collected can be used as a formative assessment and a retention tool (having students try to recall information can help it stick). The quiz should include questions about the relevance of communication and the definition as discussed in the previous lesson. If you have ready access to technology, consider using an online polling software or survey tool to receive responses immediately.

Introduction

Review the lesson objectives with students. Review the quiz and address any misunderstandings or errors before beginning.

Main Activities

1. Have students complete the What Is Effective Interpersonal Communication? activity (page 119).
2. Review skill cues for each aspect of communication covered in the unit: self-expression, refusal, and conflict resolution. Reference student ideas from the brainstorm they will conduct in the activity whenever possible to connect to the cues. You may even change a word or phrase to integrate their ideas into the final versions. It is beneficial to have a handout for students with the skill cues or to have a guided notes sheet to help them remember the cues. **(skill cues)**

Closure

If students completed the homework from lesson 1, ask them to share the skill cues observed in their interaction. If they did not, ask them to discuss in small groups or share in pairs what might be the challenges to effectively communicating in their lives. Discuss as a large group and make note of their ideas for use later in the unit. End by letting students know that even though there are challenges, communication is essential for helping keep us healthy, especially in maintaining healthy relationships. Let them know they will be practicing skills to help them feel more confident and overcome communication challenges.

(continued)

Differentiation

Provide skill cue cards for students or have posters hanging around the room for easy reference.

Homework

Have students share the skill cues with a parent or guardian and see what they think about the skill cues. Would they add anything? How often do they communicate in this way?

What Is Effective Interpersonal Communication?

LESSON 2

NHES Performance Indicators

None addressed

Objective

Students will be able to describe characteristics of effective communication.

Skill Development Step

Step 1: introduction (relevance)

Duration

15 to 20 minutes

Materials

Effective Communication Brainstorm worksheet for students to record ideas

Description

1. Put students into small groups. Tell students that in their groups, they should brainstorm what effective communication in relationships looks like, feels like, and sounds like. Students should complete the Effective Communication Brainstorm worksheet provided.
2. Ask each group to share their ideas for each aspect. Record their ideas on the board. You will use student ideas in the next part of the lesson when you review the skill cues for each aspect of interpersonal communication.

Tips and Extensions

- Try to use as many ideas from the students when reviewing the skill cues as possible.
- Encourage students to come up with at least four ideas for each aspect (looks like, feels like, sounds like).

Modifications

This could be a gallery walk activity where students go around in small groups and write their ideas on flip chart paper. Each flip chart page has *looks like, feels like,* or *sounds like* written on it.

Effective Communication Brainstorm

Effective communication in a relationship . . .

Looks like . . .	Feels like . . .	Sounds like . . .

LESSON 3: Identifying Effective Communication

Purpose

Before students begin their practice, they must have an opportunity to see the skill cues in action. This lesson is focused on providing examples of both effective and ineffective communication in a variety of relationship scenarios.

NHES Performance Indicators

Grades 6 Through 8

- Describe characteristics and benefits of healthy relationships, including healthy behaviors in a relationship (indicator 1.8.7).

Grades 9 Through 12

- Discuss the importance of healthy relationships on students' social, emotional, intellectual, and physical health (adapted from indicators 1.12.1 and 1.12.2).
- Discuss the possible implications of unhealthy relationships on personal health and wellness (adapted from indicators 1.12.5, 1.12.7, and 1.12.8).

Objective

Students will be able to identify effective and ineffective communication in relationship scenarios.

Skill Development Step

Step 3: modeling

Materials

Materials needed for the Do You See What I See? activity

Instant Activity

Before or when students enter the classroom, they are assigned to groups. Each group receives a set of skill cues with each skill cue written on a separate piece of paper for each of the three types of communication that are all jumbled. Students need to correctly sort the skill cues for each type of communication.

Introduction

Review the lesson objectives and the skill cues with students. Tell students that today they will be watching different videos to determine whether effective communication or ineffective communication is present and to see if they can identify the skill cues when they see them (or which are missing).

Main Activities

1. Have students complete the Do You See What I See? activity (page 122). **(modeling)**
2. Debrief the activity: Discuss with students which videos demonstrated effective or ineffective communication. You will likely find that this was not easy for students to determine. Be sure to ask them to justify their responses by referring to the skill cues. Provide a space for other students from other groups to respond and agree or disagree. End the debriefing by telling students that they will be spending a lot of time working on demonstrating and identifying the skill cues so that they are able to more clearly demonstrate the skills, so that they can be more aware of their communication styles, and so that they can more effectively communicate in a variety of situations.

Closure

Review the key takeaways of the lesson. Preview the next lesson by telling students that communication is a key aspect of healthy relationships and will be discussed in the next lesson.

Differentiation

- Include videos with closed captions.
- Provide scripts for the videos.

Homework

Have students find their own video clips of an effective communication or an ineffective communication situation and explain why it is effective or what would make it more effective based on the skill cues. You could then use these in future classes.

Do You See What I See?

LESSON 3

NHES Performance Indicators

Grades 6 Through 8

- Describe characteristics and benefits of healthy relationships, including healthy behaviors in a relationship (indicator 1.8.7).

Grades 9 Through 12

- Discuss the importance of healthy relationships on students' social, emotional, intellectual, and physical health (indicators 1.12.1 and 1.12.2).
- Discuss the possible implications of unhealthy relationships on personal health and wellness (indicators 1.12.5, 1.12.7, and 1.12.8).

Objective

Students will be able to identify effective and ineffective communication in relationship scenarios.

Skill Development Steps

- Step 2: steps of the skill (reinforcing this step in the activity)
- Step 3: modeling

Duration

20 to 25 minutes (can vary depending on the number of videos included)

Materials

- Quick response (QR) codes with videos embedded (if using QR codes)
- Copies of the Do You See What I See? worksheet

Description

1. Before the lesson, prepare video clips illustrating ineffective and effective communication in relationship situations. It would be most relevant to use clips from shows or movies that students can relate to (or that they watch). Have at least four videos, two with effective examples and two with ineffective examples. Have examples of each aspect of communication: self-expression, refusal, and conflict resolution.

2. Put students into small groups. Students watch the videos on tablets or other devices. Students complete the Do You See What I See? worksheet for each video.

3. Have students bring their skill cues handout from lesson 2 so they can use the correct language and reinforce the skill cues.

Tips and Extensions

Remind students that it might be challenging to determine the effectiveness of the interaction, and that is OK.

Modifications

- This activity could be done as stations with a video at each station.
- Have students work in pairs rather than in small groups.
- Create a QR code with a link to each video. Place the QR codes around the room if you want to include movement in the lesson or distribute them to each group.
- Have each student fill out the worksheet individually with the videos playing in front of the classroom.

After you watch each video, work together as a group to answer the questions about each video. Don't forget to use the communication vocabulary that we went over (use your skill cues handout for help).

Video 1

Was the interaction effective or ineffective? Why?

What skill cues were demonstrated in the interaction?

If the interaction was ineffective, what could have been done to make it more effective?

Video 2

Was the interaction effective or ineffective? Why?

What skill cues were demonstrated in the interaction?

If the interaction was ineffective, what could have been done to make it more effective?

Video 3

Was the interaction effective or ineffective? Why?

What skill cues were demonstrated in the interaction?

If the interaction was ineffective, what could have been done to make it more effective?

Video 4

Was the interaction effective or ineffective? Why?

What skill cues were demonstrated in the interaction?

If the interaction was ineffective, what could have been done to make it more effective?

LESSON 4: Fishing for Healthy Relationships

Purpose

In addition to learning about the skills, students need to acquire information about characteristics of healthy relationships and ways to support healthy relationships. This lesson focuses on characteristics of potential partners in dating relationships. This information will then be discussed as it relates to other types of relationships in the next lessons.

NHES Performance Indicators

Grades 6 Through 8

- Discuss the importance of healthy relationships on their social, emotional, intellectual, and physical health (indicators 1.8.1 and 1.8.2).
- Describe characteristics and benefits of healthy relationships, including healthy behaviors in a relationship (indicator 1.8.7).
- Apply effective verbal and nonverbal communication skills in small groups to enhance relationship health (indicator 4.8.1).

Grades 9 Through 12

- Discuss the importance of healthy relationships on their social, emotional, intellectual, and physical health (indicators 1.12.1 and 1.12.2).
- Describe characteristics and benefits of healthy relationships, including healthy behaviors in a relationship (indicators 1.12.1 and 1.12.7).
- Discuss the possible implications of unhealthy relationships on personal health and wellness (indicators 1.12.5, 1.12.7, and 1.12.8).
- Use skills for communicating effectively with peers within small groups to prioritize characteristics of healthy relationships (indicator 4.12.1).

Objectives

See the NHES performance indicators in the previous list. There are no additional lesson objectives.

Skill Development Step

Step 4: skill practice (but note that the focus is on practicing communication during group work rather than a structured practice activity)

Materials

Materials needed for the Fishing for Healthy Relationships activity

Instant Activity

Interpersonal Communication Quiz (page 126). This is used as a review technique, not a graded quiz.

Introduction

After reviewing the quiz and the skill cues, introduce the lesson objectives. Tell students that today you will be focusing on characteristics of potential partners in romantic relationships.

Main Activities

1. Fishing for Healthy Relationships (page 128) (Be sure to collect each group's list as you will be using their ideas in the next lesson.)
2. Large-group discussion about how healthy relationships affect health and how communication is an essential component to healthy relationships

Closure

Preview the next lesson by telling students to think about how some of these characteristics might be important in other types of relationships in our lives (e.g., family or peers). Let students know that you will be discussing these other types of relationships in the next lesson.

Differentiation

- Include visuals for the relationship words.
- Include definitions for terms students may be unfamiliar with.
- Include words in students' native languages.

Resources

Search for *a great catch* at http://flippedhealth.blogspot.com/

Interpersonal Communication Quiz

LESSON 4

NHES Performance Indicators

Grades 6 Through 8

- Discuss the importance of healthy relationships on their social, emotional, intellectual, and physical health (indicators 1.8.1 and 1.8.2).
- Describe characteristics and benefits of healthy relationships, including healthy behaviors in a relationship (indicator 1.8.7).

Grades 9 Through 12

- Discuss the importance of healthy relationships on their social, emotional, intellectual, and physical health (indicators 1.12.1 and 1.12.2).
- Describe characteristics and benefits of healthy relationships, including healthy behaviors in a relationship (indicators 1.12.1 and 1.12.7).
- Discuss the possible implications of unhealthy relationships on personal health and wellness (indicators 1.12.5, 1.12.7, and 1.12.8).

Objective

Students will be able to apply information learned in a formative assessment.

Skill Development Step

Not applicable; this activity focuses on the functional information.

Duration

10 minutes

Materials

Copies of the Interpersonal Communication Quiz

Description

Students should take the quiz individually at the start of class. Review the answers as a class, and review the skill cues for effective communication, refusal, and conflict resolution. An answer key for the quiz is provided in the web resource.

Modifications

Have students act out the statements in different communication styles and have students identify the style they used.

Submitted by Terri Bowman, middle school health teacher in Massachusetts.

Name: _____ Class: _____

Part 1

In the statements provided, determine if each statement is assertive, passive, or aggressive.

1. _____ "No, I don't feel like going out tonight. Maybe we can go out next week."

2. _____ "Why bother asking? My Dad never lets me do anything anyway."

3. _____ "What is wrong with you? You are such an idiot sometimes."

4. _____ "You better get my name out of your mouth or I'll slap you!"

5. _____ "I don't really want to, but I will if that is what you want."

6. _____ "I feel loved when you say that I look nice."

7. _____ "You are so fake! Get out of my face!"

8. _____ "Thank you for asking, but no, I don't want any McDonald's food."

Part 2

Read the situation, and then write how you would tell your friend "no."

Your friend wants you to steal $20 from your father's wallet. Your friend says that your parents will never know, but you know that it's wrong to steal—and if your parents ever found out you would lose your phone and be grounded for at least a month. You don't want to lose their trust.

Write no in a passive way:

Write no in an aggressive way:

Write no in an assertive way:

Fishing for Healthy Relationships

LESSON 4

NHES Performance Indicators

Grades 6 Through 8

- Discuss the importance of healthy relationships on their social, emotional, intellectual, and physical health (indicators 1.8.1 and 1.8.2).
- Describe characteristics and benefits of healthy relationships, including healthy behaviors in a relationship (indicator 1.8.7).
- Apply effective verbal and nonverbal communication skills in small groups to enhance relationship health (indicator 4.8.1).

Grades 9 Through 12

- Discuss the importance of healthy relationships on their social, emotional, intellectual, and physical health (indicators 1.12.1 and 1.12.2).
- Describe characteristics and benefits of healthy relationships, including healthy behaviors in a relationship (indicators 1.12.1 and 1.12.7).
- Discuss the possible implications of unhealthy relationships on personal health and wellness (indicators 1.12.5, 1.12.7, and 1.12.8).
- Use skills for communicating effectively with peers within small groups to prioritize characteristics of healthy relationships (indicator 4.12.1).

Objectives

See the NHES performance indicators in the previous list. There are no additional lesson objectives.

Duration

30 minutes

Materials

- Fishing rods or dowels with strings attached to resemble fishing poles
- Cards (You can find the cards in the web resource or make your own based on the characteristics in the Characteristics for Cards list.)
- Healthy Relationship Characteristics worksheet (see page 130)

Description

1. Working in small groups, students "fish" by using a fishing pole (dowel rod with a magnet that can pick up the cards that also have magnets on them) to pick up various cards with a relationship quality or personal characteristic on it.

2. The students then have to fill in a Healthy Relationship Characteristics worksheet by writing each quality in one of three columns (must have, significant, or not necessary for a healthy relationship). Students need to work together to decide as a group where the characteristics belong. This is an added challenge for students to have to collaborate with others to come to group decisions about what really matters in dating relationships. Their experience with this will also serve as a good discussion point after the activity.

3. Once the groups have a list of various qualities, stop the activity and ask questions such as:
   - How does this activity resemble real-life relationships?
   - What do you think are the two most important qualities to having a successful healthy relationship? Why do you think this?
   - What are two qualities you are missing from your current list?
   - Was it easy or challenging to decide where to place the characteristics? Did you often agree in your group? Disagree?

Tips and Extensions

- Assign roles in the groups or suggest taking turns in fishing and recording.
- Remind students to practice their effective communication skills as they decide where the characteristics should go.

Modifications

- This doesn't need to involve fishing. Students could just pick a card from a pile.
- Students could brainstorm the characteristics ahead of time (without knowing why). Their ideas could then be used in this activity.

Adapted from a submission by Andy Horne, high school health teacher in Illinois.

Characteristics for Cards

Same religion

Enjoys the outdoors

Shy and quiet

Handles stress

Smart

Committed to relationship

Happy most of the time

Short

Slim

Good provider

Values a beautiful home

Sense of humor

Likes your family

Independent

Wants to live in the suburbs

Nice body

Virgin (no other sexual partners)

Cigarette smoker

Life of the party

About the same age

Cooks

Wants to live in the country

Faithful

Respectful

Very health conscious

Money saver

Money spender

Hard worker

Tall

Loves to talk

Humble

Confident

Good with kids

Has a lot of education

Risk taker

Spontaneous

Pet lover

Has a lot of friends; is sociable

Easy going

Passionate

Ambitious

Unselfish

Good listener

Likes sports

Musical

Sexually experienced

Considerate

Likes to gamble with money

Rude

Jealous

Trustworthy

Opinionated

Into politics

Independent

Loves to travel

Same interests

Good hygiene

Wealthy

Athletic and fit

Punctual

Has a good job

Healthy Relationship Characteristics

As your group "catches fish" or picks up cards, discuss which category they belong in. You must come to an agreement as a group. Record the characteristic in the appropriate column.

Crucial (a must-have)	Important (a big deal but not a must-have)	Not necessary

Purpose

In the previous lesson, students discussed characteristics of dating relationships. It is important that students see how certain characteristics are critical for any kind of relationship in their life, whether it is a peer, a family member, a coworker, etc. This lesson focuses on the functional information of relationships in nondating situations—what is similar and what is different.

NHES Performance Indicators

Grades 6 Through 8

- Discuss the importance of healthy relationships on their social, emotional, intellectual, and physical health (indicators 1.8.1 and 1.8.2).
- Describe characteristics and benefits of healthy relationships, including healthy behaviors in a relationship (indicator 1.8.7).

Grades 9 Through 12

- Discuss the importance of healthy relationships on their social, emotional, intellectual, and physical health (indicators 1.12.1 and 1.12.2).
- Describe characteristics and benefits of healthy relationships, including healthy behaviors in a relationship (indicators 1.12.1 and 1.12.7).
- Discuss the role of effective communication in supporting healthy relationships (indicators 1.12.5 and 1.12.7).

Objectives

See the NHES performance indicators in the previous list. There are no additional lesson objectives.

Skill Development Step

Step 4: skill practice (but note that the focus here is on practicing communication during group work rather than a structured practice activity)

Materials

- A list of the crucial and significant characteristics from all the groups from lesson 4; students will use this in the Relationship Stations activity
- Materials needed for the Relationship Stations activity

Instant Activity

As students take their seats, they should respond to the following prompt: "List at least three people who are not a significant other, with whom you have a relationship. For each of those people, write how you most often communicate with that person and how that person affects your health."

Introduction

Tell students that they were asked to think about other relationships in their lives for the instant activity because even though the last lesson focused on dating relationships, there are many other relationships that influence our health. Tell students that you are going to discuss characteristics of these relationships and how communication can affect these relationships.

Main Activities

1. In a large-group discussion, ask students to share people from their list to create a big list on the board. Ask students to see if they can categorize the people on the board (i.e., friends, family, etc.).
2. Have the class complete the Relationship Stations activity (page 133).

(continued)

3. In a large-group discussion, ask students how many of the characteristics discussed during the Relationship Stations activity overlapped. What are some of the characteristics of relationships with multiple people? How would communication affect these relationships?

4. Students brainstorm a list of potential situations in each type of relationship that they have been discussing, with a focus on family, friends, and partner. You will be using these ideas at the start of lesson 6. Some ideas include:

   - *Family:* moving, divorce, chores, bathroom time, transportation, shared space
   - *Friends:* exclusion, new friends, new school, drug use, eating disorders, grades
   - *Partner:* time spent together, time spent apart, ways of showing affection, clinginess, cheating

Closure

Review by summarizing that we have many different relationships in our lives that can affect different aspects of our health. These relationships may all be very different, but there are certain characteristics that are important for supporting healthy relationships with a variety of people. One of the factors that can support healthy relationships is communication. Tell students that they will be using their brainstormed ideas in the next lesson to write stories that will be used in their final unit assessment.

Differentiation

- Provide students a written list of examples and have them classify the scenarios into categories.
- Ask students to focus on one or two categories and write ideas down around the room.

Relationship Stations

LESSON 5

NHES Performance Indicators

Grades 6 Through 8

- Discuss the importance of healthy relationships on their social, emotional, intellectual, and physical health (indicators 1.8.1 and 1.8.2).
- Describe characteristics and benefits of healthy relationships, including healthy behaviors in a relationship (indicator 1.8.7).

Grades 9 Through 12

- Discuss the importance of healthy relationships on their social, emotional, intellectual, and physical health (indicators 1.12.1 and 1.12.2).
- Describe characteristics and benefits of healthy relationships, including healthy behaviors in a relationship (indicators 1.12.1 and 1.12.7).
- Discuss the role of effective communication in supporting healthy relationships (indicators 1.12.5 and 1.12.7).

Objectives

See the NHES performance indicators in the previous list. There are no additional lesson objectives.

Skill Development Step

Not applicable; the focus is on functional information.

Duration

15 to 20 minutes

Materials

- Characteristics for Cards list (lesson 4)
- Relationship Stations worksheet

Description

1. Assign students to a station. Each station is one of the categories that students created earlier in the lesson. Also, include at least the following categories: friends, family, and trusted adults. Add other categories as appropriate based on student ideas.
2. At the stations, students use the handout that you created from their ideas generated in lesson 4 to determine which characteristics from romantic partner relationships would also apply to the type of relationship at their station. For example, if they were at the friend station, discuss which characteristics from their sheet would also be appropriate for a friend relationship. Next, discuss how these relationships can affect different areas of their health. They then rotate to the next station. Plan on approximately five minutes at each station.

Modifications

- Students use technology rather than a worksheet to record their responses.
- This activity can be done in a large group with discussion occurring for each type of relationship.
- Provide students with time to think about their responses individually before being put into groups or participating in the discussion.

Relationship Stations

Station Name: _____

Characteristics of healthy relationships:

How can your relationships affect your health?

Station Name: _____

Characteristics of healthy relationships:

How can your relationships affect your health?

Station Name: _____

Characteristics of healthy relationships:

How can your relationships affect your health?

Purpose

Students have discussed characteristics of healthy relationships and how communication can affect relationships. However, they have not had a chance to practice the aspects of communication covered in this unit: self-expression, refusal, and conflict resolution. This lesson provides an opportunity for skill practice before they begin working on their final assessments in the unit.

NHES Performance Indicators

Grades 6 Through 8

■ Apply effective verbal and nonverbal communication skills to enhance health (indicator 4.8.1).

■ Demonstrate refusal and negotiation skills that avoid or reduce health risks (indicator 4.8.2).

■ Demonstrate effective conflict management or resolution strategies (indicator 4.8.3).

Grades 9 Through 12

■ Use skills for communicating effectively with family, peers, and others to enhance health (indicator 4.12.1).

■ Demonstrate refusal, negotiation, and collaboration skills to enhance health and avoid or reduce health risks (indicator 4.12.2).

■ Demonstrate strategies to prevent, manage, or resolve interpersonal conflicts without harming self or others (indicator 4.12.3).

Objectives

See the NHES performance indicators in the previous list. There are no additional lesson objectives.

Skill Development Step

Step 4: skill practice

Materials

■ The Relationship Stations worksheet that was started in the previous lesson

■ Materials needed for the Skill Practice activity

Instant Activity

As students take their seats, have them try to recall the skill cues for each aspect of communication. You may want to scaffold this activity by providing the acronyms if you used them or other clues to help them remember. Remind students that it is OK if they can't remember, tell them to do the best they can.

Introduction

Review the skill cues with students. Tell students the objectives for the lesson are to finish their relationship stories and to practice some of the skills that they will be using in the rest of the unit.

Main Activities

1. Provide students time to write stories using their ideas from lesson 5. You could have students write these by hand or type them. You may need to provide scaffolding for the stories. Make sure students know that the stories should not have an ending. These will be used as scenarios in future lessons. Be sure that students write three stories; one for friends, one for family, and one for partners.

2. Skill Practice (page 137).

(continued)

Closure

Preview the next lessons by telling students that they will be using the stories and skills in role-plays in the next lessons. Also let them know that you will be describing their final assessment in the next class.

Differentiation

- Provide a handout that scaffolds the assignment for students.
- Provide a checklist for students with the skill cues and assignment criteria to allow students to self-check their work.

Skill Practice

NHES Performance Indicators

Grades 6 Through 8

- Apply effective verbal and nonverbal communication skills to enhance health (indicator 4.8.1).
- Demonstrate refusal and negotiation skills that avoid or reduce health risks (indicator 4.8.2).
- Demonstrate effective conflict management or resolution strategies (indicator 4.8.3).

Grades 9 Through 12

- Use skills for communicating effectively with family, peers, and others to enhance health (indicator 4.12.1).
- Demonstrate refusal, negotiation, and collaboration skills to enhance health and avoid or reduce health risks (indicator 4.12.2).
- Demonstrate strategies to prevent, manage, or resolve interpersonal conflicts without harming self or others (indicator 4.12.3).

Objectives

See the NHES performance indicators in the previous list. There are no additional lesson objectives.

Skill Development Step

Step 4: skill practice

Duration

15 to 20 minutes

Materials

- Scripts for the stations
- Checklists if you choose to modify the activity

Description

Preparation

- Set up three stations, one for each type of communication: self-expression, refusal, and conflict resolution. Assign students to a station.
- Create scripts for each station. You should create two different scripts that include examples of effective communication (self-expression, refusal, and interpersonal communication) for each station. The scripts will be most effective if you can make them relevant and appropriate for your students and situations they deal with. The more closely related to their experiences these can be, including using language they would use, the more useful this activity will be for students.

Activity Procedure

- Working in small groups or with partners depending on numbers, students should use the scripts to practice effective communication. Each student should have the chance to practice with at least one script at each station. Remind students that an important part of practice is their nonverbal communication as well. You may want to review the skill cues before beginning this activity.
- Students will have five to six minutes at each station. Students should rotate to each station so that they can practice each aspect of the skill.

Tips and Extensions

Circulate as students are practicing and provide feedback.

Modification

You could create a checklist for students to evaluate each other and provide feedback during their practice.

Purpose

Students have covered relationship content and practiced the skills. In these lessons, students will continue to develop the skill and then will perform a role-play for the final assessment and evaluation of the skill.

NHES Performance Indicators

Grades 6 Through 8

- Apply effective verbal and nonverbal communication skills to enhance health (indicator 4.8.1).
- Demonstrate refusal and negotiation skills that avoid or reduce health risks (indicator 4.8.2).
- Demonstrate effective conflict management or resolution strategies (indicator 4.8.3).

Grades 9 Through 12

- Use skills for communicating effectively with family, peers, and others to enhance health (indicator 4.12.1).
- Demonstrate refusal, negotiation, and collaboration skills to enhance health and avoid or reduce health risks (indicator 4.12.2).
- Demonstrate strategies to prevent, manage, or resolve interpersonal conflicts without harming self or others (indicator 4.12.3).

Objective

Students will be able to observe and evaluate peers' communication.

Skill Development Steps

- Step 4: skill practice
- Step 5: feedback and reinforcement

Materials

- Materials needed for the Relationship Role-Plays activity
- Props for the role-plays (if desired)

Instant Activity

An instant activity is not applicable for these lessons because students will be working during the entire lessons. However, if you would like, you could add instant activities to maintain consistency in class flow.

Introduction

Tell students that the next four lessons will involve writing, practicing, and performing role-plays for the different stories that they wrote in the previous lesson. Explain the final assessment (should be a review from lesson 1).

Main Activity

Relationship Role-Plays (page 141) **(feedback and reinforcement)**

Closure

At the end of the four lessons, introduce the next unit.

(continued)

Differentiation

- Employ typical accommodations to support all learners.
- Assign group roles.
- Modify the peer evaluation to include skill cues covered in the unit.
- You could make the worksheets and other materials electronic rather than hard copy.

Resources

- *Activities That Teach, More Activities That Teach,* and *Still More Activities That Teach,* by Tom Jackson
- *Personal & Social Skills,* by Joyce V. Fetro

Relationship Role-Plays

LESSONS 7, 8, 9, AND 10

NHES Performance Indicators

Grades 6 Through 8

- Apply effective verbal and nonverbal communication skills to enhance health (indicator 4.8.1).
- Demonstrate refusal and negotiation skills that avoid or reduce health risks (indicator 4.8.2).
- Demonstrate effective conflict management or resolution strategies (indicator 4.8.3).

Grades 9 Through 12

- Use skills for communicating effectively with family, peers, and others to enhance health (indicator 4.12.1).
- Demonstrate refusal, negotiation, and collaboration skills to enhance health and avoid or reduce health risks (indicator 4.12.2).
- Demonstrate strategies to prevent, manage, or resolve interpersonal conflicts without harming self or others (indicator 4.12.3).

Objective

Students will be able to observe and evaluate peers' communication.

Skill Development Step

- Step 4: skill practice
- Step 5: feedback and reinforcement

Duration

120 to 180 minutes (works great with three to four 50-minute classes)

Materials

- Relationship Role-Play worksheet (one per group)
- Role-Play Peer Evaluation worksheet (The number of worksheets you will need will depend on the number of students in the class and how many students you plan to have evaluate each role-play.)
- Props (Allow students to use materials in the classroom, but all other props must be provided by the group.)

Description

In lesson 5, students brainstormed a list of common situations in each type of relationship (family, friends, partner) and in lesson 6 took one of those situations and wrote a realistic fiction story without an ending pertaining to that relationship and the situation:

- *Family:* moving, divorce, chores, bathroom time, transportation, shared space
- *Friends:* exclusion, new friends, new school, drug use, eating disorders, grades
- *Partner:* time spent together, time spent apart, ways of showing affection, clinginess, cheating

Inform students that they are to use the communication skills they've been working on as they work in small groups to create role-plays based on their unfinished scripts. Use the Relationship Role-Play worksheet. Students should use assertiveness, appropriate body language, and other communication skills not only in their performances but also as they work as a team to complete the assignment.

Give each group three stories (one from each relationship type); groups write an ending and work on a cast of characters on days 1 and 2. Have students practice their role-plays on days 2 and 3. On days 3 and 4, groups record and perform role-plays, and students do peer evaluations of the performances using the Role-Play Peer Evaluation worksheet.

On day 4, return evaluations back to the groups and allow them to discuss. In large or small groups, talk about the communication that occurred within each group. Tell the students that you are going to fill them in on a little secret—that the role-plays weren't the only important part of the last few days! They are often shocked! Then ask them what they think *was* another important part. Often they realize and understand that the group collaboration and communication were more important and more true to life than a performance. This can lead to a rich discussion about working with others, what our individual communication strengths and weaknesses are, and how group dynamics and communication affect a final product or outcome.

Have students independently complete a written reflection, perhaps as homework. They should reflect on the experience of working with a group to complete the role-play. Instruct them to discuss strengths and weaknesses as well as overall lessons you learned about communication in relationships. Also, ask them how they would've rated themselves if they had used the evaluation chart to grade themselves during the whole process.

Tips and Extensions

- Observe students for assertiveness skills while working in groups. This is equally, if not more, important as the role-play is because it demonstrates skills in action! Provide guidance and assistance as needed. Provide written or verbal feedback to each individual student. By having a rubric of communication expectations and observing your students throughout the planning, performing, and processing of this activity, you can provide students some written feedback of their communication skills.

- Consider not requiring everyone to act. Rather, require that everyone has to participate in some way (direct, narrate, handle props or sound, etc.) for the in-class performances. Everyone should demonstrate the skills in the recorded role-plays.

- Make the evaluation sheets quarter-sheet size and then collect and staple together after each performance as the next group prepares to perform.

- On performance day, set up a stage with an audience. For each performance, choose one person per group in the audience (four to five people total) to fill out an evaluation form. If you have every student do one for every performance, their evaluation becomes rote and lazy.

- Have each group perform at least one practiced role-play. Choose randomly and base it on time available. If there is extra time, perhaps they'll perform more than one. Although learning is occurring as they perform, this is the fun aspect of the learning activity. The *true* learning and what you want to be more focused on is allowing an opportunity for peers to work together to solve a problem—a much more authentic learning activity that the students don't often realize they're engaging in! As stated in the Assessment section of this chapter, using a rubric of communication expectations and observing your students throughout the planning, performing, and processing of this activity, you can provide students some written feedback on their personal communication skills.

Modifications

- Employ typical accommodations to support all learners.
- Assign group roles.
- Modify the peer evaluation to include skill cues covered in the unit.
- You could make the worksheets and other materials electronic rather than hard copy.

Resources

- *Activities That Teach, More Activities That Teach,* and *Still More Activities That Teach,* by Tom Jackson
- *Personal & Social Skills,* by Joyce V. Fetro
- New York state health education standards guidance document

Modified from a submission by Lindsay Armbruster, middle/high school health teacher in New York.

Relationship Role-Play

With your group, you are going to plan, practice, and perform role-plays pertaining to relationships.

1. Plan: Fill in the chart.

Relationship	Healthy ending of the story	Character and actor
Family		
Friends		
Partner		

2. Practice three role-plays that
   - provide *some* background information about the characters and their relationship(s);
   - describe the situation, remembering that you need to have a role-play where you can demonstrate effective communication (self-expression), refusal, and conflict resolution; and
   - resolve situation in a healthy way!

   Be sure to demonstrate assertive body language, speaking, and listening.
   Be sure to demonstrate care and respect.
   Remember that the people in these role-plays are important to each other.

3. Perform:
   You will not perform *all* the role-plays you prepared. You will be chosen randomly to perform one of your role-plays. Be ready! However, for the assessment for the unit, you need to record each of the role-plays that I will use for grading. Make sure you plan your time so you can do this in class! Your classmates will be evaluating the role-plays that you perform in class.

Role-Play Peer Evaluation

For each criterion, circle Yes or No.

Yes	No	Acted out the conflict safely
Yes	No	Demonstrated a realistic situation
Yes	No	Resolved the situation healthfully
Yes	No	Showed assertive body language
Yes	No	Showed assertive listening
Yes	No	Showed assertive speaking
Yes	No	Demonstrated care and respect

Write one compliment about the role-play:

Provide one suggestion for improving the role-play:

BONUS ACTIVITY

This activity is not included in the unit plan, but it could be added to this unit or used as a supplemental activity for your developing interpersonal communication skills for health and wellness unit.

Interruptions Are Time for Learning

NHES Performance Indicators

- *Grades 6 through 8:* Apply effective verbal and nonverbal communication skills to enhance health (indicator 4.8.1).
- *Grades 9 through 12:* Use skills for communicating effectively with family, peers, and others to enhance health (indicator 4.12.1).

Objectives

See the NHES performance indicators in the previous list. There are no additional lesson objectives.

Skill Development Step

Step 4: skill practice

Duration

Will vary

Materials

None needed

Description

It is important that the skill of interpersonal communication is introduced and that students are familiar with the steps of the skill and its performance indicators.

Teachers are often faced with interruptions during classes for a variety of school-day happenings, such as taking heights and weights during health education class. Instead of considering this (or any other interruption) lost time on learning, use these experiences to practice the real-life skill of interpersonal communication in an authentic setting!

When recording heights and weights, tell students ahead of time that you will not share the information with them unless they ask. Wait patiently while they gather the courage to inquire. When they do, congratulate them enthusiastically on their ability to ask for information that supports their health.

Students could also practice in other settings such as waiting in line. For example, students can practice refusal skill cues for a variety of scenarios while waiting in line or before an assembly or other down times.

Encourage students to practice in other situations, such as during vision testing with the school nurse. Tell students that once in the medical office, students should (1) greet the nurse, (2) ask for their own results, and (3) thank the nurse for his or her time and service.

Tips and Extensions

Be sure to have introduced and modeled the skill prior to asking students to implement the skill cues.

Extensions outside the classroom have been outlined previously but could go so much further! Students could practice while fundraising, eating dinner with family, working out issues with siblings (who is using the car, the shower, etc.), making appointments, establishing boundaries in relationships, and while at the doctor's office.

Modifications

- For students who struggle with this activity, ask them to practice privately with you, a trusted adult, or a school counselor.
- For English language learners, cue cards can be used.

Modified from a submission from Claudia T. Brown, former high school health teacher in Massachusetts.

CHAPTER 6

Making Decisions That Improve Health Outcomes

This chapter focuses on the skill of decision making, which is Standard 5 of the National Health Education Standards. Within this chapter you will see examples of the skill in action. Together, the sample assessments, lesson plans, and learning activities can be used in your classroom to guide students as they develop this skill.

The materials presented here are designed to support each step of the skill development model (see chapter 1) and are presented and organized to reflect a backward-design approach (see chapter 2). We begin with the end in mind by looking at the big picture of what the skill is and what students should be able to do once they develop the skill, including the specific performance indicators from the National Health Education Standards. We also include sample skill cues for teaching the skill, and then the rest of the chapter includes assessments, lesson plans, and learning activities that you can implement in your classroom as is or with modifications to meet the needs of your program and your students. We have included both sets of the NHES performance indicators (grades 6-8 and grades 9-12) in the unit overview and each lesson as appropriate. Take the materials provided and make them your own in order to meet the needs of your students. Our goal is to provide a usable framework that is also easily modifiable.

Throughout this chapter, we use the topic of alcohol and other drugs as the context. As with all of the lessons in this book, you can use the lessons and activities in this chapter in their current format or modify them to meet your needs. While the topic of alcohol and other drugs is used in this example, there are many health topics that could be relevant and appropriate when teaching this skill. We encourage you to use any other health topic that you need to address, that fits into your overall scope and sequence, and that works in your course and curriculum.

SKILL OVERVIEW

Making decisions is a routine part of each and every day. From the time you wake up to the time you go to bed, you are making decisions about a variety of things—such as what to eat, what to wear, or what song to listen to. For many of these day-to-day decisions, you will choose an option quickly, act on the decision, and will not think about it again. However, all of our decisions—big and small—have consequences. Some of these consequences might be short term and not very significant, some might be longer term and very significant, and others are somewhere in between with consequences that can be positive, negative, or neutral. The overall impact of the consequences of our decisions depends on the situation we are in. For example, if we choose to rush out of the house without brushing our teeth, we run the risk of bad breath or longer term tooth decay, but if we get to school or work on time, we avoid the penalties associated with being late. In this case, the negative consequences (bad breath and possible tooth decay) are likely outweighed by getting to work or school on time, which could have long-lasting consequences. Another example is skipping lunch or choosing unhealthy snacks throughout the day. We might feel sluggish, be unable to concentrate, or find ourselves at an unhealthy weight, but we might also have been able to put more time into a project or arrived in time to pick our kids up from their activities. For some, feeling sluggish might be worse than having more time on the project, and for others, the project isn't as important as feeling good. As you can see, while the decisions we make might often seem simple, there is a complex set of interactions that play out for each and every one of these decisions.

The skill of decision making requires students to think critically about their decisions in terms of the potential impact on their health and the health of others. The skill also requires that students thoughtfully employ a decision-making process as they make decisions. It's not only about the impact of the decisions but also about the process of making them. While each skill of the National Health Education Standards requires students to demonstrate their learning, decision making is one of a few skills that specifies a process for students to follow. The performance indicators for elementary school students are aimed at having students begin to think about the when and why of their decisions and move slowly into considering potential outcomes based on their options. The performance indicators for students in middle school and high school, as you would expect, prescribe a more sophisticated decision-making approach, having students work through a process to arrive at a health-enhancing decision, predict the impact of each option, select the healthy alternative, and then reflect on or evaluate the decision. For secondary students, the skill becomes less about whether the student can make a decision and more about using a process to think critically about how the options would affect one's health and determine whether or not the consequences would lead one toward a health-enhancing outcome.

While the skill is prescriptive in the sense that students must work through a decision-making process, it's also flexible in that the standards don't specify one particular decision-making model to use. For example, various social competency or socio-emotional learning curricula have acronyms for decision making, and many schools have a well-established decision-making model that is taught to all students and is often referenced for students to consider before they make decisions about a variety of topics. If your school uses such a model, we encourage you to build your decision-making unit around that. Before doing so, compare the school-wide model with the performance indicators of the National Health Education Standards. If you find that most of the steps align, then you have a match. If you find that many of the steps align, but perhaps the model is missing the reflective piece, you still might be able to use the school-wide model and then build in the additional reflection step (or other identified modification) so that students can apply that piece of the process as well. Ideally, students will always make the health-enhancing choice. In reality, though, that isn't always the case, and it would be unrealistic to assume that they would. Instead, we strive to have our students reflect and think critically about the potential consequences and identify the health-enhancing choice to help them recognize how a decision ultimately might affect future goals, relationships, health, or even daily tasks.

Table 6.1 shows the performance indicators from the National Health Education Standards, which outline what students should be able to do within each grade span grades 6 through 8 and 9 through 12.

SKILL CUES

Skill cues are used during step 2 of the skill development model to highlight the critical elements of the skill; in this case, decision making. We have included the sample skill cues to explain to students the process of working through decision making. Be sure to adjust the language to meet the needs of your students. This is also where you would substitute your school-wide decision-making model. Just keep in mind that you want the skill cues to represent the critical aspects of the skill, be memorable for students, and serve as reminders of the steps they need to implement when using the skill. Figure 6.1 shows some sample skill cues for decision making that may be used for grades 6 through 12.

TABLE 6.1   Performance Indicators for Standard 5 of the NHES (Grades 6-12)

	6-8		9-12
5.8.1	Identify circumstances that can help or hinder healthy decision making.	5.12.1	Examine barriers that can hinder healthy decision making.
5.8.2	Determine when health-related situations require the application of a thoughtful decision-making process.	5.12.2	Determine the value of applying a thoughtful decision-making process in health-related situations.
5.8.3	Distinguish when individual or collaborative decision making is appropriate.	5.12.3	Justify when individual or collaborative decision making is appropriate.
5.8.4	Distinguish between healthy and unhealthy alternatives to health-related issues or problems.	5.12.4	Generate alternatives to health-related issues or problems.
5.8.5	Predict the potential short-term impact of each alternative on self and others.	5.12.5	Predict the potential short-term and long-term impact of each alternative on self and others.
5.8.6	Choose healthy alternatives over unhealthy alternatives when making a decision.	5.12.6	Defend the healthy choice when making decisions.
5.8.7	Analyze the outcomes of a health-related decision.	5.12.7	Evaluate the effectiveness of health-related decisions.

Reprinted, with permission, from the American Cancer Society. *National Health Education Standards: Achieving Excellence,* Second Edition (Atlanta, GA: American Cancer Society, 2007), 24-36, cancer.org/bookstore

Decision Making

STANDARD 5

Students will demonstrate the ability to use decision-making skills to enhance health.

DECIDE

Determine the decision
- What is it?
- Does it require thought?
- Does it require help?

Examine options

Consider consequences

Identify values and possible influences that may affect the situation

Decide on the healthiest option and act on the decision

Evaluate the outcome

FIGURE 6.1   Decision-making skill cues for grades 6 through 12.

UNIT OUTLINE

This section includes an outline of the unit for Standard 5; table 6.2 shows this outline, including lesson titles, lesson objectives, the step(s) of the skill development model that are addressed in each lesson, and the titles of the main learning activities in each lesson.

Students begin the unit by exploring the skill of decision making; the steps involved; and considerations to making a sound, health-enhancing decision. Following that, students explore the topic of alcohol, tobacco, and other drugs, and go on a "webquest," or web search, to find information. The unit wraps up with students applying their learning to scenarios requiring thoughtful decision making in regard to their use of alcohol, tobacco, and other drugs.

The performance indicators for Standard 5 for grades 6 through 12, appropriate performance indicators from Standard 1, Core Concepts, and additional content form the foundation for the objectives for this unit. The topic of alcohol, tobacco, and other drugs is a good fit for the health topic in this unit because many students will face decisions about whether or not to use those substances.

Unit Objectives, Grades 6 Through 8

By the end of this unit, students will be able to

- identify circumstances that can help or hinder healthy decision making in ATOD (alcohol, tobacco, and other drugs) situations (indicator 5.8.1);
- determine when ATOD situations require the application of a thoughtful decision-making process (indicator 5.8.2);
- distinguish when individual or collaborative decision making is appropriate in ATOD situations (indicator 5.8.3);
- distinguish between healthy and unhealthy alternatives to ATOD issues or problems (indicator 5.8.4);
- predict the potential short-term impact of each alternative on self and others (indicator 5.8.5);
- choose healthy alternatives over unhealthy alternatives when making a decision about ATOD (indicator 5.8.6);
- analyze the outcomes of an ATOD decision (indicator 5.8.7); and
- describe the consequences associated with using alcohol, tobacco, and illegal drugs (indicator 1.8.8).

Unit Objectives, Grades 9 Through 12

By the end of this unit, students will be able to

- examine barriers that can hinder healthy decision making in ATOD situations (indicator 5.12.1);
- determine the value of applying a thoughtful decision-making process in ATOD situations (indicator 5.12.2);
- justify when individual or collaborative decision making is appropriate in ATOD situations (indicator 5.12.3);
- generate alternatives to ATOD issues or problems (indicator 5.12.4);
- predict the potential short-term and long-term impact of each alternative on self and others (indicator 5.12.5);
- defend the healthy choice when making ATOD-related decisions (indicator 5.12.6);

TABLE 6.2 Standard 5 Unit Outline

Lesson title	Lesson objectives (indicators in parentheses) *By the end of this lesson, students will be able to:*	Steps of the skill development model addressed in the lesson	Main learning activities
Lesson 1: Decisions? What Decisions?	• Determine when situations require the application of a thoughtful decision-making process (5.8.2) • Identify circumstances that can help or hinder healthy decision making in ATOD situations (5.8.1) *or* • Determine the value of applying a thoughtful decision-making process in ATOD situations (5.12.2) • Examine barriers that can hinder healthy decision making in ATOD situations (5.12.1) • Justify when individual or collaborative decision making is appropriate in ATOD situations (5.12.3) All grades: • Define the term *decision making* • Discuss the relevance of decision making	Skill introduction (step 1)	• Step Forward or Step Back Decision-Making Activity (p. 156) • Small-group discussion
Lesson 2: How Do I DECIDE What to Do?	• List the steps of the DECIDE model (decision-making skill cues) • Discuss effective application of the DECIDE model • Evaluate decisions based on ethics and values	Steps of the skill and modeling (steps 2 and 3)	Introducing Dan the Man's party (p. 158)
Lesson 3: Using Ethical Tests to Make Decisions	• List the steps of the DECIDE model (decision-making skill cues) • Discuss effective application of the DECIDE model • Examine the role that values can play in decision making	Skill practice (step 4)	Hip Hypothetical Party (p. 162)
Lessons 4 and 5: Alcohol, Tobacco, and Illegal Drug Webquest	• Describe the consequences associated with using alcohol, tobacco, and illegal drugs (1.8.8 *or* 1.12.8 and 1.12.9) • Describe the differences between use, misuse, and abuse • Apply aspects of the DECIDE model to scenarios related to alcohol, tobacco, and illegal drug use (5.12.2-5.12.7 or 5.8.2-5.8.7)	Health topic focus (no skill development in these lessons)	Alcohol, Tobacco, and Illegal Drug Webquest (p. 166)
Lesson 6: Revisiting the Scene of the Party	• Apply the DECIDE decision-making model (5.8.2-5.8.7 or 5.12.2-5.12.7)	Skill practice (step 4)	Hip Hypothetical Party Revisited (p. 170)
Lessons 7 and 8: Let's Make a Decision	• Apply the DECIDE decision-making model (5.8.2-5.8.7 or 5.12.2-5.12.7) • Describe the consequences associated with using alcohol, tobacco, and illegal drugs (1.12.8 and 1.12.9)	Skill practice (step 4)	Decision-Making Comic Strip (p. 178)
Lesson 9: Let's Enjoy Some Comics	• Evaluate and analyze the outcomes of health-related scenarios • Provide appropriate peer feedback based on the provided parameters	Feedback and reinforcement (step 5)	Comic Gallery Walk

Performance indicators are from: Joint Committee on National Health Education Standards. (2007). *National Health Education Standards: Achieving Excellence* (2nd ed.). Atlanta, GA: American Cancer Society.

- evaluate the effectiveness of ATOD-related decisions (indicator 5.12.7); and
- describe the consequences associated with using alcohol, tobacco, and illegal drugs (indicators 1.12.8 and 1.12.9).

Additional Unit Objectives Grades 6 Through 12

By the end of this unit, students will be able to

- define the term *decision making*;
- discuss the relevance of decision making;
- list the steps of the DECIDE model (decision-making skill cues);
- discuss effective application of the DECIDE model;
- evaluate decisions based on ethics and values and describe the differences between use, misuse, and abuse;
- apply aspects of the DECIDE model to scenarios related to alcohol, tobacco, and illegal drug use;
- apply the DECIDE decision-making model (indicators 5.8.2-5.8.7 *or* indicators 5.12.2-5.12.7);
- evaluate and analyze the outcomes of health-related scenarios;
- provide appropriate peer feedback based on the provided parameters.

ASSESSMENT

Here is a sample assessment that will evaluate the extent to which students can meet the objectives identified for this unit. In this assessment, students are required to design a comic strip where the characters work through the DECIDE model related to alcohol, tobacco, and other drugs.

Objectives

Through this assessment, students will demonstrate their ability to

- apply the DECIDE decision-making model (indicators 5.8.2 through 5.8.7 *or* 5.12.2 through 5.12.7); and
- describe the consequences associated with using alcohol, tobacco, and illegal drugs (indicator 1.8.8) (grades 6-8); or
- describe the consequences associated with using alcohol, tobacco, and illegal drugs (indicators 1.12.8 and 1.12.9) (grades 9-12).

Description

The final assessment asks students to apply their decision-making skills through the comic strips assignment from lessons 7 and 8 in a scenario specific to alcohol, tobacco, and other drugs. Students will complete a self-assessment checklist that students will hand in with the assignment. The checklist allows students to monitor their progress toward completing the assignment. You will use the checklist to provide the summative evaluation of the assessment (the self-assessment checklist is also the scoring rubric).

Modifications

This assessment is based on information and activities contained in this chapter and, as with the lessons, should be modified to address changes to the objectives or as necessary for your students. Modifications to the assessment may include:

■ While the included scenarios are all still ATOD related, each contains unfamiliar elements that are not previously introduced in the unit. To raise the level of assessment rigor, consider changing the scenarios to address non-ATOD topics. A change to the current scenarios requires students to demonstrate a deeper level of thought and will allow students to demonstrate proficiency (rather than just competence).

■ Have students work through a decision-making process on a topic of interest to them (not necessarily ATOD related). Do this either as skill practice or as a part of the assessment. Once students have practiced and gained experience applying the skill in ATOD-related situations, explain to students that the skill process will be the same and have them work through and solve a different scenario.

Implementation Tips

The scenarios include a variety of ATOD situations that are different from those that students worked with previously in class. Changing the scenarios and providing a new context for students to consider is important because it will enhance students' ability to demonstrate proficiency and apply their learning in a different way.

Decision-Making Comic Strip Self-Checklist

Concerns (not yet) Areas that need work with comments	Criteria (proficient) Standards for performance (with indicators in parentheses)	Advanced (above and beyond) Evidence of exceeding standard with comments
	A character in the comic strip identifies the decision to be made (5.8.1, 5.8.2, and 5.8.3).	
	A character in the comic strip examines three options that can be made (5.8.4).	
	A character in the comic strip considers a pro and a con for each option (5.8.5).	
	A character in the comic strip identifies an internal and an external influence that might affect the decision.	
	A character in the comic strip decides and takes action regarding the healthiest decision (5.8.6).	
	A character in the comic strip evaluates the decision by explaining if it was a good or bad decision and why (5.8.7).	
	Three facts regarding the appropriate ATOD product are included in the comic strip (1.8.1 and 1.8.9).	
	The comic strip is creative, colorful, and unique. There are minimal spelling and grammatical errors. The comic strip shows pride in work.	

Grade and Comments:

Assessment and worksheets modified from a submission from Jeff Bartlett, middle school health teacher in Massachusetts.

LESSON PLANS

The lesson plans included here are the ones detailed in the unit outline earlier in the chapter and that will advance students toward achieving unit objectives and being able to successfully demonstrate the skill (evaluated in the assessment). The included lessons assume a 50-minute class period. Consider this prior to implementation.

Lesson plans include suggested activities, and those activities follow the lesson plans. Lesson plans and activities can be used together or independently to meet the needs of your classes.

Throughout the lesson plans, you will see the steps of the skill development model in **boldface type** after activities that address each skill development step.

Purpose

Taking the time to think critically about how everyday decisions can affect one's health is an important tool for adolescents. As students consider the bigger picture when making decisions, they become empowered to take ownership of their own health by making decisions that support healthy outcomes.

NHES Performance Indicators

Grades 6 Through 8

- Determine when situations require the application of a thoughtful decision-making process (indicator 5.8.2).
- Identify circumstances that can help or hinder healthy decision making in ATOD situations (indicator 5.8.1).

Grades 9 Through 12

- Determine the value of applying a thoughtful decision-making process in ATOD situations (indicator 5.12.2).
- Examine barriers that can hinder healthy decision making in ATOD situations (indicator 5.12.1).
- Justify when individual or collaborative decision making is appropriate in ATOD situations (indicator 5.12.3).

Objectives

Students will be able to

- define the term *decision making* and
- discuss the relevance of decision making.

Skill Development Step

Step 1: definition, relevance, and educational outcomes

Materials

Handouts for notes, if using

Instant Activity

After students take their seats, they write their responses to the prompt: "What decisions have you made today? Write a list of the decisions you have had to make today. Place an X next to the decisions you needed help making and a checkmark next to the ones that had an impact on your health in some way."

Introduction

Let students know that today is the first day in the decision-making unit. Review the lesson objectives and then begin the first activity.

Main Activities

1. Small-group discussions: Ask students to share their list of decisions from the instant activity in their groups. Next, have the members of the group identify three decisions that members of the group made today that relate to their health.
   - Discuss whether it was easy or difficult to make the health-enhancing choice. Are there any decisions that were difficult to make even if they would be health enhancing?
   - Did any of these decisions require a lot of thought? Why or why not? What kinds of health decisions require thought? Why?
   - Ask groups to share their responses to the last question and write them on the board. **(relevance)**

2. Complete the Step Forward or Step Back Decision-Making Activity (page 156).

3. Review a definition of decision making. **(definition)**

Closure

Preview the next lesson for students by explaining that next time they will be learning the steps to decision making.

Differentiation

- Select groups ahead of time.
- Provide a worksheet with the directions for each section.

Homework

Before the next class, students must write down two decisions that teens have to make that will affect their health and that require thoughtful consideration.

Step Forward or Step Back Decision-Making Activity

LESSON 1

NHES Performance Indicators

Grades 6 Through 8

- Determine when situations require the application of a thoughtful decision-making process (indicator 5.8.2).
- Identify circumstances that can help or hinder healthy decision making in ATOD situations (indicator 5.8.1).

Grades 9 Through 12

- Determine the value of applying a thoughtful decision-making process in ATOD situations (indicator 5.12.2).
- Examine barriers that can hinder healthy decision making in ATOD situations (indicator 5.12.1).
- Justify when individual or collaborative decision making is appropriate in ATOD situations (indicator 5.12.3).

Objectives

Students will be able to

- define the term *decision making* and
- discuss the relevance of decision making.

Skill Development Step

Step 1: introduction

Duration

10 minutes

Materials

No materials needed

Description

1. Have students line up horizontally across the room. Explain to students that they are now on a continuum from 1 to 10 with 1 being an easy choice and 10 being a decision that requires a lot of consideration.
2. Read each of the following decisions. With each decision that is read, have students move to a space that aligns with how they would classify the decision. That is, they move closer to 1 if they think the decision is an easy choice and requires little thought and move closer to 10 if the decision is a difficult one that might require a lot of consideration and weighing of options.
   - Brushing their teeth
   - Eating breakfast
   - Getting a job
   - Applying to college
   - Choosing a college
   - Drinking alcohol
   - Kissing a partner
   - Engaging in sexual activity (more than kissing) with a partner
   - Choosing fruit at lunch

- Getting to sleep at a reasonable hour
- Recycling
- Wearing a helmet while riding a bike
- Using drugs

3. After reading the statements, ask what makes that decision easy or hard? What would make it harder or easier?

Tips and Extensions

- Change up the aforementioned decisions to those that are relevant based on student-need data.
- This activity is intended to spur conversation. While students should individually make their choice for where to stand on the continuum, make note of differences and use as teachable moments when appropriate.

Purpose

In lesson 1, students are introduced to the definition and relevance of using a process to make decisions. In this lesson, students will learn the skill cues associated with decision making (DECIDE) and will discuss how to apply the model in an effective manner in a realistic scenario.

NHES Performance Indicators

None addressed (the decision-making process outlined in the performance indicators are being modeled, however).

Objectives

Students will be able to

- list the steps of the DECIDE model (decision-making skill cues) and
- discuss effective application of the DECIDE model.

Skill Development Steps

- Step 2: steps of the skill
- Step 3: modeling

Materials

None (unless you want to create a worksheet or handout for the skill cues)

Instant Activity

As students take their seats, they will respond to the following prompt: "Making a sound decision takes thought and consideration. What steps do you think are important when making a big decision?"

Introduction

Once students have settled in and have had a chance to answer the instant activity prompt, introduce the lesson for the day and inform students that over the next series of lessons, they will be asked to think about the decisions they are making. Review the lesson objectives.

Main Activities

1. Read this scenario aloud to students:

   Mountain Town High School has a long-standing reputation for excellence. Student test scores are high and the school's athletic teams rank among the best in the state. Both athletic and nonathletic students are involved in the many clubs and activities available at the school, and students are generally proud to say they go to school here. Over the past few years, however, there has been an alarming increase in marijuana and alcohol use and abuse among even the best students. You recently heard about a party this coming Friday night at Dan the Man's house. His parents are out of town (not that they would care if he threw a party anyway). Dan's parents are not exactly connected with his life. Dan is on his own most of the time. They pay attention to his school calendar, but leave him alone as long as he checks in with them about where he is going. Heck, they are busy with work and other commitments and sometimes go away for the weekend. He doesn't really have too many rules to follow; as long as he's a star on the lacrosse team and his grades are decent, life is good. During school, you personally get invited to the party by Dan. You are excited because you know someone you really like will be there, too. You hear that there will probably be beer and weed and maybe some other drugs. Dan has a reputation for having some crazy parties where kids have gotten into trouble before. Your friends are encouraging you to go. You don't want to disappoint your friends and the person you like either. Will you go?

2. Have students write down whether or not they would go to the party and explain why.

3. Circle back to the question posed in the instant activity. Ask students for the steps they feel are important. Write them on the board.

4. Once the large group has had a chance to brainstorm and get ideas on the board, introduce the DECIDE acronym (see figure 6.1). Point out to students that while not all decisions require this level of thought, it is worthwhile to use this process when considering decisions that could have an impact on their health, that might have significant or long-lasting consequences, or that are important to them. You might want to create a worksheet for students to record the skill cues. You could also provide a handout with the skill cues for student reference. **(skill cues)**

5. Model the DECIDE process as a whole group using the hip hypothetical party scenario. **(modeling)** Because this is a modeling activity, be sure to explain what the *effective* application of the DECIDE model would be while still allowing students to share their ideas (great discussions can arise when students can share ideas, even if they aren't giving you the ideal answers).

Closure

At the end of lesson 2, ask students to turn to a partner and discuss what barriers might prevent teens from making health-enhancing decisions around ATOD.

Differentiation

- Provide hard copies of the scenario for students to have at their seats.
- Partner low-proficiency English language learners with another student to help them understand the language within the scenario.
- Change the scenario to better reflect your own community—this will allow students to better see themselves within the scenario.

Resources

- "8 Ethical Tests" in *Character Matters,* by Dr. Tom Lickona, available at www2.cortland.edu/dot-Asset/299013.pdf
- *TED Talk: How to Make Hard Choices*, by Ruth Chang
- *Activities That Teach, More Activities That Teach*, and *Still More Activities That Teach,* by Tom Jackson
- *Personal & Social Skills,* by Joyce V. Fetro

Lesson modified from submission by Lindsay Armbruster, middle/high school health teacher in New York.

LESSON 3: Using Ethical Tests to Make Decisions

Purpose

Lesson 2 introduced skill cues to students and modeled the skill of decision making. In this lesson, students will take a deeper look at the "Identifying Values" step of the DECIDE model.

NHES Performance Indicators

None addressed

Objectives

Students will be able to

- list the steps of the DECIDE model (decision-making skill cues),
- discuss effective application of the DECIDE model, and
- examine the role that values can play in decision making.

Skill Development Steps

Step 4: skill practice

Materials

Hip Hypothetical Party worksheet

Instant Activity

When students enter the classroom, the DECIDE acronym is on the board. When class begins, ask students to fill in the steps that they learned in the previous lesson.

Introduction

Review the objectives for the lesson. Review the skill cues with students. Let them know that today, you will be returning to the hip hypothetical party scenario and focusing on the *I* step of the DECIDE model, where you are looking at values and ethics as they relate to the decision-making process.

Main Activity

1. Introduce the concept of ethical tests and suggest six short questions to ask yourself when making a decision (derived from "8 Ethical Tests" in *Character Matters,* by Dr. Tom Lickona, and found on the SUNY Cortland website: www2.cortland.edu/dotAsset/299013.pdf):

   - The golden rule test (Would I want people to do this to me?)
   - The religion test (If I have religious beliefs, would a respected member of my religion agree with this choice?)
   - The parent and grandparent test (Would my parents and grandparents approve if they found out about this?)
   - The conscience test (Does the little voice inside my head approve?)
   - The Twitter test (Would I want this broadcasted on social media?)
   - The What if everyone did this? test (Would I want to live in a world where everyone did this?)

2. Share the following additional details about the hip hypothetical party with the students:

   - Dan lives *far* out in the country; there are no neighbors around.
   - Dan knows people from other schools. It's safe to assume that there will be lots of people at the party—many of whom you don't know and who don't know you.

3. Have students complete questions 1 through 3 on the Hip Hypothetical Party worksheet. **(practice)**

4. Discuss as appropriate, perhaps discussing that we are not always given the opportunity to revise our decisions before acting upon them.

Closure

At the end of lesson 3, ask students to turn to a partner and discuss which of the six ethical tests resonated the most with them, and why.

Differentiation

- Provide hard copies of the scenario for students to have and read silently at their seats.
- Read the scenario aloud to the class.
- Partner low-proficiency English language learners with another student to help them understand the language within the scenario.
- Change the scenario to better reflect your own community; this will allow students to better see themselves within the scenario.

Resources

- "8 Ethical Tests" in *Character Matters,* by Dr. Tom Lickona; available at www2.cortland.edu/dot-Asset/299013.pdf
- *TED Talk: How to Make Hard Choices,* by Ruth Chang
- *Activities That Teach, More Activities That Teach,* and *Still More Activities That Teach,* by Tom Jackson
- *Personal & Social Skills,* by Joyce V. Fetro

Lesson modified from submission by Lindsay Armbruster, middle/high school health teacher in New York.

Hip Hypothetical Party

Name: _____

1. Fill in the following table.

Ethical test name	Details and notes	Does going to the party pass this test?

2. Revised decision

   Yes, I'm going.   No, I'm not going.

3. How does this decision compare to the ones you made in lesson 2?

4. Why is it important to consider ethics and values when making a decision?

Purpose

In the previous lessons, students have learned about the skill of decision making. In this lesson, which spans two class periods, students will take time to review topic information related to alcohol, tobacco, and illegal drugs. This information will then be used to further make a decision in the scenario.

NHES Performance Indicators

Grades 6 Through 8

- Identify circumstances that can help or hinder healthy decision making (indicator 5.8.1).
- Determine when health-related situations require the application of a thoughtful decision-making process in ATOD situations (indicator 5.8.2).
- Distinguish when individual or collaborative decision making is appropriate in ATOD situations (indicator 5.8.3).
- Distinguish between healthy and unhealthy alternatives to health-related issues or problems in ATOD situations (indicator 5.8.4).
- Predict the potential short-term impact of each alternative on self and others in ATOD situations (indicator 5.8.5).
- Choose healthy alternatives over unhealthy alternatives when making a decision in ATOD situations (indicator 5.8.6).
- Analyze the outcomes of a health-related decision in ATOD situations (indicator 5.8.7).

Grades 9 Through 12

- Examine barriers that can hinder healthy decision making (indicator 5.12.1).
- Determine the value of applying a thoughtful decision-making process in ATOD situations (indicator 5.12.2).
- Justify when individual or collaborative decision making is appropriate in ATOD situations (indicator 5.12.3).
- Generate alternatives to health-related issues or problems in ATOD situations (indicator 5.12.4).
- Predict the potential short-term and long-term impact of each alternative on self and others in ATOD situations (indicator 5.12.5).
- Defend the healthy choice when making decisions in ATOD situations (indicator 5.12.6).
- Evaluate the effectiveness of health-related decisions in ATOD situations (indicator 5.12.7).

Objective

Students will be able to describe the differences between use, misuse, and abuse.

Skill Development Step

None; the focus is on functional information

Materials

- Desktop computers, laptops, or tablets
- Internet capability
- Slide show presentation or hard copies of the slides

(continued)

Instant Activity

After students take their seats, they write their responses to the prompt: "Write down your own definition of the following terms: *drug use, drug misuse,* and *drug abuse."*

Introduction

In this lesson, students will be using predetermined sites to access valid and reliable information about alcohol, tobacco, and illegal drugs. (*Note:* Use this activity only if students have completed an accessing information unit as this is an opportunity to apply the skill.) It is important that students use the sites listed and work through the slides to answer all of the questions. This lesson will span two class periods.

Before sending students off to complete their packet of information (a sample packet is included in the web resource), discuss the instant activity and give the appropriate definitions for drug use, misuse, and abuse, as shown in the following list. Be sure to include how misuse and abuse can lead to serious complications or negative consequences.

- *Drug use:* Using a substance for its intended (or prescribed) purpose. This includes following a prescription, labeled instructions, or health care provider's instruction.
- *Drug misuse:* Taking a medication or substance for reasons other than prescribed or appropriate though not for the purposes of getting high or for fun. This might include taking an additional dose of a medication, accidentally taking a medication, using someone else's prescription, or self-medicating.
- *Drug abuse:* Using any substance for the purpose of feeling good or getting high. Abuse might also include the use of a substance for purposes outside of the recommended dosage for the purpose of creating an intensified response—either euphoric or depressed. This might include using a prescription medication too frequently in order to achieve the desired results (thereby developing a tolerance to the substance), repeated, chronic use of a substance, or exceeding the recommended dose.

Have students open up their laptop computers or take out their tablets (if students do not have personal devices arrange for them to be available from the school) and open the following websites to prepare for the lesson:

- In the know zone, http://www.intheknowzone.com/substance-abuse-topics.html
- National Institutes of Health, National Institute on Drug Abuse for Teens, http://teens.drugabuse.gov/drug-facts
- Foundation for a Drug-Free World, http://www.drugfreeworld.org/drugfacts.html

Main Activities

Alcohol, Tobacco, and Illegal Drug Webquest (page 166)

Closure

At the end of the assignment, ask students to complete a 3-2-1 reflection about what they have learned.

- Three things students learned that will affect their decision making
- Two things they still have questions about
- One thing they will do differently as a result of learning this information

Differentiation

- Have students work in groups to complete the assignment.
- Print materials for students to read if you do not have access to the Internet or computers.
- Print PowerPoint slides for students to use as a hard copy.
- Reduce the number of substances looked at.

Resources

- Parent Talk Kit, http://medicineabuseproject.org/assets/documents/parent_talk_kit.pdf
- In the know zone, www.intheknowzone.com/substance-abuse-topics.html
- National Institutes of Health, National Institute on Drug Abuse for Teens, http://teens.drugabuse .gov/drug-facts
- Foundation for a Drug-Free World, www.drugfreeworld.org/drugfacts.html

Lesson adapted from a submission by Danielle Petrucci, middle school health teacher in Massachusetts.

Alcohol, Tobacco, and Illegal Drug Webquest

LESSONS 4 AND 5

NHES Performance Indicators

Grades 6 Through 8

- Identify circumstances that can help or hinder healthy decision making (indicator 5.8.1).
- Determine when health-related situations require the application of a thoughtful decision-making process in ATOD situations (indicator 5.8.2).
- Distinguish when individual or collaborative decision making is appropriate in ATOD situations (indicator 5.8.3).
- Distinguish between healthy and unhealthy alternatives to health-related issues or problems in ATOD situations (indicator 5.8.4).
- Predict the potential short-term impact of each alternative on self and others in ATOD situations (indicator 5.8.5).
- Choose healthy alternatives over unhealthy alternatives when making a decision in ATOD situations (indicator 5.8.6).
- Analyze the outcomes of a health-related decision in ATOD situations (indicator 5.8.7).

Grades 9 Through 12

- Examine barriers that can hinder healthy decision making (indicator 5.12.1).
- Determine the value of applying a thoughtful decision-making process in ATOD situations (indicator 5.12.2).
- Justify when individual or collaborative decision making is appropriate in ATOD situations (indicator 5.12.3).
- Generate alternatives to health-related issues or problems in ATOD situations (indicator 5.12.4).
- Predict the potential short-term and long-term impact of each alternative on self and others in ATOD situations (indicator 5.12.5).
- Defend the healthy choice when making decisions in ATOD situations (indicator 5.12.6).
- Evaluate the effectiveness of health-related decisions in ATOD situations (indicator 5.12.7).

Objective

Students will be able to describe the differences between use, misuse, and abuse.

Skill Development Step

Step 4: skill practice

Duration

90 to 100 minutes (approximately two class periods)

Materials

- Slide show presentation or hard copies of the slides (referred to as "the packet" in the lesson plan)
- Desktop computers, laptops, or tablets
- Internet capability

Description

Have students open up their laptops or take out their tablets (if students do not have personal devices arrange for them to be available from the school) and open the following websites to prepare for the lesson:

- In the know zone, www.intheknowzone.com/substance-abuse-topics.html
- National Institutes of Health, National Institute on Drug Abuse for Teens, http://teens.drugabuse .gov/drug-facts
- Foundation for a Drug-Free World, www.drugfreeworld.org/drugfacts.html

Tips and Extensions

- Have students work in groups to complete the assignment.
- Print materials for students to read if you do not have access to the Internet or computers.
- Print slides for students to use as a hard copy.
- Reduce the number of substances looked at.

LESSON 6: Revisiting the Scene of the Party

Purpose

In this lesson, students will revisit the hip hypothetical party from lessons 2 and 3 and will learn new information that will have an impact on the outcome of their actions.

NHES Performance Indicators

Grades 6 Through 8

- Identify circumstances that can help or hinder healthy decision making (indicator 5.8.1).
- Determine when health-related situations require the application of a thoughtful decision-making process in ATOD situations (indicator 5.8.2).
- Distinguish when individual or collaborative decision making is appropriate in ATOD situations (indicator 5.8.3).
- Distinguish between healthy and unhealthy alternatives to health-related issues or problems in ATOD situations (indicator 5.8.4).
- Predict the potential short-term impact of each alternative on self and others in ATOD situations (indicator 5.8.5).
- Choose healthy alternatives over unhealthy alternatives when making a decision in ATOD situations (indicator 5.8.6).
- Analyze the outcomes of a health-related decision in ATOD situations (indicator 5.8.7).

Grades 9 Through 12

- Examine barriers that can hinder healthy decision making (indicator 5.12.1).
- Determine the value of applying a thoughtful decision-making process in ATOD situations (indicator 5.12.2).
- Justify when individual or collaborative decision making is appropriate in ATOD situations (indicator 5.12.3).
- Generate alternatives to health-related issues or problems in ATOD situations (indicator 5.12.4).
- Predict the potential short-term and long-term impact of each alternative on self and others in ATOD situations (indicator 5.12.5).
- Defend the healthy choice when making decisions in ATOD situations (indicator 5.12.6).
- Evaluate the effectiveness of health-related decisions in ATOD situations (indicator 5.12.7).

Objective

Students will be able to apply the DECIDE decision-making model to a realistic scenario.

Skill Development Step

Step 4: skill practice

Materials

Hip Hypothetical Party Revisited worksheet

Instant Activity

After students enter the room, have them review the hip hypothetical party scenario and worksheet from lessons 2 and 3. This is intended to reorient them to the scenario and the class activities. Ask students to consider if, to this point, they would do anything different.

Introduction

As you welcome students back to class, highlight all of the learning that has taken place so far. Review the lesson objectives. Let students know that today they will come to the end of the party scenario and will have to make a final determination about whether or not they will attend the party.

Main Activities

Hip Hypothetical Party Revisited (page 170) **(practice)**

Closure

Each situation we put ourselves into has the potential to have good, bad, or neutral outcomes.

Differentiation

Employ typical accommodations to support all learners.

Resources

- "8 Ethical Tests" in *Character Matters*, by Dr. Tom Lickona, available at www2.cortland.edu/dot-Asset/299013.pdf
- *TED Talk: How to Make Hard Choices*, by Ruth Chang
- *Activities That Teach, More Activities That Teach*, and *Still More Activities That Teach,* by Tom Jackson
- *Personal & Social Skills,* by Joyce V. Fetro

Lesson adapted from a submission by Lindsay Armbruster, middle/high school health teacher in New York.

Hip Hypothetical Party Revisited

LESSON 6

NHES Performance Indicators

Grades 6 Through 8

- Determine when health-related situations require the application of a thoughtful decision-making process in ATOD situations (indicator 5.8.2).
- Distinguish when individual or collaborative decision making is appropriate in ATOD situations (indicator 5.8.3).
- Distinguish between healthy and unhealthy alternatives to health-related issues or problems in ATOD situations (indicator 5.8.4).
- Predict the potential short-term impact of each alternative on self and others in ATOD situations (indicator 5.8.5).
- Choose healthy alternatives over unhealthy alternatives when making a decision in ATOD situations (indicator 5.8.6).
- Analyze the outcomes of a health-related decision in ATOD situations (indicator 5.8.7).

Grades 9 Through 12

- Determine the value of applying a thoughtful decision-making process in ATOD situations (indicator 5.12.2).
- Justify when individual or collaborative decision making is appropriate in ATOD situations (indicator 5.12.3).
- Generate alternatives to health-related issues or problems in ATOD situations (indicator 5.12.4).
- Predict the potential short-term and long-term impact of each alternative on self and others in ATOD situations (indicator 5.12.5).
- Defend the healthy choice when making decisions in ATOD situations (indicator 5.12.6).
- Evaluate the effectiveness of health-related decisions in ATOD situations (indicator 5.12.7).

Objective

Students will be able to apply the skill of decision making in a real-life situation.

Skill Development Step

Step 4: skill practice

Duration

50 to 60 minutes

Materials

- Hip Hypothetical Party Revisited worksheet
- Outcomes (two for each student, one for going and one for not going; available in the web resource)

Description

1. Reread the original story of the hip hypothetical party provided in lesson 2 and lesson 3, and share the following additional details:
   - One person was drugged and raped.
   - Gateway drugs were present at the party.

- The people at the party were a wide range of users, from never used to dependent users.
- It was *really* cold the night of the party.
- A parent of one of the people at the party is a police officer.

2. Have students complete the DECIDE model for the updated scenario.

3. Referring to table 6.3, which lists many potential outcomes of the scenario, randomly assign each student two outcomes: one for going to the party and one for not going to the party. Do not let the students view them until all have been distributed. When ready, have students independently read the outcome of their final decision. Then have each student read their outcome aloud. When all have been read aloud, have students independently read their other outcome and then share each one with the entire class again. By doing this, every student hears the *full* ending of the story.

4. Then read the ending of Dan's story:

   A teacher overheard invitations to the party. She informed the principal because the school has been asked to help mitigate the problems that the town has seen recently with drug abuse. The principal called the local police to inform them of the suspected party. Officers arrived at the party at about 11 p.m. The driveway was filled with cars, and, as the officers approached the house, they heard loud voices and music. As one of the officers was about to knock on the door, a teenager emerged holding a beer can and smelling like pot. This gave the officers probable cause to enter the home. When they entered, they found about 15 kids in a smoke-filled living room, and liquor and soda bottles were on the table. A few individuals snuck out the back door. Officers took the names of everyone present to be recorded in each of their personal records and assisted in calling their parents to pick them up. During this time, the officers discovered some pills on the table, which lab tests later determined to be Xanax (alprazolam) and OxyContin (oxycodone). While this was going on at the home, two students who snuck out were in a car accident that injured them both seriously. One teen, who had only one drink at the party, decided to let another teen, who had had several beers, drive. The driver, as police found out later, had drugs in his system, which impaired his driving, resulting in his driving off the road and hitting a small tree. Doctors say the driver will recover from his injuries, whereas the passenger suffered a traumatic brain injury that will keep him in a nursing facility for years to come.

5. Discuss outcomes and the whole learning activity using questions from the reflection for guidance. Students independently complete a reflection on the worksheet.

Tips and Extensions

- Incorporate this learning activity into an entire learning experience or unit about decision making (including internal and external influences) and substance use and abuse; students are expected to use their knowledge of these topics to engage fully in the Hip Hypothetical Party learning activity.

- It is great to use Poll Everywhere on the first and last days of this learning activity. It shows everyone's decisions anonymously. This is a great way to spark discussion about social norms, and, at the end, why people do or don't change their minds.

- Adjust the details of Mountain Town High School to resemble your school community.

- Change *Dan the Man* to another name if you have a Dan in your class.

- Copy the going to the party and not going to the party outcomes onto different-colored heavy weight paper. Put the going to the party outcomes on green paper and not going on red paper. That way, you can instruct students to turn over the green outcome if they're going to the party and the red one if they're not. Heavy weight paper is important so that students can't read through and find out the outcomes before it is time. The anticipation is a great teaching moment; they won't know the outcome until it happens.

Modifications

Employ typical accommodations to support all learners.

TABLE 6.3 Outcomes of Dan's Party

Didn't go	Did go
You stayed home and were very bored. A sense of inspiration struck, though, and you cooked a fantastic meal, inspiring you to become a master chef overnight.	You had one drink. You're not sure what was in it, though. When the police showed up at the party, you snuck out the door with some other kids. You decided to drive because you only had one drink. You ended up driving off the road because, as they find out later at the hospital, your drink was drugged and you were incapacitated. You only had minor scratches, but your passenger experienced a traumatic brain injury.
Your best friend was at the party, got arrested, and is now grounded for three months.	You drank a bunch of beers. As you stumbled out the back door of Dan's house when the police showed up, a friend shoved you into the passenger seat of his car. The driver was drunk and drove off the road. You ended up with a traumatic brain injury that will require you to stay in a physical rehabilitation facility, relearning how to do everything as if you were a baby, for years.
You were not affected by the party at all.	You snuck out the back door of Dan's house but didn't have a ride, a car, a coat, or your phone. You ended up staying in the woods overnight; the weather was in the 30s and rainy.
You were driving home from the movies and got cut off by the drunk driver from the party.	You snuck out the back door of Dan's house. You had nothing with you but your phone (not even the keys to you dad's car that he let you borrow for the night). You called your parents, who picked you up at the end of Dan's driveway. Even though they knew you had been drinking and had smoked pot, they didn't yell at you . . . right then. The next morning, you felt terrible, physically and emotionally, but your parents forced you to talk with them for a long time. You are grounded for three months and lost all car privileges.
You were not affected by the party at all.	You drank a lot at Dan's party. You and a classmate had a presentation due in English on Monday that you both had planned to work on all day Sunday. Instead, you were unable to get out of bed or think clearly. As a result, your presentation received a failing grade.
You were riding home from a friend's house and got rear-ended by a driver who had left the party high.	The person you like was at the party, and you had a great time hanging out. Someone else who likes you spent a lot of time talking with you too. You all smoked pot together. You ended up hooking up with the person who likes you—whom you don't really like.
You were not affected by the party at all.	You were in the living room when the police came. Officer Renet helped you call your parents to pick you up. Your mom was the first person to show up, and she came in her pajamas.
As you were driving home from a friend's house, you glanced down at a text message from your mom, and hit someone whom you hadn't noticed was walking down the street dressed all in black. You called 9-1-1. An ambulance and police officers came. You were brought to the police station and charged with vehicular manslaughter.	You were in the living room when the police came. They recognized your name from the sports section of the newspaper and made sure that you knew that they would be contacting the school about your choice to drink and smoke at Dan's party. This is your second offense, so you'll be suspended for the rest of your season.
You were not affected by the party at all.	You were at the party but had no intention of drinking or doing any drugs. When everyone around you, including most of your friends, decided to drink, you called your parents to get you out of the situation. Your parents sent your older brother to pick you up.
You were walking home from your neighbor's house and got hit by a car leaving the party. You did not suffer major injuries, but you're pretty banged up and can't play in your sectional final game tomorrow because of it.	You were at the party and had one beer. You decided it wasn't for you and wanted to get out. Another friend had the same thought and called a family member for a ride. You asked to ride with him too. The next morning you called your coach to tell him that you were at the party. You have to have a meeting with your coach, parents, and other people from school to determine what your consequences will be.
You were not affected by the party at all.	You drank a significant amount and tried some pills that someone had. You remember heading to a bed to sleep for a while. When you woke up, your clothes were gone. You were raped.

Didn't go	Did go
Two of the key players on your team were at the party. Your teammates got caught by the police while smoking pot. The school was notified, and now they are suspended for the rest of the season.	You did not drink or do drugs at the party. You have *many* pictures from that night though. You were in the living room when the police came. Your parents refused to pick you up at the party but were willing to meet you at the police station. You were questioned by the police because you were sober. They requested to see your iPhone, and your parents agreed to let them hold it as evidence. The pictures you took will be used against several of your friends and classmates.
Instead of going to the party, you and your parents went out for dinner. After dinner you stopped for ice cream and your parents got a couple of scratch-off lottery tickets. They let you scratch a few and said that if the ones you scratched were winners, the money would be yours. You scratched the first one; it was a loser. You scratched the second one; you won $2. You scratched the third one; you won $20.	You drank a significant amount. As a result of your drunkenness, you said some very hurtful things toward your partner and your best friend. You also shared some very personal information about both of them with random people.
You were working with a partner on a major project for English. Your partner went to the party. When you come into class the Monday after the party, your part was ready to go, but your partner hadn't done anything. This is a group grade, and you and your partner received a failing grade. This makes it impossible for you to pass the course; you'll have to repeat it in the summer or next year. Since you're a senior, this also means you can't graduate with your class.	You were drunk and smoking pot when the police arrived. They notified the school, and you're now suspended from your team for the rest of the season.
You were not affected by the party at all.	You called your parents when the police arrived; they came to get you. Your parents used to trust you to make good decisions, and you always have made good decisions. They are happy that you're safe, but you've lost their trust now.
You were not affected by the party at all.	You drank at the party and spent a lot of time showing off your new iPhone. Somehow you lost track of it and now it's lost. You don't have an extra $700 to get another one. Your parents are not happy at all.
Your brother was at the party, got very drunk, and decided to spend the night at Dan's house. He texted you to cover for him with your parents, and you did. Your parents found out. Now you're in trouble too.	You drank excessively (four drinks in about two hours) at Dan's party. You became very confused and were vomiting before the police arrived. The police called an ambulance for you because your breathing slowed and then you lost consciousness. You had alcohol poisoning and had to receive several treatments in the emergency department.
You were not affected by the party at all.	You had one drink and were among the people who the police "helped" call parents. Your parents picked you up and reamed you out on the way home. You lost all social privileges for the rest of the school year.
You were not affected by the party at all.	You don't drink because of a family history of alcoholism; however, you were convinced by some people at the party that pot is harmless, so you tried it. The police came while you were high and forced you to call your parents while you were obviously high. Your parents are pretty smart and knew exactly what was going on. They picked you up and expressed their deep disappointment in your decision. You will not be allowed to take your driver's test next week as scheduled. They don't know when they'll allow it.
You were not affected by the party at all.	You and your significant other attended the party together. You decided to drink, while your partner chose to remain completely sober. You were not acting like yourself, and it upset your partner, resulting in a breakup.

(continued)

TABLE 6.3 *(continued)*

Didn't go	Did go
The person who drives you to school each morning was at the party. This student was driving drunk and got into a major accident.	You attended the party with your best friend, who drove you there. The original plan for the night was to spend the night at her house—that's what you told your parents. She convinced you to go to the party just for a little while. At the party, she ran out of the house when the police arrived, leaving you stranded. You didn't drink or use any other drugs, but you still had to call your parents while the police listened to ask them to pick you up.
You were not affected by the party at all.	You attended the party with your best friend, who needed convincing to come to the party just for a little while. When the police arrived, you sprinted out of the house with the people you were talking to, leaving your friend there to get in trouble for something that she didn't even want to do.
You were not affected by the party at all.	You were in the living room when the police showed up. You're in the process of applying to college, so you begged them not to record your information. They declined and assisted you in calling your parents to come get you.
Your step-sister was at the party. She took your mom's OxyContin (which your mom needs as a result of her recent back surgery) to the party. Your mom can't get a refill now for several weeks, since it's a controlled substance. Your mom basically can't move, which means you won't be going on the trip you and she had planned for next weekend.	You attended the party with your long-term significant other. You both decided to drink and use other drugs, with the agreement that you would watch out for each other. You stuck together for the entire night and had a great time. You hadn't previously gone very far in terms of a physical relationship, but after leaving Dan's party, you went a lot farther than either of you wanted to.
You were not affected by the party at all.	You went to the party for a little while but didn't drink or use other drugs. As the evening progressed, you noticed that it was getting a little out of control. You and a few friends decided to leave before anything bad happened. You made it home safely.
You were not affected by the party at all.	You went to the party with some friends who weren't interested in drinking or doing any other drugs. You were curious what it would be like since you've never done anything like that before. As you were about to give in to the pressure to have a beer, the friend who drove you said he was leaving because the party was getting a little out of control. Begrudgingly, you said you'd go with him. You made it home safely.
You were not affected by the party at all.	You were in the living room, with a drink in your hand, when the police showed up. There was no hiding that you were drunk and no use in running, since your parents are friends with Officer Renet. He called your parents before any other parents, filling them in personally about what he had witnessed. Your parents arrived, and you rode home with your mom, who expressed her extreme disappointment in you, especially since they had to wake up your little sister to come get you, and she was sitting in the backseat seeing you act like a fool. Your dad drove your car home, using your keys, which he has taken, indefinitely.
The person who you like was disappointed that you weren't at the party but hooked up with someone else anyway.	You had fun at the party but left earlier than most people because you had a gut feeling that things were going to get out of hand. While on your walk home, you were hit by a car and are in critical condition at the hospital. It is unclear if you're going to survive.
You were not affected by the party at all.	You had fun at the party and spent most of your time with the person you like. You both decided to leave the party early so you could have one-on-one time at your house. You both had been drinking some and you ended up having sex. You're not sure if anything was used to prevent pregnancy or sexually transmitted infections.

Name: _____

1. The situation involving Dan's party is fictional, but the process of making a choice, gathering information, and the outcomes are real. Discuss how the whole activity mimics making decisions in real life (from the very beginning when you made a quick decision to the end when you discovered all the outcomes and everything in between).

2. You heard many different outcomes. Which one or ones really struck you? Why?

3. Based on table 6.3, we know how the story ends for you and your classmates, but what about Dan? Write the ending to his story. Consider plot lines that include his own decisions and actions, his parents' reactions, his involvement in lacrosse, his schooling, the legal consequences, and the like.

Purpose

Students have had a chance to work through the DECIDE model for a scenario that was predetermined. In an effort to promote transfer of the skill to another area of your students' lives, this assignment will ask them to use the DECIDE model in a novel way.

NHES Performance Indicators

Grades 6 Through 8

- Identify circumstances that can help or hinder healthy decision making (indicator 5.8.1).
- Determine when health-related situations require the application of a thoughtful decision-making process in ATOD situations (indicator 5.8.2).
- Distinguish when individual or collaborative decision making is appropriate in ATOD situations (indicator 5.8.3).
- Distinguish between healthy and unhealthy alternatives to health-related issues or problems in ATOD situations (indicator 5.8.4).
- Predict the potential short-term impact of each alternative on self and others in ATOD situations (indicator 5.8.5).
- Choose healthy alternatives over unhealthy alternatives when making a decision in ATOD situations (indicator 5.8.6).
- Analyze the outcomes of a health-related decision in ATOD situations (indicator 5.8.7).

Grades 9 Through 12

- Examine barriers that can hinder healthy decision making (indicator 5.12.1).
- Determine the value of applying a thoughtful decision-making process in ATOD situations (indicator 5.12.2).
- Justify when individual or collaborative decision making is appropriate in ATOD situations (indicator 5.12.3).
- Generate alternatives to health-related issues or problems in ATOD situations (indicator 5.12.4).
- Predict the potential short-term and long-term impact of each alternative on self and others in ATOD situations (indicator 5.12.5).
- Defend the healthy choice when making decisions in ATOD situations (indicator 5.12.6).
- Evaluate the effectiveness of health-related decisions in ATOD situations (indicator 5.12.7).

Objectives

See the NHES performance indicators in the previous list. There are no other objectives for this lesson.

Skill Development Step

Step 4: skill practice

Materials

Materials needed for the Decision-Making Comic Strip activity

Instant Activity

After students take their seats, they write their responses to the prompt: "How would you explain the importance of decision making to a peer who has never had a health class?"

Introduction

In the next two lessons, students will be using what they have learned throughout the unit to apply the DECIDE process to a decision of their choice. While there will be two scenarios presented, students will also have the option to use a topic that is of personal interest to them. Perhaps it will be a decision they are already thinking about.

Main Activity

Decision-Making Comic Strip (page 178) **(practice, feedback and reinforcement)**

Closure

Lesson 7 does not need a specific closing. You can let students know that they will continue the activity in the next lesson. For lesson 8, you should close by letting students know that they will be presenting their comics the next time the class meets.

Differentiation

Have students work in pairs to complete the assignment.

Adapted from a submission by Jeff Bartlett, middle school health teacher in Massachusetts.

Decision-Making Comic Strip

LESSONS 7 AND 8

NHES Performance Indicators

Grades 6 Through 8

- Determine when health-related situations require the application of a thoughtful decision-making process in ATOD situations (indicator 5.8.2).
- Distinguish when individual or collaborative decision making is appropriate in ATOD situations (indicator 5.8.3).
- Distinguish between healthy and unhealthy alternatives to health-related issues or problems in ATOD situations (indicator 5.8.4).
- Predict the potential short-term impact of each alternative on self and others in ATOD situations (indicator 5.8.5).
- Choose healthy alternatives over unhealthy alternatives when making a decision in ATOD situations (indicator 5.8.6).
- Analyze the outcomes of a health-related decision in ATOD situations (indicator 5.8.7).

Grades 9 Through 12

- Determine the value of applying a thoughtful decision-making process in ATOD situations (indicator 5.12.2).
- Justify when individual or collaborative decision making is appropriate in ATOD situations (indicator 5.12.3).
- Generate alternatives to health-related issues or problems in ATOD situations (indicator 5.12.4).
- Predict the potential short-term and long-term impact of each alternative on self and others in ATOD situations (indicator 5.12.5).
- Defend the healthy choice when making decisions in ATOD situations (indicator 5.12.6).
- Evaluate the effectiveness of health-related decisions in ATOD situations (indicator 5.12.7).

Objectives

Students will be able to

- apply aspects of the DECIDE model to scenarios related to alcohol, tobacco, and illegal drug use; and
- apply the DECIDE decision-making model (application of indicators 5.8.2 through 5.8.7 or indicators 5.12.2 through 5.12.7).

Skill Development Step

Step 4: skill practice

Duration

90 to 100 minutes (approximately two class periods)

Materials

- Decision-Making Comic Strip planning sheet
- Paper for comic strip development
- Pens, colored pencils, markers, and other drawing supplies

Description

In this activity, students create a comic strip that shows a character going through each step of the decision-making process. Two example scenarios each for middle school and high school are provided here. You can give your students these sample scenarios to work with, or you or your students can create scenarios. The comic strip should demonstrate students' background knowledge of alcohol, tobacco, or other drugs as discussed in the unit. The planning sheet provided here will guide students through the process of designing and finalizing their comic strip. A self-checklist is also provided to hand out so students know what their finished comic strip should demonstrate. The rubric covers the following project requirements:

- The *complete* decision-making protocol (DECIDE acronym)
  - Decision to be made (indicators 5.8.1, 5.8.2, and 5.8.3)
  - Examination of three different options (indicator 5.8.4)
  - Consideration of one pro and one con for each option (indicator 5.8.5)
  - Identification of one internal and one external influence that might affect the decision
  - Decision and action (indicator 5.8.6)
  - Evaluation of the decision (indicator 5.8.7)
- Three facts regarding the appropriate product depending on the prompt (indicators 1.8.1 and 1.8.9)

Students follow these steps in completing the project:

1. Review the project description.
2. Review the self-checklist.
3. Complete the planning sheet.
4. Get the planning sheet approved by your teacher.
5. Complete the draft (the templates are provided for quick sketches and dialogue).
6. Complete the final copy (construction paper is provided to create a final piece with final pictures and dialogue).

Decision-Making Comic Strip Scenarios (High School)

1. You're at a fireworks display during the summer when your friends sneak off into the woods behind the school. You follow them there and start feeling a little nervous because you don't know many people there. Some people are smoking cigarettes and drinking. An upperclassman comes over and starts talking to you. He can tell that you are nervous because you don't know many people. He asks if you smoke and you say, "No." He doesn't smoke either; he talks about how smoking is so bad for you and is so noticeable to your parents. He can't afford to get in trouble for that. Instead, he asks if you are interested in trying this stuff he took from his mom; he says it is great to relax your nerves and will help you have fun. You have never taken pills before and are not sure about what to do. You look around and notice another group of people who are just talking, laughing, and not smoking. What do you do?

2. You and your friends are going to see the release of the newest comedy. You are excited because you have been waiting for this movie to come out for weeks and haven't been able to get tickets until now. There is a group of you going and while you are in the car on the way to the theater, one of your friends asks the driver to make a quick stop because he has to pick something up from a friend. The driver makes the stop and after your friend gets back in the car he asks if anyone wants to smoke a joint before heading into the movie. What do you do?

1. You and your friends are playing on a co-ed baseball team. This is your third year playing with your team and having the same coach. This year, one of the older players on the team chews tobacco regularly during the games. You have actually noticed your coach doing it as well. Your teammate asks you if you want to try it during the next game. You aren't sure if you should because you learned about the smokeless nicotine product in health class and know it's not the greatest thing for your health. What do you do?

2. You go to your friend's house after school one day to check out the new puppy she just got! You notice that there are no adults home. While playing with the dog, you see your friend's older sibling walk into the room drinking a beer. Your friend's sibling asked if you and your friend wanted to try it because it tasted really good. What do you do?

Decision-Making Comic Strip Self-Checklist

Concerns (not yet) Areas that need work with comments	Criteria (proficient) Standards for performance (with indicators in parentheses)	Advanced (above and beyond) Evidence of exceeding standard with comments
	A character in the comic strip identifies the decision to be made (5.8.1, 5.8.2, and 5.8.3).	
	A character in the comic strip examines three options that can be made (5.8.4).	
	A character in the comic strip considers a pro and a con for each option (5.8.5).	
	A character in the comic strip identifies an internal and an external influence that might affect the decision.	
	A character in the comic strip decides and takes action regarding the healthiest decision (5.8.6).	
	A character in the comic strip evaluates the decision by explaining if it was a good or bad decision and why (5.8.7).	
	Three facts regarding the appropriate ATOD product are included in the comic strip (1.8.1 and 1.8.9).	
	The comic strip is creative, colorful, and unique. There are minimal spelling and grammatical errors. The comic strip shows pride in work.	

Grade and Comments:

Assessment and worksheets modified from a submission from Jeff Bartlett, middle school health teacher in Massachusetts.

Decision-Making Comic Strip Planning Sheet

Directions: The following document serves as your planning/brainstorm sheet for this project. Please make sure that you include everything in this planning sheet in your comic strip. This *must* be approved by your teacher before you begin your draft!

Step 1. Identify the decision to be made. In a complete sentence, identify the specific decision you need to make based on the situation you selected. Be specific!

Step 2. Examine your options. Create a list of options for your decision. What are your choices in this situation?

Step 3. Consider the pros and cons for each option listed. Fill in the chart below, making notes of at least one positive and negative for each option.

Positives	Negatives

Step 4. Identify influences. What are the different influences (internal and external) that might affect the decision?

   Internal:

   External:

Step 5. Decide and take action! Identify which option you went with and, in a complete sentence, explain *why* you think this is the *best* decision to make!

Step 6. Evaluate your decision. Was your decision a good decision or a bad decision? Why?

Step 7. The facts: Please list three facts about the substance in the scenario that you will put into your comic strip.

Comic box planning: In the table below, please describe what characters, setting, and dialogue (what your characters are going to say to each other) will be in each of your boxes within your actual comic strip. Use the answers in steps 1 through 7 to help you. *Suggestion:* It will be helpful to make a separate box for each part to the decision-making process—a box for the D, a box for the E, a box for the C, a box for the I, a box for the D, a box for the E.

Box no.	Characters, setting, and dialogue
1	
2	
3	
4	
5	
6	
7	
8	
9	
10	

Submitted by Jeff Bartlett, middle school health teacher in Massachusetts.

LESSON 9: Let's Enjoy Some Comics

Purpose

After the comic strips are completed, students will hang them up around the room. This lesson provides an opportunity for students to discuss and receive feedback on their decision-making process.

NHES Performance Indicators

None addressed

Objectives

Students will be able to

- evaluate and analyze the outcomes of health-related scenarios and
- provide appropriate peer feedback based on the provided parameters.

Skill Development Step

Step 5: feedback and reinforcement

Materials

- Student comic strips
- Decision-Making Comic Strip Peer Evaluation Form (enough copies for students to evaluate three comics each)

Instant Activity

After students take their seats, they write their responses to the prompt: "What is the most important thing you have learned in this unit. Why?"

Introduction

Let students know that today they will be evaluating their peers' work and getting a chance to see the other comic strips and how their classmates worked through a decision-making process. Additionally, students will use a peer-assessment tool to evaluate each other's work.

Main Activities

Preparation

Post student comic strips around the room.

Comic Gallery Walk

Students have 10 to 15 minutes to walk around the room and review the comic strips. They must complete evaluations on three of the comic strips using the Decision-Making Comic Strip Peer Evaluation Form.

Closure

- Ask the following questions in a large-group discussion: How can the skill of decision making be applied to other situations in your life? With what other health-related behaviors will you use this skill?
- Let students know what the next unit will be and how decision making will be applied in the next unit.

Differentiation

Each student could present his or her comic strip to the class prior to the gallery walk.

Decision-Making Comic Strip Peer Evaluation Form

Concerns (not yet) Areas that need work with comments	Criteria (proficient) Standards for performance (with indicators in parentheses)	Advanced (above and beyond) Evidence of exceeding the standard with comments
	A character in the comic strip identifies the decision to be made (5.8.1, 5.8.2, and 5.8.3).	
	A character in the comic strip examines three options that can be made (5.8.4).	
	A character in the comic strip considers a pro and a con for each option (5.8.5).	
	A character in the comic strip identifies an internal and an external influence that might affect the decision.	
	A character in the comic strip decides and takes action regarding the healthiest decision (5.8.6).	
	A character in the comic strip evaluates the decision by explaining if it was a good or bad decision and why (5.8.7).	
	Three facts regarding the appropriate substance are included in the comic strip (1.8.1 and 1.8.9).	
	The comic strip is creative, colorful, and unique. There are minimal spelling and grammatical errors. The comic strip shows pride in work.	

Comments:

CHAPTER 7

Setting Goals for a Health-Enhancing Lifestyle

In this chapter, we offer materials that will help you support students' development of goal-setting skills, which is associated with Standard 6 of the National Health Education Standards. All activities are designed to be used in your classroom. In this chapter, you will find a summative assessment, lessons plans, and learning activities to help you implement a goal-setting unit in your classroom.

The materials presented here are designed to support each step of the skill development model (see chapter 1) and are presented and organized to reflect a backward-design approach (see chapter 2). We begin with the end in mind by looking at the big picture of what the skill is and what students should be able to do once they develop the skill, including the specific performance indicators from the National Health Education Standards. We also include sample skill cues for teaching the skill, and the rest of the chapter includes assessments, lesson plans, and learning activities that you can implement in your classroom. We have included both sets of the National Health Education Standards performance indicators (grades 6 through 8 and grades 9 through 12) in the unit overview and each lesson as appropriate. Take the materials here and make them your own in order to meet the needs of your students or to adequately address the objectives. Our goal is to provide a usable framework that is also easily modifiable.

Throughout this chapter, we highlight 10 dimensions of wellness to provide the context for goal setting. While a search related to dimensions of wellness will result in a variety of definitions and models, this chapter applies a 10-component model. The use of 10 dimensions is intended to provide a comprehensive and broad look at our health and the concept of wellness. We urge you to thoughtfully consider each dimension and the role it plays in your students' lives. While not all dimensions may seem immediately relevant, over time each will play a role in overall health outcomes. Consider including some of the nontraditional dimensions included in the model presented here to show students that there are many ways to be healthy. The more we can connect our students to various aspects of their health, the more likely they become to consider their health in a holistic manner. Goal setting is the perfect skill to allow students to evaluate their personal health and then use the results of their self-assessment to determine a goal they are willing to work on that will improve their health.

SKILL OVERVIEW

We have all been told that if we want to achieve something we need to set our minds to it and work to achieve it. We need to focus, try hard, and not give up. While it is true that we must work hard and be dedicated to reaching our target, there is more to the process. Simply working hard and staying focused does not guarantee that we will reach our target; instead we must be thoughtful in *how* we are going to reach the target by making a plan, considering the potential obstacles that could get in our way, strategies to overcome those barriers, and people who can support us along the way. When we do this and work through a process to achieve our goal, we set ourselves up for greater success and an increased likelihood that we will achieve what we have set out to accomplish.

The performance indicators of the National Health Education Standards consider the skill of goal setting, like decision making, to be a process that students must work through. This skill places less emphasis on whether students are able to achieve their goal and a greater emphasis on a student's ability to apply the process in a thoughtful and meaningful way. This skill requires students to envision what is possible and then make a plan to work toward an aspect of their health in a way that will maintain or improve their health outcomes. The process that they learn in health class is also relevant in all other areas of their lives. This unit provides an opportunity for students to maintain or improve their health and will also give them tools to set goals and make changes in any area of their lives.

The National Standards have students, beginning in elementary school, think about what a goal is and consider the possibility of taking ownership of their own health by setting a goal and also identifying the people and resources they will need in order to achieve the goal. This foundation allows students to recognize that health doesn't just happen to them, but rather that they play an important and key role in determining their health outcomes. As students progress into middle school, the process of goal setting is expanded. Here, students must first assess their personal health and overall health status in order to identify the best area to focus on. Keep in mind that students do not necessarily need only to improve areas in which they have found deficiencies, but it is important for them to have experience in self-assessment in order to make informed decisions about their goals. Next, they will set a goal and develop a plan to reach their goal. Following this, they must consider the strategies and skills needed to achieve the goal, and then determine how they will monitor their progress. Finally, after working on their goal, they will reflect on their progress and determine next steps for maintaining their current progress or altering their path in order to solidify this goal for a long-term duration.

Each step of the goal-setting process is important for students to consider because the process and the accompanying critical thinking help students better understand themselves and how their goals will influence their future. In addition, it is also through students working through the goal-setting process that we are able to measure student proficiency. It is common for students to set the goal. Or, we might have them report on achievement of the goal, but we do not ask them to consider the factors that support or hinder their success, to reflect on their progress, or what they have learned as a result of the process. In this chapter, we advocate for implementing a process through which students thoughtfully consider their personal needs, select a meaningful and appropriate goal based on their own health status and needs, consider how the goal fits into their life, state specific strategies for achieving the goal, and reflect on the process of working toward the goal. While not all students will be able to achieve their goal, failure, too, is an important learning process. Having students see that just setting a goal doesn't guarantee success is an important lesson, because we can also show them that we have the ability to adjust goals, that working toward one change can lead to other changes and that sometimes, making a change isn't easy, but it is worth it. While goal setting can seem like a relatively straightforward skill, it is actually complex and has intricacies that really need to be experienced to be understood.

The topic used in this goal-setting unit is based on the dimensions of wellness. We do not focus on one specific health behavior; rather, we provide a forum for students to explore multiple areas to determine those most meaningful for them to improve. The 10 dimensions included here are emotional, environmental, financial, intellectual, multicultural, occupational, physical, sexual, spiritual, and social (see figure 7.1).

The concept of wellness dimensions is used in a variety of settings and also, depending on the source, references a varying number of dimensions. For example, some models include 6 dimensions while others include 8 or 10. While the dimensions of sexual health and multicultural health are newer to the mix, we have included them here because they carry important considerations for our health. We all live within and among a variety of cultures, and each of these cultural experiences shapes our health choices. The same is true for sexual health; this is a dimension that encourages us to think about how our sexuality affects and is affected by our health. Helping our students to have thoughtful and structured conversations about this dimension helps them to better understand their own sexuality and to make health-enhancing choices to avoid or reduce health risk.

We encourage you to be as broad as possible when having your students think about their own health. We recognize that some dimensions may not feel immediately relevant to your students. For example, occupational or financial wellness may feel like issues that older students and adults would consider. Your role is to help students see how these dimensions are relevant to their health by giving them an opportunity to learn about themselves and how each of the dimensions can have a long-term impact on or be affected by health decisions they make now. Throughout the unit, students will have the opportunity to explore multiple dimensions, though it may not be feasible to have every student explore every dimension in detail. When students move on to determining the goals they want to set for themselves, encourage them to review at least three dimensions before deciding which goals they want to work on. This will help students to explore areas they may not readily consider. We have found that it is common for students

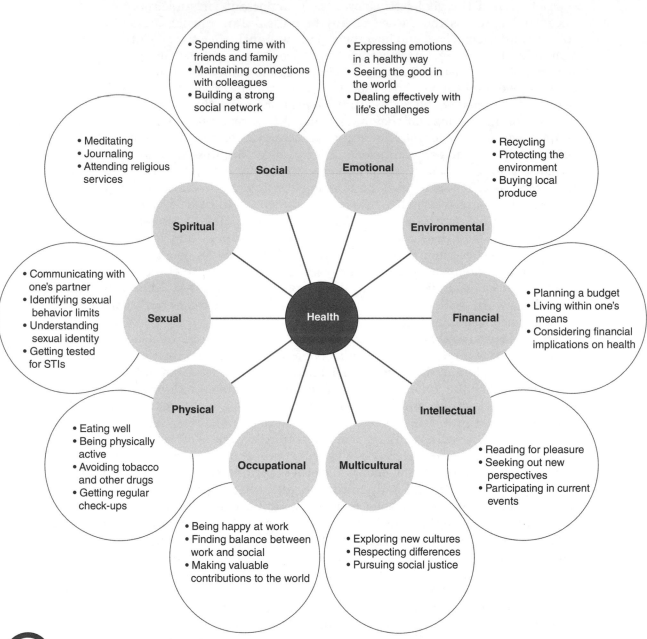

FIGURE 7.1   The 10 dimensions of wellness.

Adapted, by permission, from S. Benes and H. Alperin, 2016, *The essentials of teaching health education* (Champaign, IL: Human Kinetics).

(and adults for that matter) to default to getting more physically active and eating better as their health goals. While we are not diminishing the importance of these behaviors, we feel it is important for students to broaden their understanding of health and health behaviors.

Table 7.1 shows the performance indicators from the National Health Education Standards, which outline what students should be able to do within grades 6 through 8 and 9 through 12.

TABLE 7.1   Performance Indicators for Standard 6 of the NHES (Grades 6-12)

	6-8		9-12
6.8.1	Assess personal health practices.	6.12.1	Assess personal health practices and overall health status.
6.8.2	Develop a goal to adopt, maintain, or improve a personal health practice.	6.12.2	Develop a plan to attain a personal health goal that addresses strengths, needs, and risks.
6.8.3	Apply strategies and skills needed to attain a personal health goal.	6.12.3	Implement strategies and monitor progress in achieving a personal health goal.
6.8.4	Describe how personal health goals can vary with changing abilities, priorities, and responsibilities.	6.12.4	Formulate an effective long-term personal health plan.

Reprinted, with permission, from the American Cancer Society. *National Health Education Standards: Achieving Excellence*, Second Edition (Atlanta, GA: American Cancer Society, 2007), 24-36, cancer.org/bookstore

SKILL CUES

Skill cues are used during step 2 of the skill development model to highlight the critical elements of the skill. Here we include sample skill cues and provide an explanation for students. Be sure to adjust the language to meet the needs of your students. If you modify the skill cues, be sure to include all aspects of the skill and performance indicators. Figure 7.2 shows some sample skill cues for goal setting that may be used for grades 6 through 12.

UNIT OUTLINE

This section includes an outline of the unit for Standard 6; table 7.2 shows this outline, including lesson titles, lesson objectives, the step(s) of the skill development model that are addressed in each lesson, and the titles of the main learning activities in each lesson.

The dimensions of wellness serve as the basis for the topics included in this goal-setting unit. It is appropriate to identify health topics and behaviors such as sleep, time management, environmental health, mental health, or healthy relationships that are relevant for your students within these dimensions. You may need to provide more functional information related to these topics than you have included in other units. We leave the specific topic detail to your determination. Be sure to add objectives as necessary.

The unit objectives included are based on the performance indicators for both Standard 6, Goal Setting, and Standard 1, Core Concepts, of the National Health Education Standards. Because this skill is sequential and is a process, we have included all of the performance indicators for Standard 6, and students must demonstrate them to show they are proficient in the skill. We integrate Standard 1 objectives into the unit as there are performance indicators directly applicable in the unit we present here. We also have added additional learning objectives. While some of the topic information aligns with the Standard 1 performance indicators, not all of it does, leading to the need for the additional objectives.

Goal Setting

STANDARD 6 — Students will demonstrate the ability to use goal-setting skills to enhance health.

Goal-Setting Skill Cues

Assess current health (strengths and areas for improvement)

Identify an area that you want to work on

Create a SMART goal to maintain or improve your health

Apply strategies and skills to accomplish the goal

Record, reflect on, and evaluate goal progress and outcome

HUMAN KINETICS

From S. Benes and H. Alperin, 2019, *Lesson planning for skills-based health education* (Champaign, IL: Human Kinetics). Reprinted, by permission, from S. Benes and H. Alperin, 2016, *The essentials of teaching health education* (Champaign, IL: Human Kinetics).

 FIGURE 7.2 Skill cues for the skill of goal setting.

Unit Objectives Grade 6 Through 8

By the end of this unit, students will be able to

- assess personal health practices (indicator 6.8.1);
- develop a goal to adopt, maintain, or improve a personal health practice (indicator 6.8.2);
- apply strategies and skills needed to attain a personal health goal (indicator 6.8.3); and
- describe how personal health goals can vary with changing abilities, priorities, and responsibilities (indicator 6.8.4).

Unit Objectives Grades 9 Through 12

By the end of this unit, students will be able to

- assess personal health practices and overall health status (indicator 6.12.1);
- develop a plan to attain personal health goals that addresses strengths, needs, and risks (indicator 6.12.2);
- implement strategies to monitor goal progress (indicator 6.12.3); and
- formulate an effective long-term personal health plan (indicator 6.12.4).

Additional Unit Objectives Grades 6 Through 12

By the end of this unit, students will be able to

- describe how setting goals can affect their health;
- explain how health is affected across a variety of dimensions;
- list the steps of effective goal setting;
- analyze the relationship between healthy behaviors and personal health (indicator 1.8.1);
- describe the interrelationships of emotional, intellectual, physical, and social health in adolescence (indicator 1.8.2);
- predict how health behaviors can affect health status (indicator 1.12.1);
- describe the interrelationship of emotional, intellectual, physical, and social health (indicator 1.12.2);
- identify two dimensions of their health to improve;
- determine SMART (specific, measurable, adjustable, realistic, and timely) goals for improving their health;
- develop a plan to attain personal health goals that addresses strengths, needs, and risks;
- identify strategies to monitor goal progress;
- create a vision board to support goal achievement;
- identify three individuals to support the goal process;
- assess goal progress and refine as necessary;
- apply a goal-setting process to improve health outcomes through health-related scenarios;
- explain their personal goal-setting process and celebrate success;
- formulate an effective long-term personal health plan.

TABLE 7.2 Standard 6 Unit Outline

Lesson title	Lesson objectives (indicators in parentheses) *By the end of this lesson, students will be able to:*	Step of the skill development model addressed in the lesson	Main learning activities
Lesson 1: There Is life After High School . . . Where Do You Want It to Lead?	• Describe how setting goals can affect their health • Explain how health is affected across a variety of dimensions • List the steps of effective goal setting	• Skill introduction (step 1) • Steps of the skill (step 2)	Goal-Setting Pre-assessment (p. 200)
Lesson 2: Introduction to the Dimensions of Wellness	• Assess personal health practices (6.8.1) • Develop a goal to adopt, maintain, or improve a personal health practice (6.8.2) *or* • Assess personal health practices and overall health status (6.12.1) • Develop a plan to attain a personal health goal that addresses strengths, needs, and risks (6.12.2) • Analyze the relationship between healthy behaviors and personal health (1.8.1) • Predict how health behaviors can affect health status (1.12.1) • Describe the interrelationships of emotional, intellectual, physical, and social health in adolescence (1.8.2) • Describe the interrelationship of emotional, intellectual, physical, and social health (1.12.2)	None addressed	Introduction to the Dimensions of Wellness (p. 204)
Lesson 3: Dimensions of Wellness Self-Assessment	• Assess personal health practices and overall health status (6.12.1) • Predict how health behaviors can affect health status (6.12.1) • Analyze the relationship between healthy behaviors and personal health (1.8.1) • Describe the interrelationship of emotional, intellectual, physical and social health (6.12.2) • Describe the interrelationships of emotional, intellectual, physical, and social health in adolescence (1.8.2)	Skill practice (step 4)	Dimensions of Wellness Self-Assessment (p. 208)
Lesson 4: Got Goals?	• Develop a goal to adopt, maintain, or improve health practices (6.8.2) *or* • Develop a plan to attain a personal health goal that addresses strengths, needs, and risks (6.12.2) • Identify two dimensions of their health to improve • Determine SMART goals to improve their health • Develop a plan to attain personal health goals that addresses strengths, needs, and risks	Modeling and skill practice (steps 3 and 4)	Determining Your SMART Goal (p. 215)
Lesson 5: Creating a Vision	• Apply strategies and skills needed to attain a personal health goal (6.8.3) *or* • Implement strategies and monitor progress in achieving a personal health goal (6.12.3) • Identify strategies to monitor goal progress • Create a vision board to support goal achievement	Skill practice (step 4)	Creating Your Vision (p. 219)
Lesson 6: Recruit Your Champions	• Apply strategies and skills needed to attain a personal health goal (6.8.3) *or* • Implement strategies and monitor progress in achieving a personal health goal (6.12.3) • Identify three individuals to support the goal process • Assess current progress on their goal	Skill practice (step 4)	Goal Champions and Progress (p. 221)

Lesson 7: Goal Check—Revisit, Reevaluate, and Revise (if Needed)	• Apply strategies and skills needed to attain a personal health goal (6.8.3) • Describe how personal health goals can vary with changing abilities, priorities, and responsibilities (6.8.4) *or* • Implement strategies and monitor progress in achieving a personal health goal (6.12.3) • Formulate an effective long-term personal health plan (6.12.4) • Assess goal progress and refine as necessary	Skill practice (step 4)	Recheck, Reevaluate, and Revise (p. 224)
Lessons 8 and 9: One SMART Celebration	• Assess personal health practices (6.8.1) • Develop a goal to adopt, maintain, or improve health practices (6.8.2) • Apply strategies and skills needed to attain a personal health goal (6.8.3) • Describe how personal health goals can vary with changing abilities, priorities, and responsibilities (6.8.4) *or* • Assess personal health practices and overall health status (6.12.1) • Develop a plan to attain a personal health goal that addresses strengths, needs, and risks (6.12.2) • Implement strategies and monitor progress in achieving a personal health goal (6.12.3) • Formulate an effective long-term personal health plan (6.12.4) • Apply a goal-setting process to improve health outcomes through health-related scenarios • Explain their personal goal-setting process and celebrate success	Feedback and reinforcement (step 5)	Goal-Setting Postassessment (p. 228)

Performance indicators are from: Joint Committee on National Health Education Standards. (2007). *National Health Education Standards: Achieving Excellence* (2nd ed.). Atlanta, GA: American Cancer Society.

ASSESSMENT

The assessment for goal setting is two parts, a preassessment (lesson 1) and a postassessment (lessons 8 and 9). Both assessments use the same worksheet and assess students' ability to apply a SMART goal-setting process. The personal goal-setting activities included in the unit have students apply the goal-setting steps; the preassessment gauges students' understanding of the goal-setting process before they learn the steps, and the postassessment will tap into student's ability to recall the process and apply it to a unique situation. The assessment is scored using a rubric (see table 7.3) that looks at each component of the process and ensures appropriate completion.

Objective

Through this assessment, students will be demonstrate their ability to apply a goal-setting process to improve health outcomes through health-related scenarios.

Description

Students complete a Goal-Setting Preassessment at the beginning of the unit to determine baseline knowledge, which can be used to determine student growth during the unit. After completing the goal-setting process for individual goals, the postassessment provides an opportunity for students to demonstrate their learning of the goal-setting process related to a new scenario. Similar to the preassessment, students will use a Goal-Setting Postassessment worksheet and included rubric to score their work and determine the level of student achievement. Analysis of results will guide further teaching and discussion around this skill.

Tips and Extensions

■ Allow students ample time. For the postassessment, consider allowing students as much time as they need, but require them to complete it without the use of notes and assistance from others. Some students work slower, but that doesn't mean that they are having trouble.

■ Self-grading using the rubric is a great opportunity for students to become critical of their work and really see their strengths and areas of growth related to this skill. We suggest this with the postassessment only; it will only cause confusion with the preassessment.

■ A comparison of a student's pre- and postassessments is another great learning tool for students. It may be helpful to the learning process as well to review the preassessment and associated rubric as the students study each of the elements of goal setting.

TABLE 7.3   Rubric for Goal-Setting Worksheets

	4 Distinguished	3 Proficient	2 Basic	1 Unsatisfactory
Writing a SMART goal	Contains all 5 requirements	Contains 4 requirements	Contains 2-3 requirements	Contains one requirement
Identifying roadblocks and solutions	Identifies 3 or more realistic roadblocks and provides 2 or more plausible solutions for each	Identifies 3 or more realistic roadblocks and provides 1-2 plausible solutions for each	Identifies 1-2 realistic roadblocks and provides 1 plausible solution for each	Identifies 1-3 realistic roadblocks, but does not provide plausible solutions
Creating an action plan	Contains all 4: • 3 or more steps • Reasonable and well-spaced due dates • Steps directly relate to SMART goal • Logical and sequential steps	Contains 3 steps • Reasonable and somewhat well-spaced due dates • Steps relate to SMART goal • Mostly logical and sequential steps	Contains 2 steps • Dates are included but are not well-spaced or not reasonable • Steps demonstrate limited connection to SMART goal • Somewhat logical and sequential steps	Contains 1 step • Steps do not directly relate to SMART goal • The steps are not logical or sequential
Identifying support systems	Identifies a health-enhancing reward that is related to the goal and a motivation buddy who has expertise in the goal area	Identifies a health-enhancing reward and a motivation buddy who has expertise in the goal area, but the reward is not related to the goal	Identifies a health-enhancing reward that is related to the goal and a motivation buddy who does not have expertise in the goal area	Identifies a reward that is not health enhancing or related or Is missing either the motivation buddy or reward
Creating a plan for recording progress	Explains a specific method of recording progress that includes a quick indicator (e.g., smiley face) and narrative on progress	Explains a specific method of recording progress that includes a quick indicator or a narrative on progress	Explains a general method of recording progress that includes a quick indicator or a narrative on progress	Explains a general method of tracking that does not include a quick indicator or a narrative on progress

Submitted by Lindsay Armbruster, middle/high school health teacher in New York. This assessment was created under the guidance of National Health Education Standards and New York State Health Education Standards/Guidance Document.

Goal-Setting Preassessment

Name: _____

Read the scenario below and then complete the worksheet.

Julian is an eighth grader who stays after school for activity period each day and arrives home just after 4 p.m. When he gets home, he grabs a snack and heads to the family room in the basement. He turns on the TV, opens his phone to Snapchat, and frequently texts with his friends. His mom has suggested in the past that he do his homework as soon as he gets home, but Julian feels that he needs a bit of a break before tackling that. Around 7 p.m. each night, his family has dinner together, and no electronics are allowed. After dinner, Julian's chores are to clear the table and take out the trash. Julian loves TV and has something to watch each night at 8 p.m.; he does his homework while he watches.

He has recently discovered that eighth grade is much harder than seventh, even though his methods of doing what he's supposed to in class and doing his homework haven't changed at all. Julian received 90s last year, but his grades are quickly slipping to 80s and 70s now. As a result, he'd like to make a change in his life.

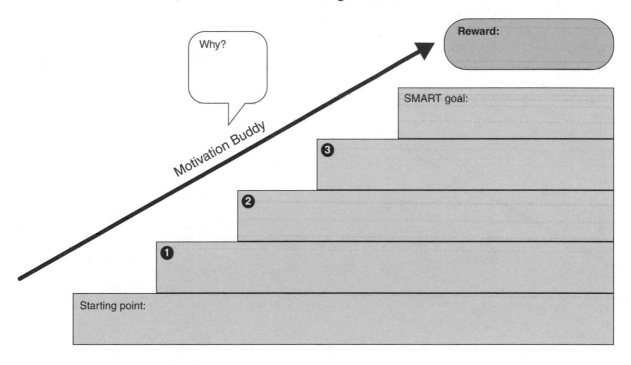

Roadblock	Solution

How will Julian make progress toward this goal?

Goal-Setting Postassessment

Name: _____

Read the scenario below and then complete the worksheet.

Rebecca considers herself a regular eighth grader. She aims to earn an average in the high 80s or low 90s in each class. She plays volleyball three out of four seasons a year. Rebecca also plays the trumpet in 8th grade band as well as jazz band. Each night, after she gets dropped off at home by a friend's mom or dad, she is responsible for getting dinner started and setting the table, since her parents work late. They eat as soon as her mom and dad get home around 7 p.m. She's a busy girl who finds herself exhausted each night when she finally gets to bed around 11:30 p.m. Life has been particularly busy recently and she's been falling asleep in her fourth period class. As a result, she'd like to make a change in her life.

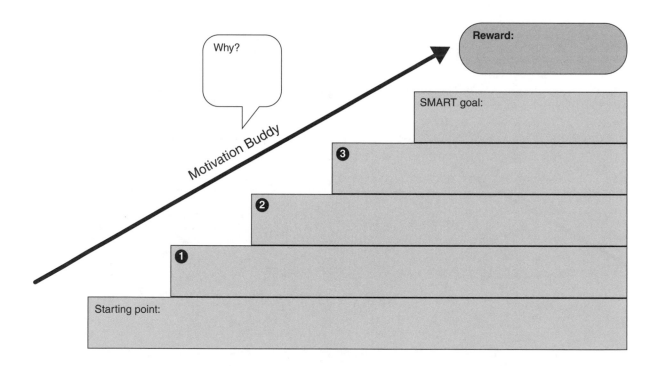

Roadblock	Solution

How will Rebecca make progress toward this goal?

LESSON PLANS

The lesson plans included here are the ones outlined in the unit outline earlier in the chapter and that will advance students toward achieving unit objectives and being able to successfully demonstrate the skill (evaluated in the assessment). The included lessons assume a 50-minute class period. Consider this prior to implementation.

Lesson plans include suggested activities, and those activities follow the lesson plans. Lesson plans and activities can be used together or independently to meet the needs of your classes.

Throughout the lesson plans, you will see the steps of the skill development model in **boldface type** after activities that address each skill development step.

LESSON 1: There Is Life After High School . . . Where Do You Want It to Lead?

Purpose

Life accomplishments don't just happen, they take planning and hard work. This lesson helps students to consider their hopes for the future and the importance of setting goals to help them get where they want to be. This lesson starts by having students complete a preassessment to help you get a better sense of their ability to set SMART goals and then introduces the goal-setting process.

NHES Performance Indicators

No performance indicators are covered in this introductory lesson. See the lesson objectives.

Objectives

Students will be able to

- describe how setting goals can affect their health,
- explain how health is affected across a variety of dimensions, and
- list the steps of effective goal setting.

Skill Development Steps

- Step 1: definition, relevance, and educational outcomes
- Step 2: steps of the skill

Materials

Materials for the Goal-Setting Preassessment

Instant Activity

After students take their seats, they write their responses to the prompt: "Achieving your goals takes thought and consideration. What steps do you feel are involved in setting and accomplishing a goal?"

Introduction

Let students know that today is the first day in the goal-setting unit. Review the lesson objectives and then begin the first activity.

Main Activities

1. Goal-Setting Preassessment activity (page 200). Allow time for students to complete the assessment and for you to collect them.

2. Think-Pair-Share:
   - Ask students to imagine they are about to graduate from high school. What do they hope happens next? What goals do they have? What do they envision themselves doing? Is it college, the military, an apprenticeship, a job, or something else?
   - Next, what would they need to do to make sure their post-high school goals happen? Have them list at least two short-term goals they would set to be sure they reach that outcome.
   - Have students form pairs to share their postgraduation goals. Students explain how their goals will lead to the desired outcomes for the next step after high school.
   - Have pairs share with the rest of the class and write goals on the board. Discuss how short-term goals can help us achieve our long-term, future goals and help us to be successful. **(relevance)**

3. Highlight the reasons for setting goals: to help the students reach their dreams and to set up a plan to make sure they can get there. **(definition)** Review the steps of setting a goal. **(steps of the skill)**

Closure

Preview the next lesson for students by explaining that next time they will be assessing personal health practices and considering goals that will help them to improve their health.

Differentiation

- Give students the option to complete the preassessment at home.
- Include a handout for the steps of goal setting with visuals to help them recall the critical elements of the skill.

Resources

Use a search engine to find information on SMART goals (for example, sites like www.edutopia.org often have good resources).

Goal-Setting Preassessment

LESSON 1

NHES Performance Indicators

None addressed

Objective

Students will be able to demonstrate their level of goal setting prior to the start of the unit.

Skill Development Step

Step 1: introduction

Duration

15 to 20 minutes

Materials

Copies of the Goal-Setting Preassessment worksheet

Description

1. Let students know that this activity is a preassessment to determine what they know about goal setting. Remind them that it is OK if they do not know the answers or are unsure. They should do the best they can and they are not being graded on their performance.
2. Distribute the worksheet. Read the scenario as a group.
3. Allow time for students to complete the preassessment individually.

Modifications

- Provide language supports for students who need it.
- Revise the scenario as necessary to be appropriate for your students.

Goal-Setting Preassessment

Name: _____

Read the scenario below and then complete the worksheet.

Julian is an eighth grader who stays after school for activity period each day and arrives home just after 4 p.m. When he gets home, he grabs a snack and heads to the family room in the basement. He turns on the TV, opens his phone to Snapchat, and frequently texts with his friends. His mom has suggested in the past that he do his homework as soon as he gets home, but Julian feels that he needs a bit of a break before tackling that. Around 7 p.m. each night, his family has dinner together, and no electronics are allowed. After dinner, Julian's chores are to clear the table and take out the trash. Julian loves TV and has something to watch each night at 8 p.m.; he does his homework while he watches.

He has recently discovered that eighth grade is much harder than seventh, even though his methods of doing what he's supposed to in class and doing his homework haven't changed at all. Julian received 90s last year, but his grades are quickly slipping to 80s and 70s now. As a result, he'd like to make a change in his life.

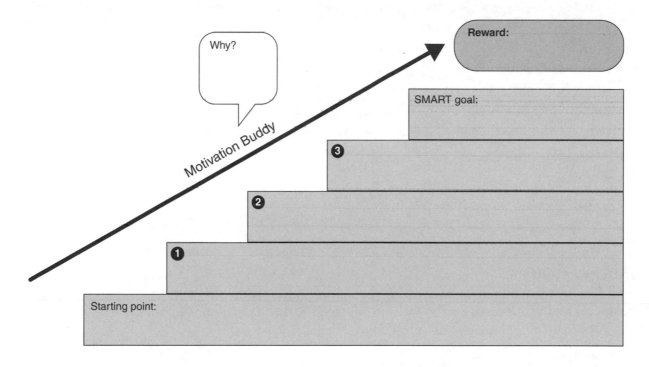

Roadblock	Solution

How will Julian make progress toward this goal?

Purpose

In lesson 1, students were introduced to the concept of setting goals to support them in being able to achieve their ambitions. In lessons 2 and 3, students will use the dimensions of wellness to assess their personal health and select two areas where they will set goals for the purpose of improving their health.

NHES Performance Indicators

Grades 6 Through 8

- Assess personal health practices (indicator 6.8.1).
- Develop a goal to adopt, maintain, or improve a personal health practice (indicator 6.8.2).

Grades 9 Through 12

- Assess personal health practices and overall health status (indicator 6.12.1).
- Develop a plan to attain a personal health goal that addresses strengths, needs, and risks (indicator 6.12.2).

Objectives

Students will be able to

- assess personal health practices and overall health status;
- predict how health behaviors can affect health status; and
- describe the interrelationship of emotional, intellectual, physical, and social health.

Skill Development Step

None addressed

Materials

- Scenario with the 10 dimensions of wellness appropriate and relevant to your students
- Materials needed for the Introduction to the Dimensions of Wellness activity

Instant Activity

After students take their seats, they write their responses to the prompt: "Write down two health behaviors you try to do every day to keep yourself healthy and one behavior you think is important to do more often than you already do."

Introduction

1. Once students have settled in and have had a chance to answer the instant activity prompt, introduce the lesson of the day and inform students that over the next two lessons they will be asked to look at different health behaviors and to think critically about how various health choices affect their overall health.

2. Review the lesson objectives.

3. To get students started, explain that you are going to read them a short passage to highlight some of the different dimensions of our health. Ask them to see if they can identify the 10 dimensions of wellness in the paragraph. Note, consider writing your own scenario based on the 10 dimensions of wellness that will be relevant for your students. We provide an example here that may work better at the high school level and encourage you to modify as needed for your grade level and students. Read the following (avoid reading parenthetical text):

    Imagine you are just waking up. Already your health is being affected. As you rub your eyes and press snooze, you realize that you didn't get as much sleep last night as you would have hoped (physical wellness). Also, you remember the fight you had yesterday with your partner and are feeling pretty bad about how the whole thing played out (social wellness). You were trying to discuss your limits and how physical you want to be together. You and your partner are not seeing eye to eye on this (sexual health). You want to call and talk things out, but you are afraid he or she will still be too mad to discuss things. This has you really stressed (emotional wellness), and you aren't sure how you are going to get through the day (mental and emotional wellness). On top of that, it's Sunday and you have to go to work. You don't really like your job, but you know that working allows you to make money; without money, you would have no car and wouldn't be able to participate in activities (financial and occupational wellness). Even though you have to go to work, you know that you will have to talk your parents about how many hours you are working, especially on a Sunday; they don't think it is right to be missing the weekly Sunday dinner with family (cultural wellness). While you are not particularly religious, you do like to set aside time on Sunday mornings to reflect on your week and to be mindful about the good things going on (spiritual wellness). With the way this day is shaping up, you aren't sure it is going to happen.

As if this wasn't enough, as you are just getting out of bed, you remember that you have a big exam tomorrow and need to factor in time to study (intellectual wellness) that doesn't require you to pull an all-nighter. But, there isn't anything you can do about it now so you get up, take a really long shower, and brush your teeth. You check the clock again because not only do you want to avoid being late for work, but also you are hoping to ride your bike because you like the exercise and that it is a good way to reduce pollutants in the air (physical and environmental wellness).

Main Activities

1. After reading the scenario, discuss with the group and identify all 10 dimensions. Relate the scenario to students' experiences.
2. Have students complete the Introduction to the Dimensions of Wellness activity (page 204).

Closure

Tell students that next class period, they will be completing a self-assessment of the dimensions of wellness.

Differentiation

- Provide hard copies of the scenario in this lesson for students to have at their seats.
- Partner English language learners with another student to help them understand the language within the scenario.
- Change the scenario to better reflect your own community or age of students; this will allow students to better see themselves within the scenario.

Resources

- Institute for Wellness Education, www.instituteforwellness.com/10-dimensions-of-wellness/
- University of New Hampshire Health and Wellness, www.unh.edu/health-services/ohep/wellness
- Substance Abuse and Mental Health Services Administration, www.samhsa.gov/wellness-initiative/eight-dimensions-wellness

Introduction to the Dimensions of Wellness

LESSON 2

NHES Performance Indicators

None addressed—the focus is on functional information.

Objectives

Students will be able to

- list the 10 dimensions of wellness and
- identify health behaviors that fit into each dimension.

Skill Development Step

None addressed

Duration

20 to 30 minutes

Materials

- Flip chart paper
- Markers
- Copies of the dimensions of wellness model (if you choose)

Description

This activity uses a 10-component dimensions of wellness model (see table 7.4 for descriptions of the dimensions). While a variety of models exist with varying numbers of components, this activity asks students to consider the 10 components in table 7.4. The inclusion of 10 components requires students to further explore areas of their health they may not have previously considered.

1. Hang poster paper around the room. Each one will have one dimension of wellness listed on it.
2. Small groups of students are assigned to each sheet of paper with one of the dimensions written on it.
3. Students are given two minutes at the poster to list health behaviors that would fall under that dimension. After two minutes, students rotate to the next dimension. Based on time, students may filter through all dimensions or only a few.
4. After the students have rotated through the dimensions, each group will report on the behaviors listed for the dimension that they have ended at. Be sure to add or correct any inaccuracies or omissions.

Tips and Extensions

- The length of time for the activity may vary based on available class time.
- Providing a definition of each dimension will assist students in considering health behaviors to include.

TABLE 7.4 Dimensions of Wellness

Multicultural wellness	Awareness and understanding of others. Recognizes that each person brings a diverse set of experiences that shapes their view of health and well-being. Recognizes the importance of tolerance, acceptance, and justice. All individuals deserve access to health and health services.
Emotional wellness	Understanding of and attention to the variety of feelings and emotions within each person. Emotionally well people have high self-esteem, ability to positively express feelings, a positive view of their body, and ability to cope with life challenges.
Environmental wellness	Recognition between one's health and connection to environmental surroundings. This includes factors such as air quality, water, living conditions, and energy usage. Encourages individuals to explore how personal behaviors to conserve and protect the environment affect individual health.
Financial wellness	The role of money and finances in the ability to access and maintain good health. Financial wellness includes financial goals, access to credit, available income, budgeting, and savings in order to achieve realistic goals and live within one's means.
Intellectual wellness	The value of learning and critical thinking over the life span. Includes a person's desire and quest to attain new information, explore beliefs and values, make reasoned decisions, and understand current events to improve their outcomes and global awareness.
Occupational wellness	The level a person engages in, receives satisfaction from, and pursues career opportunities in line with values and desired professional goals. This includes physical and emotional working conditions, ability to perform job functions, satisfaction with work role, and learning new skills that will benefit future opportunities.
Physical wellness	Maintaining health and well-being of the physical body. This includes a variety of behaviors that maintain and enhance health as well as reduce health risks. Behaviors may include diet, physical activity levels, sleep, injury prevention, proper medication usage, drug and alcohol use, and regular visits to a health care provider.
Sexual wellness	The relationship of our mental, physical, and emotional health as it relates to our sexuality and intimate partner relationships. Includes sexual identity, healthy intimate partner relationships free of violence and coercion, testing for sexually transmitted infections, use of contraception, discussion of limits within relationships, and delay and abstinence.
Social wellness	Interactions within one's community and with others. This includes being aware of social surroundings, friendships, managing conflict, social networks, participation in groups or clubs, and sharing common interests with others.
Spiritual wellness	The meaning of life's purpose that is in accordance with one's values and beliefs. It involves the use of reflection, further teaching, and connection to other like-minded individuals. May include organized religion, harmony with the universe, gratitude, or belief in a higher power.

Purpose

In lesson 1, students were introduced to the concept of setting goals to support them in being able to achieve their ambitions. In lesson 2, students were introduced to the 10 dimensions of wellness. In this lesson, students will use the dimensions of wellness to assess their personal health and then select two areas where they will set goals for the purpose of improving their health.

NHES Performance Indicators

Grades 6 Through 8

- Assess personal health practices (indicator 6.8.1).
- Develop a goal to adopt, maintain, or improve a personal health practice (indicator 6.8.2).

Grades 9 Through 12

- Assess personal health practices and overall health status (indicator 6.12.1).
- Develop a plan to attain a personal health goal that addresses strengths, needs, and risks (indicator 6.12.2).

Objectives

Students will be able to

- assess personal health practices and overall health status;
- predict how health behaviors can affect health status; and
- describe the interrelationship of emotional, intellectual, physical, and social health.

Skill Development Step

None addressed

Materials

- Dimensions of Wellness Self-Assessment activity
- Flip chart paper
- Markers

Instant Activity

After students take their seats, they write their responses to the prompt: "For each of the 10 dimensions of wellness, list and give one example what this dimension is all about."

Introduction

Tell students that you will continue the discussion of the dimensions of wellness. Review the dimensions from the last lesson.

Main Activity

Dimensions of Wellness Self-Assessment (page 208)

Closure

Ask students to write down something they learned about themselves from this activity.

Differentiation

- Provide hard copies of the scenario in lesson 2 for students to have at their seats.
- Partner English language learners with another student to help them understand the language within the scenario.
- Change the scenario to better reflect your own community or age of students; this will allow students to better see themselves within the scenario.

Resources

- Institute for Wellness Education, www.instituteforwellness.com/10-dimensions-of-wellness/
- University of New Hampshire Health and Wellness, www.unh.edu/health-services/ohep/wellness
- Substance Abuse and Mental Health Services Administration, www.samhsa.gov/wellness-initiative/eight-dimensions-wellness

Dimensions of Wellness Self-Assessment

LESSON 3

NHES Performance Indicators

Grades 6 Through 8

- Assess personal health practices (indicator 6.8.1).
- Develop a goal to adopt, maintain, or improve a personal health practice (indicator 6.8.2).

Grades 9 Through 12

- Assess personal health practices and overall health status (indicator 6.12.1).
- Develop a plan to attain a personal health goal that addresses strengths, needs, and risks (indicator 6.12.2).

Objectives

Students will be able to

- assess personal health behaviors as they relate to the 10 dimensions of wellness and
- identify areas of strength and weakness related to their health across dimensions.

Duration

20 to 30 minutes

Materials

Copies of the Dimensions of Wellness Self-Assessment

Description

This activity uses a 10-component dimensions of wellness model. While a variety of models exist with varying number of components, this activity asks students to consider the 10 components. The inclusion of 10 components requires students to further explore areas of their health they may not have previously considered.

1. Hand out the Dimensions of Wellness Self-Assessment and ask students to rate their wellness based on the questions on the handout.
2. Following the self-assessment, ask students to look at each category and add up their points and average for each category.
3. Have students fill in the wellness dimension bubbles with one health behavior in their life that they are either doing well or would like to improve.
4. Students then share with a partner at least two areas they are doing well and one or two areas they would like to improve. (Keeping this limited and not addressing all dimensions allows students to maintain some privacy in areas they are uncomfortable sharing.)
5. Have a group discussion about any ideas that were surprising or enlightening from this activity.

Tips and Extensions

Not all questions on the questionnaire will be applicable to all students. For example, if students do not work or are not in an intimate partner relationship, certain categories may not be applicable. Even if a student is not able to answer a particular question, have them consider (after the fact) how this could be relevant to them now or in the future.

Dimensions of Wellness Self-Assessment

Answer the questions to the best of your ability. Be honest and thoughtful in your responses.

Dimension	1—Rarely	2—Sometimes	Often or always
Multicultural wellness	Awareness and understanding of others. Recognizes that each person brings a diverse set of experiences that shapes their view of health and well-being. Recognizes the importance of tolerance, acceptance, and justice. All individuals deserve access to health and health services.		
1. I treat others with respect regardless of their background.			
2. I speak up when I see someone targeted because of their race, ethnicity, or cultural background.			
3. I seek to learn about other cultures, ethnicities, or races different than my own.			
4. I seek to understand when someone uses different health approaches than I do.			
5. I enjoy participating in family rituals and traditions.			
6. I try foods from other cultures.			
7. I have learned a new language.			
Emotional wellness	Understanding of and attention to the variety of feelings and emotions within each person. Emotionally well people have high self-esteem, ability to positively express feelings, a positive view of their body, and ability to cope with life challenges.		
1. I can positively express my feelings to others.			
2. I am able to adapt to new surroundings with ease.			
3. I feel good about myself and my behavior.			
4. I have a positive self-view of my body.			
5. When I am stressed, I am able to find positive ways to relax.			
6. I worry about things outside of my control.			
7. I let other people's view of me dictate how I feel about myself.			
Environmental wellness	Recognition between one's health and connection to environmental surroundings. This includes factors such as air quality, water, living conditions, and energy usage. Encourages individuals to explore how personal behaviors to conserve and protect the environment affect individual health.		
1. I recycle regularly.			
2. I try to reduce my water consumption by turning off the water while I brush my teeth or taking shorter showers.			
3. I look for products that are environmentally friendly.			
4. I wear my clothes more than once before washing.			
5. I limit the amount of paper I print off or write on.			
6. I turn off the car when no one is driving to limit the exhaust.			
7. I use refillable water bottles or containers in my lunch.			

(continued)

Dimensions of Wellness Self-Assessment *(continued)*

Dimension	1—Rarely	2—Sometimes	Often or always
Financial wellness	The role of money and finances in the ability to access and maintain good health. Financial wellness includes financial goals, access to credit, available income, budgeting, and savings in order to achieve realistic goals and live within one's means.		
1. I have a budget and stick to it.			
2. I save money for things I really want.			
3. I only spend money that I have.			
4. I do not borrow money from others to pay for things I need.			
5. I consider upcoming expenses before I purchase something.			
6. I consider how my health decisions will financially impact my long-term goals before I make a decision.			
7. I have a bank account.			
Intellectual wellness	The value of learning and critical thinking over the life span. Includes a person's desire and quest to attain new information, explore beliefs and values, make reasoned decisions, and understand current events to improve his or her outcomes and global awareness.		
1. I search out new opportunities to learn about a topic I know little about.			
2. I have a hobby that interests me.			
3. I make reasoned decisions based on what I have learned.			
4. I am up to date on current events.			
5. I read directions in order to properly complete assignments.			
6. I learn from mistakes and correct them so I don't make the same mistakes again.			
7. I look forward to trying new things.			
Occupational wellness	The level a person engages in, receives satisfaction from, and pursues career opportunities in line with values and desired professional goals. This includes physical and emotional working conditions, ability to perform job functions, satisfaction with work role, and learning new skills that will benefit future opportunities.		
1. I have a job that I like.			
2. My job helps me learn things I can use in the future.			
3. I am taking classes that will help me get a job.			
4. I have identified a career in the future that I am working toward.			
5. My job fits into my schedule and I am able to complete other responsibilities while also having a job.			
6. I feel proud of the work I do at my job.			
7. I have positive relationships with people at work.			

Dimension	1—Rarely	2—Sometimes	Often or always
Physical wellness	Maintaining health and well-being of the physical body. This includes a variety of behaviors that maintain and enhance health as well as reduce health risks. Behaviors may include diet, physical activity levels, sleep, injury prevention, proper medication usage, drug and alcohol use, and regular visits to a health care provider.		
1. I regularly receive health check-ups.			
2. I regularly see a dentist.			
3. I get at least sixty minutes of exercise on most days of the week.			
4. I sleep at least seven hours per night.			
5. I eat the recommended number of servings of fruits and vegetables.			
6. I have enough energy to get through a day.			
7. I wear protective gear to prevent injures (such as helmets and knee pads).			
Sexual wellness	The relationship of our mental, physical, and emotional health as it relates to our sexuality and intimate partner relationships. Includes sexual identity, healthy intimate partner relationships free of violence or coercion, testing for sexually transmitted infections, use of contraception, discussion of limits within relationships, and delay or abstinence.		
1. I can talk openly and without fear to my partner.			
2. I know how to access information and services to prevent the transmission of sexually transmitted infections.			
3. I have (or will) discuss limits of sexual contact with a partner.			
4. I will delay sexual intercourse (remain abstinent) until later in life.			
5. I am open about my sexual identity (whether straight, gay, lesbian, bisexual, genderqueer, or other).			
6. I have seen a health care provider and discussed my sexual health.			
7. I am open and honest in my intimate partner relationships.			
Social wellness	Interactions within one's community and with others. This includes being aware of social surroundings, friendships, managing conflict, social networks, participation in groups or clubs, or sharing common interests with others.		
1. I have a hobby or belong to a club that brings me happiness.			
2. I have meaningful friendships with at least two people.			
3. I am able to manage conflict in productive and appropriate ways.			
4. I seek out others who share common interests.			
5. I look for the good in people.			
6. I show support for my friends and their interests.			
7. My friends show support of me and my interests.			

(continued)

Dimensions of Wellness Self-Assessment *(continued)*

Dimension	1—Rarely	2—Sometimes	Often or always
Spiritual wellness	The meaning of life's purpose that is in accordance with one's values and beliefs. The use of reflection, further teaching, and connection to other like-minded individuals. May include organized religion, harmony with the universe, gratitude, or belief in a higher power.		
1. I take time alone to reflect on what is important to me.			
2. I believe in a higher power.			
3. I do good deeds and helpful acts for others without expecting anything in return.			
4. My actions reflect my personal beliefs and values.			
5. I have gratitude for what I have in my life.			
6. I seek to live life to the fullest.			
7. I share my personal beliefs and values with trusted adults or friends.			

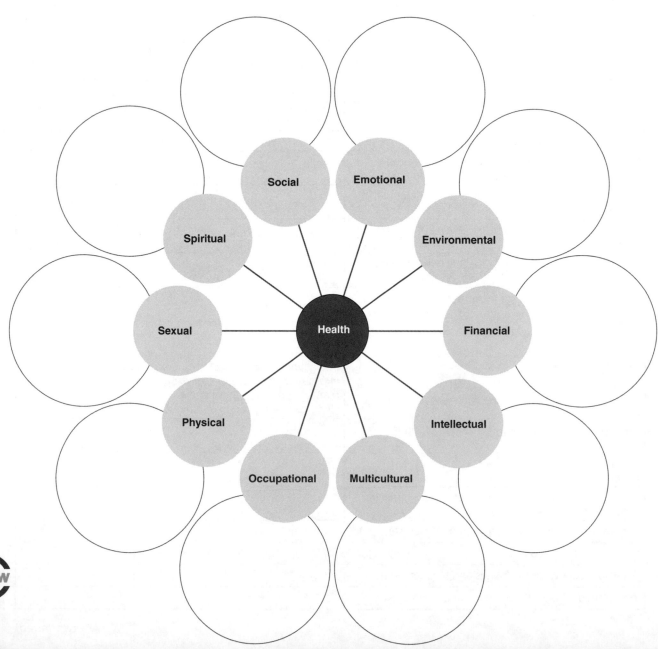

Purpose

In lesson 3, students took the time to assess their personal health and to see that health encompasses many areas (Dimensions of Wellness Self-Assessment). In this lesson, students will take time to set their personal goals in two dimensions and develop a plan to achieve them.

NHES Performance Indicators

- *Grades 6 through 8:* Develop a goal to adopt, maintain, or improve health practices (indicator 6.8.2).
- *Grades 9 through 12:* Develop a plan to attain a personal health goal that addresses strengths, needs, and risks (indicator 6.12.2).

Objectives

Students will be able to

- identify two dimensions of their health to improve;
- determine SMART goals to improve their health; and
- develop a plan to attain personal health goals that addresses strengths, needs, and risks.

Skill Development Steps

- Step 3: modeling
- Step 4: skill practice

Materials

Materials needed for the Determining Your SMART Goal activity

Instant Activity

After students take their seats, they write their responses to the prompt: "Which dimensions did you choose to work on? Why did you choose these?"

Introduction

Tell students that they will be using the SMART acronym (specific, measurable, adjustable, realistic, and timely) to set two goals that they are willing to work through in order to improve their health. Review the lesson objectives and then further explain that today they need to use their self-evaluation from the last lesson to help them choose two different dimensions of health to work on for their goal. Tell students that you will be reviewing their goals to ensure that they are health-enhancing. Review the directions for the packet that they will be completing and clarify any questions.

Main Activities

1. Model a SMART goal prior to starting the activity. While the activity has students set their own SMART goal, be sure to review the criteria and show an example of one that relates to improving health. You may also want to show examples of not SMART goals and work together as a class to make it SMARTer. **(modeling)**
2. Have students complete the Determining Your SMART Goal activity (page 215). **(practice)**

Closure

At the end of the assignment, ask students to complete a head, heart, and hands reflection about what they have learned about themselves to guide their goal development.

- *Head:* Something I learned about myself
- *Heart:* Something I am *feeling* as a result of setting these goals
- *Hands:* Action steps I am willing to take in order to ensure I reach my goal

(continued)

LESSON 4: Got Goals? *(continued)*

Differentiation

- Allow students to take home the assignment and complete it with more time.
- Break the class into groups of each of the wellness dimensions to brainstorm types of goals that would fit into that dimension. Do a gallery walk of all of the dimensions to give students ideas.

Resources

Grades 6-8 Goal Setting, www.coloradoedinitiative.org/wp-content/uploads/2014/10/GS-6-8-model.pdf

Lesson modified from a submission by Andy Horne, high school health teacher in Illinois.

Determining Your SMART Goal

LESSON 4

NHES Performance Indicators

- *Grades 6 through 8:* Develop a goal to adopt, maintain, or improve health practices (indicator 6.8.2).
- *Grades 9 through 12:* Develop a plan to attain a personal health goal that addresses strengths, needs, and risks (indicator 6.12.2).

Objectives

Students will be able to

- state a SMART goal to address a personal health issue based on their self-assessment results and
- work through a goal-setting process to enhance health outcomes.

Skill Development Steps

- Step 3: modeling
- Step 4: skill practice

Duration

50 minutes

Materials

- Copies of the SMART Goals Questionnaire
- Desktop computers, laptops, or tablets

Description

1. Provide students with copies of the questionnaire.
2. Review the instructions and grading criteria with the students. This activity could also be done without being graded. However, if you will be grading the activity, be sure to present the evaluation criteria.
3. Provide students with time to complete the worksheet.
4. Collect the worksheets in order to give feedback to the students. These should be returned to students so that they can benefit from your feedback as they begin working on their goal.

Tips and Extensions

Change the length of the goal project to meet your time parameters. While it is beneficial to allow students more time to complete the goal and to check in periodically, the duration is flexible.

Lesson modified from a submission by Andy Horne, high school health teacher in Illinois.

SMART Goals Questionnaire

During this questionnaire, you will use the results of your Dimensions of Wellness Self-Assessment to determine two goals you would like to improve. You may select only one goal per dimension (so, two goals = two dimensions). Complete the SMART Goals Questionnaire for each goal. Remember, you will be working on your goal over the next couple of weeks so be sure to select a goal that is meaningful to you and that you are willing to work toward achieving.

In no fewer than 250 words total, answer the following questions using complete sentences and including information from valid and reliable resources in your explanations.

Based on your self-assessment results, what are two health behaviors that you think *you* could improve?

1. _____

2. _____

For each goal, clearly state your goal and say why it is that you chose the goal and which dimension of wellness this goal will address.

1. _____

2. _____

Goal 1

1. *Specific:* What will your goal accomplish? How will it be accomplished?

2. *Measurable:* How will you measure whether or not your goal has been reached? List at least two indicators.

3. *Adjustable:* Will you be able to adjust this goal if needed? Once you start working on your goal, you may find it needs to be adjusted.

4. *Realistic:* Is it actually possible to achieve your goal? Have others done it successfully? Is it challenging but still achievable? Do you have the necessary skills, abilities, resources, support, and motivation to accomplish the goal?

5. *Timely:* Is our classroom timeline for the project a suitable deadline for you to be successful? If not, what is the time frame you are setting for your goal?

Action Steps

When breaking your goal down into action steps, what specific tasks will you need to complete in order to attain your goal?

1. _____

2. _____

3. _____

4. _____

5. _____

Result

How will you feel when you accomplish your goal?

Goal 2

1. *Specific:* What will your goal accomplish? How will it be accomplished?

2. *Measurable:* How will you measure whether or not your goal has been reached? List at least two indicators.

3. *Adjustable:* Will you be able to adjust this goal if needed? Once you start working on your goal, you may find it needs to be adjusted.

4. *Realistic:* Is it actually possible to achieve your goal? Have others done it successfully? Is it challenging but still achievable? Do you have the necessary skills, abilities, resources, support, and motivation to accomplish the goal?

5. *Timely:* Is our classroom timeline for the project a suitable deadline for you to be successful? If not, what is the time frame you are setting for your goal?

Action Steps

When breaking your goal down into action steps, what specific tasks will you need to complete in order to attain your goal?

1. _____
2. _____
3. _____
4. _____
5. _____

Result

How will you feel when you accomplish your goal?

Purpose

In this lesson, students will revisit the goals they have written and write up a plan to track their progress on the goal. Additionally, they will create a vision board to help keep them motivated and focused on achieving their goals.

NHES Performance Indicators

- *Grades 6 through 8:* Apply strategies and skills needed to attain a personal health goal (indicator 6.8.3).
- *Grades 9 through 12:* Implement strategies and monitor progress in achieving a personal health goal (indicator 6.12.3).

Objectives

Students will be able to

- identify strategies to monitor goal progress and
- create a vision board to support goal achievement.

Skill Development Step

Step 4: skill practice

Materials

Materials needed for the Creating Your Vision activity

Instant Activity

After students take their seats, they write their responses to the prompt: "What motivates you? Write down three things that will motivate you to accomplish your goals."

Introduction

As you welcome students back, highlight all of the learning that has taken place in the unit, so far. Let students know that today they will think about what motivates them to achieve their goal and create a vision board to support them in their efforts. Review the lesson objectives.

Main Activity

Creating Your Vision (page 219) **(practice)**

Closure

Have students share their motivational quote by writing it on a piece of paper and hanging it up in the classroom.

Differentiation

- Provide access to materials either through magazines in the room or images online.
- Pair English language learners with partners to help them to identify correct terms.

Resources

- Intermountain Health Care article on vision boards for kids, https://intermountainhealthcare.org/blogs/2014/01/helping-kids-set-goals-with-vision-boards/
- Page Turner Adventures, http://pageturneradventures.com/2012/01/1470/

Lesson modified from a submission by Andy Horne, high school health teacher in Illinois.

Creating Your Vision
LESSON 5

NHES Performance Indicators

- *Grades 6 through 8:* Apply strategies and skills needed to attain a personal health goal (indicator 6.8.3).
- *Grades 9 through 12:* Implement strategies and monitor progress in achieving a personal health goal (indicator 6.12.3)

Objectives

Students will be able to

- solidify their vision and increase motivation toward achieving their goal and
- explain personal motivation to accomplish their selected goals.

Skill Development Step

Step 4: skill practice

Duration

50 minutes

Materials

Materials will vary depending on how you choose to set up the activity

Description

In this activity, students will be creating their own vision boards to serve as motivation for achieving their goals. Remind students, that in the previous class, they thought about their health behaviors and considered which two they would like to improve by coming up with SMART goals. Explain to them that writing goals down helps create a vision and deeper level of commitment.

Next, explain the vision board activity. Their task will be to create a vision board that they can display somewhere (such as a bathroom, bedroom, or mobile device) to help remind them about their goal. Tell them to think of a vision board as a collage of pictures, words, and quotes to help motivate them to achieve a goal. What they include in the collage is up to them, but it should include the following:

1. Their goal (written somewhere)
2. Pictures and words related to the goal (minimum of 10)
3. Motivational quote(s) (minimum of 1)

The vision board can be in the form of an electronic document or poster board. For those who do a poster board, consider requiring them to take a digital picture and submitting that or converting it to a PDF file to turn in.

Provide time and materials for students to be able to complete their vision boards in class.

Tips and Extensions

- You might want to have some examples to share with students to get them thinking.
- You could have students look for quotes and pictures as homework in the lesson before this activity.

LESSON 6: Recruit Your Champions

If possible, allow one to two weeks between lessons 6 and 7. This will give students enough time to work on their goal and see if they have set an appropriate (and attainable) goal.

Purpose

We all need champions who will cheer for us and support us as we work to achieve our goals. This lesson is to help students think about who their champions will be and what supports will be most useful.

NHES Performance Indicators

- *Grades 6 through 8:* Apply strategies and skills needed to attain a personal health goal (indicator 6.8.3).
- *Grades 9 through 12:* Implement strategies and monitor progress in achieving a personal health goal (indicator 6.12.3).

Objectives

Students will be able to

- identify three individuals to support the goal process and
- assess current progress on their goal.

Skill Development Step

Step 4: skill practice

Materials

Materials needed for the Goal Champions and Progress activity

Instant Activity

After students take their seats, they write their responses to the prompt: "So far on your goal journey, what would you say has been the easiest part, and what has been hard about reaching your goal?"

Introduction

Tell students the lesson objectives. In this lesson, you will think about the people who can help you achieve your goal. Also, you will think about the progress you have made so far on your goal and how to keep the momentum moving forward.

Main Activity

Goal Champions and Progress (page 221) **(practice)**

Closure

With a classmate, share at least one person who will be your goal champion.

Differentiation

- Students can either handwrite or use computers to type their responses to the questions.
- Answers do not necessarily need to be written in complete sentences.
- Have students think in pairs before writing. This will help them to get more ideas of people who might support their process.

Goal Champions and Progress

LESSON 6

NHES Performance Indictors

- *Grades 6 through 8:* Apply strategies and skills needed to attain a personal health goal (indicator 6.8.3).
- *Grades 9 through 12:* Implement strategies and monitor progress in achieving a personal health goal (indicator 6.12.3).

Objectives

Students will be able to

- solidify their vision and increase motivation toward achieving their goal and
- explain their personal motivation to accomplish their selected goals.

Skill Development Step

Step 4: skill practice

Duration

50 minutes

Materials

- Copies of the Champions worksheet
- Copies of the What Did You Do? worksheet

Description

1. Provide students with copies of the Champions worksheet.
2. Review the instructions together as a group.
3. Provide students with time to complete the worksheet on their own.
4. Once students have finished (or time provided is up) have students share (in small or large group format) at least one person they wrote about in the worksheet.
5. Hand out copies of the What Did You Do? worksheet and provide students time to complete it before the end of the class period.

Tips and Extensions

- This activity asks students to identify champions. For students who may struggle with adult connections or peer relationships, additional support and guidance may be necessary. Where possible, help them to see adults at school, at home, or in their community who may help.
- The time that has lapsed since the initial goal setting may determine the students' ability to document progress. Take this into consideration as students are completing the assignment.

Champions

For this activity, you have to recruit three people to be a part of your goal-setting entourage. They should be people who can help you achieve your goal in whatever way you think they can. These can be the same people to support both goals, or you can identify separate people for each goal.

Name the individuals and say why it is that you chose them. What can they do to help you be successful? Thorough answers will receive full credit.

You must also complete and submit the What Did You Do? worksheet.

Individual no. 1

Individual no. 2

Individual no. 3

What Did You Do?

What did you do to achieve your goal during the past two weeks?

List at least three things that you did this week that took you one step closer to achieving your goal. Failure to list at least three things will result in a lower grade.

What did you do?	How does this help you?	Did someone help you do this? Who?	How did you feel afterwards?

LESSON 7: Goal Check—Revisit, Reevaluate, and Revise (if Needed)

Purpose

We all need to take time to reflect on our goals to see if they are meeting their intended purpose, are the right goal, or are able to be reached. This lesson allows students the opportunity to think about their goals and if they need to make any changes.

NHES Performance Indicators

Grades 6 Through 8

- Apply strategies and skills needed to attain a personal health goal (indicator 6.8.3).
- Describe how personal health goals can vary with changing abilities, priorities, and responsibilities (indicator 6.8.4).

Grades 9 Through 12

- Implement strategies and monitor progress in achieving a personal health goal (indicator 6.12.3).
- Formulate an effective long-term personal health plan (indicator 6.12.4).

Objectives

Students will be able to

- assess goal progress and refine as necessary and
- formulate an effective long-term personal health plan.

Skill Development Step

Step 4: skill practice

Materials

Materials needed for the Recheck, Reevaluate, and Revise peer interview activity

Instant Activity

After students take their seats, they write their responses to the prompt: "Write down what is working well as you implement your goal and what are you having challenges with."

Introduction

In this lesson, you will be interviewing a classmate about their goal progress. Review lesson objectives. In pairs, you will each have a chance to share and also offer feedback to your partner on their progress.

Main Activity

Recheck, Reevaluate, and Revise (page 224) **(practice)**

Closure

Following the peer interviews, the pairs share something new they learned about their goal process and what they will either keep doing or something they intend to change or modify in their goal.

Differentiation

- The closure could also be written.
- Have students write their own information and ideas about their progress prior to sharing and doing the interview with a partner.

Recheck, Reevaluate, and Revise
LESSON 7

NHES Performance Indicators

Grades 6 Through 8

- Apply strategies and skills needed to attain a personal health goal (indicator 6.8.3).
- Describe how personal health goals can vary with changing abilities, priorities, and responsibilities (indicator 6.8.4).

Grades 9 Through 12

- Implement strategies and monitor progress in achieving a personal health goal (indicator 6.12.3).
- Formulate an effective long-term personal health plan (indicator 6.12.4).

Objectives

Students will be able to

- thoughtfully consider current goal progress and make adjustments as necessary and
- revise SMART goals, as necessary, to improve personal health.

Skill Development Step

Step 4: skill practice

Duration

50 minutes

Materials

- Goal-Setting Check-In worksheet
- Goal-Setting Peer Interview worksheet
- Goal-Setting Reflection worksheet

Description

1. There are three separate worksheets to complete during this lesson. Hand out the first worksheet, the student check-in; review the instructions, and provide students with 5 to 10 minutes to complete the first worksheet.
2. The next worksheet will guide them in their peer interviews. Place students into pairs or small groups. Provide time for students to complete the interviews and record their responses to the prompts.
3. Lead a large-group discussion about failures, successes, and areas for improvement. It can be helpful for students to see that many people experience bumps along the way and that this is part of the process of goal setting.
4. Finally, in the last part of the class, provide students with the third worksheet and allow them to reflect on their own experiences.

Tips and Extensions

Not all students will feel confident reporting or presenting on the goals of their peers. Additionally, not all students will feel comfortable sharing their goals. To allow some flexibility, consider having students share just one goal.

Goal-Setting Check-In

You are hopefully closer to achieving your goal. Is it too easy? Is it too hard? Now is the time to comment on your performance so far and make the necessary changes to ensure that your goal is still challenging but ultimately achievable.

If your goal is proving to be too easy, reword it and make it more challenging but realistic.

If your goal is proving to be too hard, then word it to make it more realistic but also something worth striving to attain. Remember, SMART goals are adjustable too!

If you are confident that you have set the perfect goal, leave it as it is.

State or restate your SMART goal here:

_____

_____

_____

Goal-Setting Peer Interview

In pairs, you will interview each other. The purpose of the interview is to share your goal, goal progress, and any changes you are going to make to your goal and also to learn about your partner's goal progress. Use the following questions to guide your discussion and be prepared to share your conversation with the class.

Guiding Questions

- What is your SMART goal? Which dimension of wellness does it address?
- Why is this dimension of wellness important to you?
- How is your progress going? Is it easy or hard to try to reach your goal?
- Have you had to make any changes to your goal? How will these changes make it more likely you will succeed?
- What is one piece of advice you would give to others who might have a similar goal?

In class, we will discuss your conversations as a large group. We will share successes, failures, and strategies for improvement. Who did you interview, and how is that person doing? What advice could you give him or her? What advice, if any, did your interview partner give you?

Goal-Setting Reflection

Using the space that follows, reflect on *your* progress (was your goal too easy, just right, or too hard?), any obstacles you have encountered or things you did *not* do to achieve your goal, and possibly the progress of your peers. Please use complete sentences. More thorough answers will receive full credit.

Purpose

While setting goals and working to accomplish them is important, equally important is celebrating success. These lessons do two things. First, students will take a postassessment, and second, students share their progress and give a presentation about their personal goal-setting progress.

NHES Performance Indicators

Grades 6 Through 8

- Assess personal health practices (indicator 6.8.1).
- Develop a goal to adopt, maintain, or improve health practices (indicator 6.8.2).
- Apply strategies and skills needed to attain a personal health goal (indicator 6.8.3).
- Describe how personal health goals can vary with changing abilities, priorities, and responsibilities (indicator 6.8.4).

Grades 9 Through 12

- Assess personal health practices and overall health status (indicator 6.12.1).
- Develop a plan to attain a personal health goal that addresses strengths, needs, and risks (indicator 6.12.2).
- Implement strategies and monitor progress in achieving a personal health goal (indicator 6.12.3).
- Formulate an effective long-term personal health plan (indicator 6.12.4).

Objectives

Students will be able to

- apply a goal-setting process to improve health outcomes through health-related scenarios;
- explain their goal process and celebrate success; and
- formulate an effective long-term personal health plan.

Skill Development Step

Step 5: feedback and reinforcement

Materials

- Materials needed for the Goal-Setting Postassessment activity
- Poster-making materials (such as paper, poster board, markers, glue, and stickers)
- Desktop computers, laptops, or tablet computers (if using technology to make the poster)

Instant Activity

There is no instant activity during these lessons to allow for maximum time for the learning activities and student presentations.

Introduction

During lessons 8 and 9, we will be wrapping up our goal-setting unit. We will be sharing our accomplishments and our challenges and celebrating the work that we put into our goals and ourselves!

Main Activities

1. Have students complete the Goal-Setting Postassessment activity (page 228). **(feedback and reinforcement)**
2. Each student will make an informal presentation that should last no more than three minutes. The presentation consists of students creating a poster that shares the following information and then presenting their poster to the class:

- The SMART goals being addressed
- The names of the champions supporting their efforts and why
- How their progress is going
- Steps they will take to keep working toward or maintain their progress toward their goal

Closure

Hang the posters around the room and have students celebrate the good work everyone is doing to lead healthier lives!

Differentiation

- Presentations are optional and offer students the opportunity to share successes without presenting.
- Posters could also be made on the computer if technology is available.
- Provide students with an opportunity to present to you alone or to you with their friends.
- Students make a video recording of their presentations.

Goal-Setting Postassessment

LESSONS 8 AND 9

NHES Performance Indicators

Grades 6 Through 8

- Assess personal health practices (indicator 6.8.1).
- Develop a goal to adopt, maintain, or improve health practices (indicator 6.8.2).
- Apply strategies and skills needed to attain a personal health goal (indicator 6.8.3).
- Describe how personal health goals can vary with changing abilities, priorities, and responsibilities (indicator 6.8.4).

Grades 9 Through 12

- Assess personal health practices and overall health status (indicator 6.12.1).
- Develop a plan to attain a personal health goal that addresses strengths, needs, and risks (indicator 6.12.2).
- Implement strategies and monitor progress in achieving a personal health goal (indicator 6.12.3).
- Formulate an effective long-term personal health plan (indictor 6.12.4).

Objective

Students will be able to apply the goal-setting process in health-related scenarios.

Skill Development Step

Step 5: feedback and reinforcement

Duration

50 minutes

Materials

Goal-Setting Postassessment worksheet

Description

Have students complete the postassessment worksheet.

Resources

This assessment was created under the guidance of National Health Education Standards and the New York state health education standards guidance document.

Submitted by Lindsay Armbruster, middle/high school health teacher in New York. This assessment was created under the guidance of National Health Education Standards and New York State Health Education Standards/Guidance Document.

Name: _____

Read the scenario below and then complete the worksheet.

Rebecca considers herself a regular eighth grader. She aims to earn an average in the high 80s or low 90s in each class. She plays volleyball three out of four seasons a year. Rebecca also plays the trumpet in 8th grade band as well as jazz band. Each night, after she gets dropped off at home by a friend's mom or dad, she is responsible for getting dinner started and setting the table, since her parents work late. They eat as soon as her mom and dad get home around 7 p.m. She's a busy girl who finds herself exhausted each night when she finally gets to bed around 11:30 p.m. Life has been particularly busy recently and she's been falling asleep in her fourth period class. As a result, she'd like to make a change in her life.

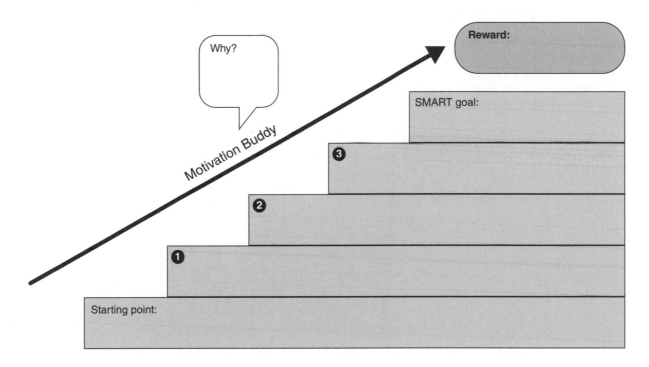

Roadblock	Solution

How will Rebecca make progress toward this goal?

CHAPTER 8

Managing Oneself to Better Health

Self-management is the skill associated with Standard 7 of the National Health Education Standards. Unlike many of the other skills and standards, the term *self-management* isn't explicitly included in the performance indicators for the standard, yet it is the skill that students will develop as they examine their role in maintaining and enhancing their health as well as practicing health-enhancing behaviors and avoiding risks to the health of themselves and others. This chapter provides you with materials for a secondary level self-management unit.

The materials for the unit reflect a backward-design approach (see chapter 2). You will first find the unit objectives (we start with the end in mind) and an assessment to evaluate the extent to which students can demonstrate their ability to address the objectives. Next you will find the lesson plans and learning activities needed to develop the skill of self-management with your secondary students. The activities included address each step of the skill development model so you can be sure that you are supporting effective skill development. The unit objectives are for grades 6 through 12, and the activities are designed for secondary students in general. Review before implementation and modify the activities to best meet the needs of your students.

This skill fits well with a variety of health topics; here we have chosen mental health as the context for developing self-management. Before beginning this unit, it might be appropriate to have a conversation with the school's counselor related to this topic. Understanding whether and where else in the school students will be discussing topics such as mental health and mindfulness will be a good understanding to have. Additionally, this will also alert the counselors in the event that students they are working with need additional support.

SKILL OVERVIEW

In many ways, self-management is exactly what we want our students to do as a result of our health courses and programs. We want them practicing behaviors that will enhance the health of themselves and others as well as engaging in behaviors that avoid or reduce health risks. The other skills and functional information we teach help support students' ability to manage their health. Some people choose to integrate self-management into other units or use the performance indicators as the outcomes for their health programs for the reasons described previously and because it can be difficult to measure the extent to which students actually practice behaviors. You also have to be careful that the behaviors that you have students practice in your self-management unit are not actually other skills! It can be hard sometimes to differentiate, so be thoughtful and purposeful in what you are including in your self-management unit. Often you are relying on student self-report of skill demonstration as a proficiency measure, and this is not always an ideal measure for skill assessment. However, one of the reasons we advocate for a self-management unit, and provide ideas here, is that this skill can be an opportunity to focus on all the positive behaviors that students might engage in to enhance their health.

Health class and dialogue around health in general often focuses on the negatives—we spend a lot of time talking about what *not* to do. Self-management can be a place to focus on what *to* do and all the many ways to be healthy. For example, the emphasis in this unit is how to maintain or enhance mental health through positive behaviors such as practicing gratitude. Even when we discuss mental illness and mental health challenges, we encourage a positive and proactive focus. Finally, the unit ends with sharing resources to help peers. We have created a unit that shows students many different strategies for enhancing mental health, all with a positive focus! You could do this with many other health topics as well. We encourage you to take this opportunity to make health about what students *can* do rather than what they *can't* (or shouldn't) do.

As previously mentioned, a challenge to implementing the skill of self-management is in how to evaluate it. When you look at the verbs in the performance indicators (table 8.1), you see that they all focus on *demonstrating* behaviors. You may be able to have some behaviors evaluated in class. For example, in this unit, students practice yoga and meditation in class—both behaviors that could be evaluated. The problem is that you do not know if they are engaging in these behaviors outside of class, and demonstrating a behavior one time isn't necessarily an indication of their ability. In this unit, we give an example of an assessment that is based on self-reported behavior. You'll note that we also ask for reflection as a way to help students internalize the experience and see the value of engaging in health-enhancing behaviors. In addition, you might consider adding some sort of external confirmation such as having a family member sign off on whether or not the student actually engaged in the behaviors or having students photograph or make a video recording of behaviors in action. However you decide to assess this skill, whether through self-report or other methods, students are showing you that they are effectively engaging in health-enhancing or risk-avoiding behaviors.

TABLE 8.1   Performance Indicators for Standard 7 of the NHES (Grades 6-12)

	6-8		9-12
7.8.1	Explain the importance of assuming responsibility for personal health behaviors.	7.12.1	Analyze the role of individual responsibility for enhancing health.
7.8.2	Demonstrate healthy practices and behaviors that will maintain or improve the health of self and others.	7.12.2	Demonstrate a variety of healthy practices and behaviors that will maintain or improve the health of self and others.
7.8.3	Demonstrate behaviors to avoid or reduce health risks to self and others.	7.12.3	Demonstrate a variety of behaviors to avoid or reduce health risks to self and others.

Reprinted, with permission, from the American Cancer Society. *National Health Education Standards: Achieving Excellence,* Second Edition (Atlanta, GA: American Cancer Society, 2007), 24-36, cancer.org/bookstore

SKILL CUES

During step 2 of the skill development model, students are presented with the critical elements of the skill. Skill cues can be an effective way to help students remember the critical elements. Sample skill cues are provided here; if necessary, modify them to meet your needs. Remember that the skill cues should highlight the aspects of the skill that need to be performed for the skill to be applied effectively. Figure 8.1 shows some sample skill cues for the skill of self-management that may be used for grades 6 through 12.

UNIT OUTLINE

This section includes an outline of the unit for Standard 7; table 8.2 shows this outline, including lesson titles, lesson objectives, the step(s) of the skill development model that are addressed in each lesson, and the titles of the main learning activities in each lesson.

All performance indicators for Standard 7, grades 6 through 12, are covered in this unit, as are select performance indicators from Standard 1. Unit objectives that are focused on the skill performance indicators are included along with additional objectives that are addressed through the unit. The health topic included in this unit is mental health with a focus on healthy practices and also recognition of warning signs for mental health issues. You may notice that step 3 of the skill development model is not explicit in the chart or the lessons. This is because you will be modeling and demonstrating self-management behaviors throughout the unit. For example, students are asked to practice healthy behaviors; these behaviors are being practiced in multiple lessons (lessons 3, 4, and 5) with you modeling the practice prior to students engaging in the action. Even though this unit does not include a specific activity that addresses modeling, you are still modeling each critical element of the skill throughout the unit.

Self-Management

STANDARD 7

Students will demonstrate the ability to practice health-enhancing behaviors and avoid or reduce health risks.

I APPEAR

Identify health behaviors, wants, or needs within your context

Access information, products, and services to support your health efforts

Practice health-enhancing behaviors

Practice avoiding risky health behaviors

Explain your role in staying healthy

Assess the outcomes of the behavior changes or of current health practices

Reflect on current health practices or changes

HUMAN KINETICS

From S. Benes and H. Alperin, 2019, *Lesson planning for skills-based health education* (Champaign, IL: Human Kinetics). Reprinted, by permission, from S. Benes and H. Alperin, 2016, *The essentials of teaching health education* (Champaign, IL: Human Kinetics).

FIGURE 8.1   Skill cues for the skill of self-management.

Unit Objectives Grades 6 Through 8

By the end of this unit, students will be able to

- explain the importance of assuming responsibility for personal health behaviors related to mental health (indicator 7.8.1);
- demonstrate healthy practices and behaviors that will maintain or improve the mental health of self and others (indicator 7.8.2);
- demonstrate behaviors to avoid or reduce mental health risks to self and others (indicator 7.8.3);
- analyze the relationship between healthy behaviors and mental health (indicator 1.8.1); and
- describe ways to reduce, prevent or address adolescent mental health conditions and illnesses (indicator 1.8.5).

Unit Objectives Grades 9 Through 12

By the end of this unit, students will be able to

- analyze the role of individual responsibility for enhancing mental health (indicator 7.12.1);
- demonstrate a variety of healthy practices and behaviors that will maintain or improve the mental health of self and others (indicator 7.12.2);
- demonstrate a variety of behaviors to avoid or reduce mental health risks to self and others (indicator 7.12.3);
- predict how healthy behaviors can affect mental health status (indicator 1.12.1); and
- propose ways to reduce, prevent or address mental health conditions and illnesses (indicator 1.12.5).

Additional Unit Objectives Grades 6 Through 12

By the end of this unit, students will be able to

- discuss the skill of self-management,
- list the steps to self-management,
- discuss the relevance of self-management,
- describe how happiness supports mental health,
- assess their own levels of happiness,
- discuss strategies for improving and enhancing their happiness,
- implement at least two strategies to improve their happiness and mental health,
- discuss the importance of mental health as a component of overall health,
- describe strategies for maintaining or enhancing mental health,
- describe (briefly) common mental health conditions,
- develop empathy for individuals with mental health conditions and illnesses,
- recognize warning signs for serious mental health conditions,
- recognize when help is needed for mental health issues,
- locate appropriate resources for supporting adolescent mental health, and
- share information about enhancing or maintaining mental health in adolescents.

TABLE 8.2   Standard 7 Unit Outline

Lesson title	Lesson objectives (indicators in parentheses) *By the end of this lesson, students will be able to:*	Steps of the skill development model addressed in the lesson	Main learning activities
Lesson 1: Developing Healthy Habits	• Discuss the skill of self-management • List the steps to self-management • Discuss the relevance of self-management • Explain the importance of assuming responsibility for personal health behaviors related to mental health (7.8.1) *or* • Analyze the role of individual responsibility for enhancing mental health (7.12.1)	Skill introduction and steps of the skill (steps 1 and 2)	Large-group discussion
Lesson 2: Happiness Is Healthy	• Describe how happiness supports mental health • Assess their own levels of happiness	Health topic (mental health)	• Happiness Wall (p. 245) • Happiness Survey (p. 246)
Lesson 3: Strategies for Increasing Happiness	• Discuss strategies for improving and enhancing their happiness • Implement at least 1 strategy to improve their happiness • Demonstrate healthy practices and behaviors that will maintain or improve the mental health of self and others (7.8.2) • Describe ways to reduce, prevent or address adolescent mental health conditions or illnesses (1.8.5) *or* • Demonstrate a variety of healthy practices and behaviors that will maintain or improve the mental health of self and others (7.12.2) • Propose ways to reduce, prevent or address mental health conditions and illnesses (1.12.5)	Health topic (mental health) and skill practice (step 4)	Practicing Gratitude (p. 250)
Lesson 4: Strategies for Increasing Happiness (Continued)	• Discuss strategies and habits that will help maintain or enhance happiness • Implement at least 2 strategies to improve or maintain their happiness • Demonstrate healthy practices and behaviors that will maintain or improve the mental health of self and others (7.8.2) *or* • Demonstrate a variety of healthy practices and behaviors that will maintain or improve the mental health of self and others (7.12.2)	Health topic (mental health) and skill practice (step 4)	Oh Happy Day! (p. 253)

Lesson title	Lesson objectives (indicators in parentheses) *By the end of this lesson, students will be able to:*	Steps of the skill development model addressed in the lesson	Main learning activities
Lesson 5: Healthy Mind, Healthy Me	• Discuss the importance of mental health as a component of overall health • Describe strategies for maintaining or enhancing mental health • Implement at least 2 strategies to maintain or improve mental health • Demonstrate healthy practices and behaviors that will maintain or improve the mental health of self and others (7.8.2) • Demonstrate behaviors to avoid or reduce mental health risks to self and others (7.8.3) • Analyze the relationship between healthy behaviors and mental health (1.8.1) *or* • Demonstrate a variety of healthy practices and behaviors that will maintain or improve the mental health of self and others (7.12.2) • Demonstrate a variety of behaviors to avoid or reduce mental health risks to self and others (7.12.3) • Predict how healthy behaviors can affect mental health status (1.12.1)	Health topic (mental health) and skill practice (step 4)	• Mental Health Jigsaw (p. 257) • Yoga for Youth (p. 258)
Lesson 6: Understanding Mental Health	• Describe (briefly) common mental health conditions • Develop empathy for individuals with mental health conditions or illnesses	Health topic (mental health) and skill practice (step 4)	• Mental Health Challenges (p. 260) • From Their Perspective (p. 261)
Lesson 7: When to Seek Help and Where to Find It	• Recognize warning signs for serious mental health conditions • Recognize when help is needed for mental health issues • Locate appropriate resources for supporting adolescent mental health • Demonstrate healthy practice and behaviors that will maintain or improve the health of self or others (7.8.2) *or* • Demonstrate a variety of healthy practices and behaviors that will maintain or improve the health of self and others (7.12.2)	Skill practice (step 4)	Locating Community Resources (p. 264)
Lesson 8: Sharing Is Caring	• Share information about enhancing or maintaining mental health in adolescents	Feedback and reinforcement (step 5)	Sharing Is Caring (p. 266)

Performance indicators are from: Joint Committee on National Health Education Standards. (2007). *National Health Education Standards: Achieving Excellence* (2nd ed.). Atlanta, GA: American Cancer Society.

ASSESSMENT

Assessment for the skill of self-management requires thoughtful planning as, per the National Health Education Standards, students need to be *demonstrating* healthy practices and behaviors—ideally in their lives, not just in the classroom. The assessment for this unit is based on student self-reporting and reflection and builds off of the activities that are introduced and practiced in class. The assessment is primarily where you will be addressing step 5 of the skill development model. Step 5 is also addressed in lesson 8, when students are creating infographics to share mental health resources with their peers.

Objectives

Through this assessment, students will be able to demonstrate their ability to

- explain the importance of assuming responsibility for personal health behaviors related to mental health (indicator 7.8.1);
- demonstrate healthy practices and behaviors that will maintain or improve the mental health of self and others (indicator 7.8.2); and
- demonstrate behaviors to avoid or reduce mental health risks to self and others (indicator 7.8.3).

Description

This is a two-part assessment using the Healthy Habits Self-Management Assessment Worksheet. In part 1 of the worksheet (preassessment), students will explain the happiness and mental health behaviors and habits they will use in their lives for the allotted amount of time. This will vary based on your needs, but we suggest allowing at least two weeks for students to practice and integrate these behaviors into their daily schedule. The second part of the worksheet (postassessment) is a reflection based on their experience trying to *practice* the healthy behaviors they chose.

Modifications

This assessment is based off of the performance indicators for middle school; however, the assessment can be easily adapted for grades 9 through 12. Other modifications may include:

- *Adding components so that additional unit objectives can be addressed:* We have focused on an assessment that demonstrates the National Health Education Standards performance indicators, and this could be modified so that students can demonstrate additional learning.
- *Having students choose a happiness habit and a healthy mind habit to practice during the unit:* If students have already had a goal-setting unit, you could modify this assessment to also include a goal-setting component. We have not added it here as it doesn't directly relate to the unit objectives or performance indicators.
- *Creating a rubric to evaluate the assessment:* You could more clearly connect the assessment to the skill cues presented. This could also be evaluated based on the depth of reflections and thoughtfulness of the responses since the questions align with the skill cues.

■ *Connecting with English Language Arts standards and expectations:* Since this assessment involves writing, it is a good opportunity to connect with the ELA teacher(s) to ensure alignment with expectations in their English courses.

Implementation Tips

■ Provide feedback to students after the first submission to support them as they work on their behaviors.

■ Have an informal check-in each lesson to remind students to continue to work on their behaviors and to have a chance to process and debrief with peers. We need to remember that integrating new habits can be difficult, so any support we provide can be helpful.

Healthy Habits Self-Management Assessment Worksheet

In class, we have been covering strategies that you can use to increase your happiness and improve or maintain your mental health. Your task for this assessment is to choose one happiness habit and one healthy mind habit to practice over the next two weeks. You will be assessed in two parts: Part 1 is this worksheet and part 2 is a reflection on your experience practicing your healthy habits. Submit part 1 next time we meet. Part 2 will be due at the end of our unit.

Part 1: Preassessment

Complete each of the following statements:
It is important that I take responsibility for my mental health because . . .
In order to improve or enhance happiness I will . . .
I am choosing this behavior or habit because . . .
Here is some information I have found about this behavior or habit and the valid and reliable source of information where I found it . . .
In order to improve or maintain my mental health I will . . .
I am choosing this behavior or habit because . . .
Here is some information I have found about this behavior or habit and the valid and reliable source of information where I found it . . .

Part 2: Postassessment

Were you able to consistently practice your habit or behavior? Why or why not?
What do you feel were your biggest successes over the past few weeks?
What do you feel were your biggest challenges over the past few weeks?
What were the results you experienced as a result of practicing the happiness and mental health behaviors or habits?
Do you think you will continue to practice these behaviors or habits? Why or why not?
What did you learn from this assessment?

LESSON PLANS

The lesson plans included here are the ones detailed in the unit outline earlier in the chapter and that will advance students toward achieving unit objectives and being able to successfully demonstrate the skill (evaluated in the assessment). The included lessons assume a 50-minute class period. Consider this prior to implementation.

Lesson plans include suggested activities, and those activities follow the lesson plans. Lesson plans and activities can be used together or independently to meet the needs of your classes.

Throughout the lesson plans, you will see the steps of the skill development model in **boldface type** after activities that address each skill development step. You will notice in this chapter, unlike the others, that step 3, modeling, is not addressed by a specific activity. This is because throughout the unit you will be modeling various self-management behaviors during the lessons rather than in one or two specific activities.

Purpose

The purpose of this lesson is to provide an overview of the skill of self-management. Students will be able to define the skill and list the steps of the skill after this lesson. This will allow them to apply and practice the skill in future lessons.

NHES Performance Indicators

- *Grades 6 through 8:* Explain the importance of assuming responsibility for personal health behaviors related to mental health (indicator 7.8.1).
- *Grades 9 through 12:* Analyze the role of individual responsibility for enhancing mental health (indicator 7.12.1).

Objectives

Students will be able to

- discuss the skill of self-management,
- list the steps to self-management, and
- discuss the relevance of self-management.

Skill Development Steps

- Step 1: definition, relevance, and educational outcomes
- Step 2: steps of the skill

Materials

Visual aid of skill cues (optional)

Instant Activity

After students take their seats, they write their responses to the prompt: "What are things in your life that you have a responsibility for? Why are you responsible for these things?"

Introduction

Tell students that today is the first day of the self-management unit. Let students know that this skill is a little different than some of the others that have been covered because it focuses on actions and behaviors that you take in order to be *responsible* for your own health. Ask students if any of them answered *health* for their instant activity. Lead a brief discussion about possible implications of this (as it is likely many students did not list health). Review the lesson and unit objectives. **(educational outcomes)**

Main Activities

1. *Large-group discussion:* Define the skill of self-management and discuss the skill cues for self-management. **(definition, skill cues)**
2. *Prompt:* Have students take two minutes to respond to the prompt: "Who helps you to be healthy?"
3. *Pair sharing:* Have students share with a partner. Have pairs discuss similarities and differences and discuss why they chose the people they did.
4. *Large group:* Bring the large group back together and have pairs share some of the people they listed. It is likely that students will not have listed themselves as a person who can help with their health (in part because of the phrasing of the question but also because we often don't think of ourselves as being in control of our health). Facilitate a discussion about why students didn't list themselves and then discuss the role we have in maintaining and enhancing our own health. You should also highlight the importance of taking personal responsibility and help students to feel empowered to take charge of their health. **(relevance)**

(continued)

Closure

Tell students that the next lesson is going to focus on happiness and how to increase or maintain happiness as a way to support mental health. Let students know that they are going to be learning and trying many different practices and behaviors that can support mental health throughout this unit.

Differentiation

- Have visual aids for students when presenting the skill cues.
- Partner English language learners with bilingual peers who speak English fluently.

Purpose

This lesson introduces students to the concept of happiness and discusses how happiness can support mental health. Students will also assess their own levels of happiness and then in the next lesson will learn about strategies for improving happiness.

NHES Performance Indicators

No performance indicators are addressed in this lesson as the focus is on the health topic.

Objectives

Students will be able to

- describe how happiness supports mental health and
- assess their own levels of happiness.

Skill Development Step

None addressed—the focus is on functional information.

Materials

- Note cards
- Materials needed for Happiness Wall activity
- Materials needed for Happiness Survey activity

Instant Activity

As students enter the classroom, they take three sticky notes (or sticky notes should be provided on their desks). Students write down one thing that makes them happy on each sticky note. They should also put their names on the sticky notes. Tell students that these ideas will be shared with classmates.

Introduction

Tell students that today's lesson is going to focus on happiness and how happiness can affect mental *and* overall health. Review the lesson objectives.

Main Activities

1. Ask students why and how happiness affects health. As students generate ideas, have them write the ideas on the board or speak out so you can record them on the board. After enough ideas have been shared, review the information in the next list item.

2. Discuss the importance of happiness in overall health and well-being (Greater Good Science Center at UC Berkeley, 2017):

   - Happiness is good for our health. Happy people are less likely to get sick, and they live longer.
   - Happiness is good for our relationships. Happy people are more likely to get married and have fulfilling marriages, and they have more friends.
   - Happy people make more money and are more productive at work.
   - Happy people are more generous.
   - Happy people cope better with stress and trauma.
   - Happy people are more creative and are better able to see the big picture.

3. Do the Happiness Wall activity (page 245).

4. Do the Happiness Survey activity (page 246).

(continued)

Closure

Tell students that in the next lesson, they are going to be *practicing* some happiness-enhancing activities! Remind students that this connects to self-management because when we are *doing* the health-enhancing behaviors we are engaging in self-management. Also remind students that they will be picking behaviors that they want to continue outside of the classroom for their assessment.

Differentiation

- Instead of starting with a large-group discussion, students could first share ideas in pairs and then come back to the large group.
- You could assign homework in lesson 1 for students to bring in pictures of things that make them happy.
- You could allow students to draw the things that make them happy rather than write words.

Homework (Optional)

Have students take a copy of the happiness survey home to do with a parent, guardian, other trusted adult, or sibling. They should discuss their results and make a plan to improve or maintain happiness as a family activity.

Resource

The Greater Good Science Center at the University of California at Berkeley, https://greatergood .berkeley.edu

Submitted by Lindsay Armbruster, middle/high school health teacher in New York.

Happiness Wall

LESSON 2

NHES Performance Indicators

None addressed

Objective

Students will be able to describe how happiness supports mental health.

Skill Development Step

None addressed—the focus is on functional information.

Duration

10 to 15 minutes

Materials

Sticky notes

Description

Preparation

Have a place in your classroom prepared for the happiness wall. As an instant activity or just as a set up for this activity, have students list things that make them happy on a sticky note (one idea per sticky note). Make sure students sign their name on each sticky note.

Activity

1. Put students into small groups and have them share the things that make them happy and explain why they make them happy.

2. In their small groups, students should begin to categorize their sticky notes into happiness themes.

3. Bring the large group together and have them work as a class to put all their sticky notes up on the space you designated for the wall. They should create happiness themes for all the sticky notes. Put the title of the theme above each section. Make sure everyone's sticky notes are put up on the wall.

4. Discuss as a group what the students learned from this activity.

Tips and Extensions

- Multicolored sticky notes would work well.
- Encourage communication and participation from all students when they bring the notes up to the wall.
- Have students bring in a picture of something that makes them happy for the wall or one that can be put on their binder or folder so that the picture can make them happy each class period!

Modifications

- Assign homework in a prior lesson for students to bring in pictures of things that make them happy.
- Allow students to draw the things that make them happy rather than write words.

Resource

The Greater Good Science Center at the University of California at Berkeley, https://greatergood.berkeley.edu

Happiness Survey

LESSON 2

NHES Performance Indicators

None addressed—the focus is on functional information.

Objective

Students will be able to assess their own levels of happiness.

Skill Development Step

None addressed—the focus is on functional information.

Duration

10 to 15 minutes

Materials

Copies of the Happiness Survey worksheet for each student

Description

1. Introduce the survey. Remind students that this is an individual activity and that honesty is important. Remind students that they shouldn't judge themselves based on their answers. This is a self-assessment to help them learn more about themselves and identify areas for growth

2. Provide time for students to complete the survey.

3. Optional: Engage in a brief discussion about their reactions to the survey.

Tips and Extensions

- Unless the responses require you to disclose student information due to mandated reporting, allow students to keep their responses confidential.

- A reflection could be added to the activity to allow students more time to process and apply their results to their own life or situation.

Resources

The Greater Good Science Center at the University of California at Berkeley, https://greatergood.berkeley.edu

Submitted by Lindsay Armbruster, middle/high school health teacher in New York.

Happiness Survey

Name: _____ Period: _____

How happy are you?

For each of the following statements or questions, please circle the point on the scale that you feel most appropriately describes you.

1. In general, I consider myself

   not a very happy person   1   2   3   4   5   6   7   a very happy person

2. Compared with most of my peers, I consider myself

   less happy   1   2   3   4   5   6   7   more happy

3. Some people are generally very happy. They enjoy life regardless of what is going on, getting the most out of everything. To what extent does this characterization describe you?

   not at all   1   2   3   4   5   6   7   a great deal

4. Some people are generally not very happy. Although they are not depressed, they never seem as happy as they might be. To what extent does this characterization describe you?

   a great deal   1   2   3   4   5   6   7   not at all

Scoring

5. Total: item 1 _____ + item 2 _____ + item 3 _____ + item 4 _____ = _____

6. Total _____ divided by 4 = _____

The result is your happiness score . . . for today!

No matter what your score is, you can always become happier.

Date	Happiness score

LESSON 3: Strategies for Increasing Happiness

Purpose

This lesson introduces students to one strategy for increasing happiness: gratitude. Students will get the chance to practice this strategy in class.

NHES Performance Indicators

Grades 6 Through 8

- Demonstrate healthy practices and behaviors that will maintain or improve the mental health of self and others (indicator 7.8.2).
- Describe ways to reduce, prevent or address adolescent mental health conditions and illnesses (indicator 1.8.5).

Grades 9 Through 12

- Demonstrate a variety of healthy practices and behaviors that will maintain or improve mental health of self and others (indicator 7.12.2).
- Propose ways to reduce, prevent or address mental health conditions and illnesses (indicator 1.12.5).

Objectives

Students will be able to

- discuss strategies for improving or enhancing their happiness and
- implement at least one strategy to improve their happiness.

Skill Development Step

Step 4: skill practice

Materials

- *Soul Pancake's the Science of Gratitude* video (www.youtube.com/watch?v=oHv6vTKD6lg)
- Materials needed for the Practicing Gratitude activity
- Desktop, laptop, or tablet computers

Instant Activity

Project the PDF file (or provide it as a handout) of the "Happy Habits" visual (https://greatergood .berkeley.edu/pdfs/happycircle-ggsc.pdf) on the board (or make sure that students can see the visuals). Have them write about which circle they feel like they could work on in order to increase their happiness and explain why.

Introduction

Tell students that today they get to practice gratitude, which is one way to increase happiness! Review the lesson objectives and the setup with the stations and then get started.

Main Activities

1. Watch *Soul Pancake's the Science of Gratitude* video together as a class. Discuss students' thoughts and reactions to the video. Discuss the importance of practicing gratitude. Transition into the stations.
2. Do the Practicing Gratitude activity (page 250). **(practice)**

Closure

Introduce the assessment and tell students that they should be thinking about behaviors that they might want to use in their own lives. Tell them they can also find their own but that over the next few lessons you will be introducing a variety of practices they can choose from for their final assessment. Encourage students to choose practices that will address the happiness circle they identified in their instant activity.

Differentiation

- You could include different activities for students to practice.
- Pair up English language learners with fluent English speakers to support their learning.

Homework (Optional)

If students did not complete the gratitude exercise, have them finish it for homework. You could also have students encourage a family member to try one of the activities from class.

Resources

- *Smiling Mind: Mindfulness Made Easy,* by Jane Martino and James Tutton
- *Yoga Calm* curriculum and curriculum supplement
- *Learning to Breathe* curriculum
- *MindUP* curriculum and curriculum supplement
- *Just One Thing: Developing a Buddha Brain One Simple Practice at a Time,* by Rick Hanson
- *Raising Happiness,* by Christine Carter
- *The How of Happiness,* by Sonja Lyubomirsky
- *Mindfulness for Teachers,* by Patricia Jennings (There is a very active Facebook group by the same name.)
- Children's book, *Mindful Monkey, Happy Panda,* by Lauren Alderfer
- Collaborative for Academic, Social, and Emotional Learning
- GoNoodle, www.gonoodle.com
- The Garrison Institute

Activities in the lesson modified from a submission by Lindsay Armbruster, middle/high school health teacher in New York.

Practicing Gratitude

LESSON 3

NHES Performance Indicators

- *Grades 6 through 8:* Demonstrate healthy practices and behaviors that will maintain or improve the mental health of self and others (indicator 7.8.2).
- *Grades 9 through 12:* Demonstrate a variety of healthy practices and behaviors that will maintain or improve mental health of self and others (indicator 7.12.2).

Objectives

Students will be able to

- discuss strategies for improving or enhancing their happiness and
- implement at least one strategy to improve their happiness.

Skill Development Step

Step 4: skill practice

Duration

20 to 30 minutes

Materials

- Books, paper, bound journals
- Supplies to decorate journals (markers, scissors, craft supplies)

Description

1. Show *Soul Pancake's the Science of Gratitude* video.
2. Students then write their own letter to a person of their choosing. When all are done, invite anyone to call the person and read it. For those who choose not to make the phone call in front of the entire class, encourage them to call the person outside of school hours or give or send them the letter.

Tips and Extensions

- Have students create their own videos about their experience reading their letters.
- Have students also create a gratitude journal to record things they are grateful for during the self-management unit.

Modifications

Have students draw or write a poem, song, or idea rather than a letter.

Modified from a submission by Lindsay Armbruster, middle/high school health teacher in New York.

Purpose

This lesson is a continuation of lesson 3. Additional strategies for increasing happiness are introduced and practiced in class.

NHES Performance Indicators

- *Grades 6 through 8:* Demonstrate healthy practices and behaviors that will maintain or improve the mental health of self and others (indicator 7.8.2).
- *Grades 9 through 12:* Demonstrate a variety of healthy practices and behaviors that will maintain or improve mental health of self and others (indicator 7.12.2).

Objectives

Students will be able to

- discuss strategies and habits that will help maintain or enhance happiness and
- implement at least two strategies to improve or maintain their happiness.

Skill Development Step

Step 4: skill practice

Materials

Materials needed for the Oh Happy Day! activity

Instant Activity

After students take their seats, have them write about their reactions to the gratitude activity. Encourage them to reflect on their own reactions as well as the reactions of the person they wrote about and spoke to.

Introduction

Tell students that today they are going to be introduced to more strategies for increasing happiness.

Main Activities

Oh Happy Day! (page 253) **(practice)**

Closure

Let students know that for the next lesson they will have a chance to do even more activities that can support their happiness and mental health.

Differentiation

- If the activity does not work well for your students, select a different activity for students to practice.
- Pair up English language learners with fluent English speakers to support their learning.

Resources

- *Smiling Mind: Mindfulness Made Easy,* by Jane Martino and James Tutton
- *Yoga Calm* curriculum and curriculum supplement
- *Learning to Breathe* curriculum
- *MindUP* curriculum and curriculum supplement
- *Just One Thing: Developing a Buddha Brain One Simple Practice at a Time,* by Rick Hanson
- *Raising Happiness,* by Christine Carter
- *The How of Happiness,* by Sonja Lyubomirsky

(continued)

LESSON 4: Strategies for Increasing Happiness   *(continued)*

- *Mindfulness for Teachers,* by Patricia Jennings (There is a very active Facebook group by the same name.)
- Children's book, *Mindful Monkey, Happy Panda,* by Lauren Alderfer
- Collaborative for Academic, Social, and Emotional Learning
- GoNoodle, www.gonoodle.com
- The Garrison Institute

Activities in the lesson modified from a submission by Lindsay Armbruster, middle/high school health teacher in New York.

Oh Happy Day!
LESSON 4

NHES Performance Indicators

- *Grades 6 through 8:* Demonstrate healthy practices and behaviors that will maintain or improve the mental health of self and others (indicator 7.8.2).
- *Grades 9 through 12:* Demonstrate a variety of healthy practices and behaviors that will maintain or improve mental health of self and others (indicator 7.12.2).

Objectives

Students will be able to

- discuss strategies and habits that will help maintain or enhance happiness and
- implement at least two strategies to improve or maintain their happiness.

Skill Development Step

Step 4: skill practice

Duration

20 to 30 minutes

Materials

- *Mindful Monkey, Happy Panda*
- Meditation app or other guided meditations
- Physical activities incorporating mindfulness

Description

1. *Mindfulness:* Read aloud *Mindful Monkey, Happy Panda* to introduce the idea of mindfulness. Prepare students to engage in a mindful meditation. There are so many options; the ones by Smiling Mind have worked really well in the classroom. This specific group has created a program for teachers to use in classrooms with students and is broken down by age group.

2. *Incorporate physical activity:* Get students moving to help them see how it makes them feel. Try out activities on GoNoodle (www.gonoodle.com) or do this:

    Spell your name and list the exercises associated with each letter of your name. Now, work out! (Repeat two times.)

A: 50 jumping jacks	N: 40 jumping jacks
B: 20 crunches	O: 25 burpees
C: 30 squats	P: 15-second arm circles
D: 15 push-ups	Q: 30 crunches
E: 1-minute wall sit	R: 15 push-ups
F: 10 burpees	S: 30 burpees
G: 20-second arm circles	T: 15 squats
H: 20 squats	U: 30-second arm circles
I: 30 jumping jacks	V: 3-minute wall sit
J: 15 crunches	W: 20 burpees
K: 10 push-ups	X: 60 jumping jacks
L: 2-minute wall sit	Y: 10 crunches
M: 20 burpees	Z: 20 push-ups

Tips and Extensions

- Have students try these at home or teach someone else. Consider having students practice these activities for a set period of days and reflect on how their body and mind feels after incorporating this into the daily routine.

- Discuss how to fit in meditation and bursts of physical activity into an often already packed schedule.

Modification

Add different activities such as coloring, making happy phrases, or doing an activity related to self-esteem.

Resources

The Greater Good Science Center at University of California at Berkeley, https://greatergood.berkeley.edu

Modified from submission by Lindsay Armbruster, middle/high school health teacher in New York.

Purpose

While learning about strategies to improve mental health and happiness is important for students, this lesson will allow students to discuss the role mental health plays on overall health and to practice (and perhaps try for the first time) techniques to help them relax and be in the moment in a non-threatening and safe environment.

NHES Performance Indicators

Grades 6 Through 8

- Demonstrate healthy practices and behaviors that will maintain or improve the mental health of self and others (indicator 7.8.2).
- Demonstrate behaviors to avoid or reduce mental health risks to self and others (indicator 7.8.3).

Grades 9 Through 12

- Demonstrate a variety of healthy practices and behaviors that will maintain or improve mental health of self and others (indicator 7.12.2).
- Demonstrate a variety of behaviors to avoid or reduce mental health risks to self and others (indicator 7.12.3).
- Predict how healthy behaviors can affect mental health status (indicator 1.12.1).

Objectives

Students will be able to

- discuss the importance of mental health as a component of overall health and
- describe strategies for maintaining or enhancing mental health.

Skill Development Step

Step 4: skill practice

Materials

- Materials needed for the Mental Health Jigsaw activity
- Materials needed for the Yoga for Youth activity

Instant Activity

Have students reflect on and respond to the following quote: "The secret of health for both mind and body is . . . live the present moment wisely and earnestly." —Buddha

Introduction

Ask students to share their responses to the quote. After a few students have shared their ideas, tell them that today they are going to build off of their happiness work and practice some other behaviors that can enhance mental health. Tell them that first you are going to discuss why mental health is important to overall health and wellness. Review the lesson objectives.

Main Activities

1. Mental Health Jigsaw (page 257)
2. Yoga for Youth (page 258) **(practice)**

Closure

Tell students that the next lesson will explore things we should look out for in ourselves and others and when to seek help for our mental health and wellness. For homework, remind students they should complete the first part of the assessment to submit next lesson.

(continued)

Differentiation

- Provide the article in students' native language and then pair English language learners up with fluent English speakers to help support understanding and engagement in the jigsaw activity.
- Provide visual aids for all of the activities.

Homework

Students should complete the first part of the assessment.

Resources

KidsHealth, www.kidshealth.org

Mental Health Jigsaw

LESSON 5

NHES Performance Indicators

None addressed—the focus is on functional information.

Objectives

Students will be able to

- discuss the importance of mental health as a component of overall health and
- describe strategies for maintaining or enhancing mental health.

Skill Development Step

None addressed

Duration

15 to 20 minutes

Materials

Copies of articles printed from the Minds section of kidshealth.org

Description

Preparation

Select a variety of articles to print out from the Minds section of kidshealth.org. Choose articles that are most appropriate and relevant for your students. Select the same number of articles as members that you want in your groups. For example, if you want groups of 5 students, select 5 articles so that each student has a different article to read.

Activity

1. Have students read articles individually.
2. Place students into groups. Each group member will read a different article.
3. Have each student provide an overview of their article for the other members of their group.

Tips and Extensions

- Have a reading guide or other worksheet for students to complete as they are reading and as they are sharing.
- Review the key aspects of each article before moving on.

Modifications

- Have students read the articles for homework prior to coming to class.
- Students create something (such as a drawing or an outline) to share with their group that highlights the key points of their article.

Resources

KidsHealth, www.kidshealth.org

Yoga for Youth

LESSON 5

NHES Performance Indicators

Grades 6 Through 8

- Demonstrate healthy practices and behaviors that will maintain or improve the mental health of self and others (indicator 7.8.2).
- Demonstrate behaviors to avoid or reduce mental health risks to self and others (indicator 7.8.3).

Grades 9 Through 12

- Demonstrate a variety of healthy practices and behaviors that will maintain or improve the mental health of self and others (indicator 7.12.2).
- Demonstrate a variety of behaviors to avoid or reduce mental health risks to self and others (indicator 7.12.3).

Objective

Students will be able to implement at least two strategies to maintain or improve mental health.

Skill Development Step

Step 4: skill practice

Duration

20 minutes

Materials

- Space (large enough for students to perform yoga)
- Yoga video
- Projector for the yoga video

Description

Preparation

In this activity, students will practice doing yoga moves for relaxation and health. Ensure there is enough space for students to move around and also a classroom environment that promotes calmness. You may want to consider finding an alternative space for this lesson (such as a gym or outside).

Activity

Play the video by the Niroga Institute found at www.youtube.com (search for "Yoga for Youth") or select another yoga video for teens.

Tips and Extensions

- Connect with the physical education teacher to see if he or she could incorporate yoga into a unit as you are working on your self-management unit.
- Use yoga resources other than a video.
- Bring in a certified yoga instructor from the community.

Resources

TeensHealth, http://kidshealth.org/en/teens/yoga.html#catmental-health

LESSON 6: Understanding Mental Health

Purpose

The purpose of this lesson is to provide students with an understanding of and empathy toward individuals with mental illness.

NHES Performance Indicators

There are no performance indicators addressed in this lesson because it focuses on a deeper understanding of mental health and encourages perspective taking.

Objectives

Students will be able to

- briefly describe common mental health conditions and
- develop empathy for individuals with mental health conditions or illnesses.

Skill Development Step

None addressed—the focus is on functional information.

Materials

- Materials for the Mental Health Challenges activity
- Materials for the From Their Perspective activity

Instant Activity

After students take their seats, they should go to www.walkinourshoes.org and create their own shoes by going to the Your Shoes section. After creating the shoes, as time allows, review the other shoes that have been posted.

Introduction

Tell students that today you will be exploring some of the common mental health challenges that teens and adults face. Review lesson objectives.

Main Activities

1. Mental Health Challenges (page 260)
2. From Their Perspective (page 261) **(practice)**

Closure

Tell students that in the next lesson they will be exploring warning signs for mental health problems and exploring available resources.

Differentiation

- Have students present the challenges they read rather than completing a gallery walk.
- Have students use headphones and listen to the stories individually.

Resources

- Walk in Our Shoes, www.walkinourshoes.org
- U.S. Department of Health & Human Services, Mental Health, www.mentalhealth.gov

Mental Health Challenges

LESSON 6

NHES Performance Indicators

None addressed—the focus is on functional information.

Objective

Students will be able to briefly describe common mental health conditions.

Skill Development Step

None addressed

Duration

15 to 20 minutes

Materials

- Printouts of the challenges
- Flip chart paper
- Markers for the flip chart

Description

Preparation

Print out mental health challenges from www.walkinourshoes.org. Have enough printouts for two or three students to have the same challenges.

Activity

1. Pass out the challenges randomly to students.
2. Have students read the challenges.
3. Have students get into groups with other students who have the same challenge as they do.
4. Students discuss what they read and come up with three to five statements about the mental health challenge they read about. At least one statement should be a positive statement about the challenge. Students record their ideas on flip chart paper. When finished, post these on the wall.
5. Have groups complete a gallery walk to review all posters. As students read about the other health challenges, they should add any statements or ideas that are similar to the challenge they read about.
6. Debrief as a large group. Highlight key points.

Tips and Extensions

- Provide the articles in students' native languages and English for English language learner students.
- Pair up English language learners with bilingual peers.

Modification

Have groups present their challenges rather than complete a gallery walk.

Resources

Walk in Our Shoes, www.walkinourshoes.org

Adapted from an activity found at walkinourshoes.org.

From Their Perspective
LESSON 6

NHES Performance Indicators
None addressed—the focus here is on developing empathy.

Objective
Students will be able to develop empathy for individuals with mental health conditions and illnesses.

Skill Development Step
None addressed

Duration
15 to 20 minutes

Materials
Devices for the videos

Description
1. Place students into small groups (partners or groups of three).
2. Have students spread out around the room and watch the stories available at www.walkinourshoes.org. Groups can choose which stories to watch.
3. Ask students to watch at least four stories.
4. After they have watched the videos, the group will reflect upon and discuss what they learned from the videos.
5. Bring the large group together and discuss the importance of listening to each other's stories and being open to experiences that are different from our own.

Tips and Extensions
- Have a reflection worksheet or question prompts for students to complete.
- Preassign selections for students to ensure adequate representation across the class.

Modifications
- Have students work individually, not in groups.
- Show the videos to the large group.
- Have students watch the stories for homework, and then discuss in class.

Resources
Walk in Our Shoes, www.walkinourshoes.org

LESSON 7: When to Seek Help and Where to Find It

Purpose

It is important for students to be able to recognize when they or someone they know might be struggling and need help with their mental health. These next lessons will use the skill of accessing valid and reliable services in order to support self-management.

NHES Performance Indicators

Grades 6 Through 8

- Explain the importance of assuming responsibility for personal health behaviors related to mental health (indicator 7.8.1).
- Demonstrate healthy practices and behaviors that will maintain or improve the health of self and others (indicator 7.8.2).

Grades 9 Through 12

- Analyze the role of individual responsibility for enhancing mental health (indicator 7.12.1).
- Demonstrate a variety of healthy practices and behaviors that will maintain or improve the health of self and others (indicator 7.12.2).

Objectives

Students will be able to

- recognize warning signs for serious mental health conditions,
- recognize when help is needed to address mental health issues, and
- locate and access resources for adolescent mental health support.

Skill Development Step

Step 4: skill practice

Materials

Computers

Instant Activity

Once all students have entered the classroom and class has begun, have students line up in the middle of the classroom in a single file line facing the front of the room. Read a statement from www.mentalhealth.gov/basics/myths-facts/index.html (or create your own myth or fact statements). After you read each statement, students should move to the left if they think it is a myth and to the right if they think it is a fact. Discuss any misconceptions as they arise. Have students return to the middle and then read the next statement.

Introduction

Tell students that today they are going to explore some of the mental health warning signs and problems that we need to look out for in ourselves and others. Review the lesson objectives.

Main Activities

1. In a large-group discussion, review the warning signs that occur that indicate students or someone the student knows should talk to a trusted adult or health professional. You can find a list at www.mentalhealth.gov/talk/young-people/.

2. Remind students that they need to be aware of their own behaviors and warning signs and should also look out for their friends and family. Discuss personal responsibility and our responsibility toward others. You may want to use additional information about the number of people who don't get treatment. Additional information may be found at www.mentalhealth.gov.

3. Have the class do the Locating Community Resources activity (page 264). **(practice)**

Closure

Tell students that in the next lesson, they will continue to explore services and will create resources to share with other teens.

Differentiation

Instead of an instant activity, have students complete the myth or fact activity individually (have the myths or facts on a piece of paper).

Resources

U.S. Department of Health & Human Services, Mental Health, www.mentalhealth.gov

Locating Community Resources

LESSON 7

NHES Performance Indicators

Grades 6 Through 8

- Locate valid and reliable health products and services (indicator 3.8.5). Note that this is not listed as a unit objective since it does not relate to the performance indicators from Standard 7, but this is a good connection to accessing valid and reliable services.
- Demonstrate healthy practices and behaviors that will maintain or improve the health of self and others (indicator 7.8.2).

Grades 9 Through 12

- Demonstrate a variety of healthy practices and behaviors that will maintain or improve the health of self and others (indicator 7.12.2).

Objective

Students will be able to locate appropriate resources for supporting adolescent mental health.

Skill Development Step

Step 4: skill practice (skill of accessing valid and reliable information, products, and services to support self-management)

Duration

30 to 40 minutes

Materials

Computers

Description

1. Place students into small groups (two or three students per group).
2. Have students find local valid and reliable services for adolescents who may be in need of mental health support.
3. For each service, have students
    - identify the service,
    - justify why it is a valid and reliable resource,
    - explain when and why someone should access this service,
    - find a map or explanation of how to get there, and
    - explain how a student could access the resource.
4. Each group should find at least three services.
5. Students should each record their findings on a piece of paper.

Tips and Extensions

- Have students place phone calls to the services and talk to staff members about what a teen would need to know in order to access services (if appropriate).
- Expand this to a project in which students actually visit the services.

Modifications

- You could assign different services for students to evaluate. However, this would not be as authentic to what they might do in real life when they are looking for support.
- Create a worksheet for groups to complete.

LESSON 8: Sharing Is Caring

Purpose

This lesson provides an opportunity for students to share resources, which will hopefully encourage students in this course and in the broader school community to be more open about mental health and support each other in getting help.

NHES Performance Indicators

None addressed—students are sharing the work they did when they were demonstrating the skill of self-management through the location of resources (which is a healthy practice).

Objective

Students will be able to share information about enhancing or maintaining mental health in adolescents.

Skill Development Step

Step 5: feedback and reinforcement

Materials

Materials needed for the Sharing Is Caring activity

Instant Activity

There is no instant activity today.

Introduction

Tell students they will be working in small groups to create infographics to be shared with their peers. Review the lesson objectives.

Main Activity

Sharing Is Caring (page 266) **(feedback and reinforcement)**

Closure

Remind students of their responsibility in their own health and the health of others.

Differentiation

- Students work individually instead of in small groups.
- If there is time, students can present their infographics.
- Students can print and post their infographics around the school.

Resources

- Canva, www.canva.com
- Piktochart, www.piktochart.com

Sharing Is Caring
LESSON 8

NHES Performance Indicators
None addressed—students are sharing the work they did when they were demonstrating the skill of self-management through the location of resources (which is a healthy practice).

Objective
Students will be able to share information about enhancing or maintaining mental health in adolescents.

Skill Development Step
Step 5: feedback and reinforcement

Duration
40 to 50 minutes

Materials
Computers

Description
1. Put students into groups. They should have previously identified services in the community.
2. Have students decide on a final list of valid and reliable resources for adolescent mental health.
3. Have students create an infographic geared toward their peers about where to go when they need mental health support. The infographics should encourage seeking help and provide students with all the information they would need to access those services or resources.
4. If there is time students should present their infographics.

Tips and Extensions
Print the infographics and post them around the school.

Modifications
- Allow students to create a different product (other than an infographic).
- Provide more specific guidelines for the product.

Resources
- Canva, www.canva.com
- Piktochart, www.piktochart.com

CHAPTER 9

Becoming an Advocate for One's Own Health

This chapter examines the skill of advocacy, Standard 8 of the National Health Education Standards. You will find a variety of activities related to the skill of advocacy that are ready to use in your classroom. An assessment, lesson plans, and learning activities for secondary health education are included here.

The materials are presented to reflect a backward-design approach (see chapter 2) with the unit objectives included first, the assessment next, followed by the lesson plans and learning activities for the unit. Items in this chapter are designed to address each step of the skill development model (see chapter 1). You might need to modify these materials in order to meet the needs of your students or to address the objectives adequately. Our goal is to provide a usable framework that also is easily modifiable.

The unit presented here has a unique feature. This unit was originally designed to span many weeks in order to allow students time to complete their work. The unit is set up as nine lessons, and while it is possible to complete all nine lessons in a block of consecutive days, you might consider how to allow for more time to complete the assignments contained within.

The unit presented here does not include any specific health topics. Instead, we encourage the use of relevant data to help students determine health topics and issues that are happening in their community and then use those topics as a basis of their advocacy efforts. This provides practice in analyzing data and ensures relevance while providing opportunities for students to choose topics of interest. However, you may decide to have students focus on a preselected health topic, have them choose any topic, or have them choose a topic that they have a personal connection to. The students will be researching and gathering information about the topic areas. This is a more organic strategy for covering health information for a variety of topics, because it will provide students with an opportunity to apply the skill of accessing valid and reliable information and finding evidence about a health topic—something that we hope they will do outside of the classroom. All students will receive the information about each of the topics when students share their projects. You could modify this unit to include more functional health information in class or to cover specific topics that need to be covered.

SKILL OVERVIEW

Advocacy is a sophisticated skill that can help us in many ways. Being able to advocate allows us to stand up for ourselves at the doctor's office, with a boss, in school, or with peers. It can help us make changes within our families, our peer groups, and in our workplaces. Advocacy can help effect change in our schools, our communities, our nation, and around the globe. Being able to advocate for ourselves and others can, quite literally, change the world.

Advocacy is a skill that requires the application of many other skills addressed in the National Health Education Standards, including accessing valid and reliable information, analyzing influences, decision making, and interpersonal communication. Depending on the setting, we also might need to set goals and apply self-management principles when advocating for something. Effective advocacy also requires some level of self-awareness so that we can identify causes that truly inspire us and about which we can be passionate. Another important aspect of advocacy is that, perhaps more than any other skill, our ability to demonstrate this skill effectively can have a broad impact on the people and environments around us. Our advocacy units should provide students with an opportunity to be interested, engaged, and inspired so that they feel empowered to be advocates for themselves and others after the course. We cannot underestimate the impact that each of our students can have. Teaching them to apply the skill of advocacy gives them the tools to make that impact.

The performance indicators (table 9.1) and application of the skill of advocacy in grades 6 through 8 and 9 through 12 are not very different. You will notice in the performance indicators that the skill remains similar. Students need to create a health-enhancing position, demonstrate how to influence others, work collaboratively, and adapt messages to a variety of audiences. Materials are included here for an advocacy unit that is appropriate for students in grades 6 to 12. While the lessons and activities could be used at any grade, if you are planning to teach the skill of advocacy in both middle school and high school (or even multiple grades in one school) we would suggest having a discussion at the local level about how the skill is assessed, the topics used for students to apply the skill, and also considerations for altering the activities to keep them fresh for students and to avoid redundancy.

While the end result will be skill demonstration each time the skill is taught, you can easily adapt to keep your advocacy relevant and engaging for your students. Depending on your students, there is much you can do to keep this unit interesting and advance their skill even if they explore advocacy in multiple grades. For example, students may focus on environmental justice, social issues, injury prevention, or even personal health behaviors. All of these areas are appropriate, providing they help students to make the connection to positive health outcomes. Students may use what they learned from exploring the dimensions of wellness, and while one group of students focuses on creating an advocacy campaign around improved environmental health concerns, another group focuses on the connection between being financially healthy and overall health outcomes.

When you consider the many ways that students can advocate, the many topics for which they can advocate, and the audiences to whom they can advocate, we realize that students can do more, go bigger, and reach new audiences, all while using the same skill cues. While we suggest an infographic as an assessment, there are many other ways that students can be advocates. As long as students are demonstrating the performance indicators and skill cues, their final advocacy message and campaign can take many forms.

SKILL CUES

Step 2 of the skill development model is when skill cues, or critical steps, of the skill are presented to students. Skill cues are intended to highlight the key aspects of the skill that students need to execute in order to apply the skill effectively. We provide sample skill cues to support your efforts to teach the skill. Modify these skill cues or create your own to best support your students in their efforts to demonstrate skill proficiency. We encourage you to be willing to adjust the skill cues if students use a different language or have ideas that still align with the intended outcome of the original skill cues. The more opportunity for student input and ownership, the better. Figure 9.1 shows some sample skill cues for the skill of advocacy that may be used for grades 6 through 12.

UNIT OUTLINE

This section includes an outline of the unit for Standard 8; table 9.2 shows this outline, including lesson titles, lesson objectives, the step(s) of the skill development model that are addressed in each lesson, and the titles of the main learning activities in each lesson.

All performance indicators for Standard 8 for grades 6 through 12 are covered in this unit, as are objectives from Standard 1. Unit objectives that are focused on the skill performance indicators are included along with additional learning objectives that include performance indicators from Standard 1 and other intended learning outcomes.

TABLE 9.1   Performance Indicators for Standard 8 of the NHES (Grades 6-12)

	6-8		9-12
8.8.1	State a health-enhancing position on a topic and support it with accurate information.	8.12.1	Utilize accurate peer and societal norms to formulate a health-enhancing message.
8.8.2	Demonstrate how to influence and support others to make positive health choices.	8.12.2	Demonstrate how to influence and support others to make positive health choices.
8.8.3	Work cooperatively to advocate for healthy individuals, families, and schools.	8.12.3	Work cooperatively as an advocate for improving personal, family, and community health.
8.8.4	Identify ways in which health messages and communication techniques can be altered for different audiences.	8.12.4	Adapt health messages and communication techniques to a specific target audience.

Reprinted, with permission, from the American Cancer Society. *National Health Education Standards: Achieving Excellence,* Second Edition (Atlanta, GA: American Cancer Society, 2007), 24-36, cancer.org/bookstore

Advocacy

STANDARD 8

Students will demonstrate the ability to advocate for personal, family, and community health.

I CARE

Identify and research a relevant and meaningful health issue

Create a health-enhancing position or message supported by facts and evidence and geared toward the audience

Act passionately and with conviction

Relay your health-enhancing message to your audience

Examine the effectiveness of the advocacy effort

From S. Benes and H. Alperin, 2019, *Lesson planning for skills-based health education* (Champaign, IL: Human Kinetics). Reprinted, by permission, from S. Benes and H. Alperin, 2016, *The essentials of teaching health education* (Champaign, IL: Human Kinetics).

HUMAN KINETICS

FIGURE 9.1 Skill cues for the skill of advocacy.

Unit Objectives Grades 6 Through 8

By the end of this unit, student will be able to

■ state a health-enhancing position on a topic and support it with accurate information (indicator 8.8.1);

■ demonstrate how to influence and support others to make positive health choices (indicator 8.8.2);

■ work cooperatively to advocate for healthy individuals, families, and schools (indicator 8.8.3); and

■ identify ways in which health messages and communication techniques can be altered for different audiences (indicator 8.8.4).

Unit Objectives Grades 9 Through 12

By the end of this unit, students will be able to

■ utilize accurate peer and societal norms to formulate a health-enhancing message (indicator 8.12.1);

■ demonstrate how to influence and support others to make positive health choices (indicator 8.12.2);

■ work cooperatively as an advocate for improving personal, family, and community health (indicator 8.12.3); and

■ adapt health messages and communication techniques to a specific target audience (indicator 8.12.4).

Additional Unit Objectives Grades 6 Through 12

By the end of this unit, students will be able to

■ define the skill of advocacy;

■ explain the relevance of advocacy related to personal and community health;

■ list the skill cues for advocacy;

■ describe characteristics of effective advocacy;

■ analyze the Youth Risk Behaviors Survey (YRBS) to identify critical issues in the community;

■ identify a topic of personal interest to advocate for;

■ research information about a health topic of choice;

■ use evidence to support a health-enhancing position on a health topic;

■ examine the likelihood of injury or illness if engaging in unhealthy behaviors (indicator 1.8.8); and

■ examine the potential seriousness of injury or illness if engaging in unhealthy behaviors (indicator 1.8.9);

or

■ analyze the potential severity of injury or illness if engaging in unhealthy behaviors (indicator 1.12.9);

■ advocate for a topic of choice by . . .;

■ work collaboratively with peers to provide feedback on advocacy projects;

■ design and create an advocacy project;

■ advocate for a health-enhancing position; and

■ describe ways to reduce or prevent injuries and other adolescent health problems (indicator 1.8.8);

or

▪ propose ways to reduce or prevent injuries and health problems (indicator 1.12.5); and

▪ describe the benefits of and barriers to practicing healthy behaviors (indicator 1.8.7).

TABLE 9.2   Standard 8 Unit Outline

Lesson title	Lesson objectives (indicators in parentheses) *By the end of this lesson, students will be able to:*	Step of the skill development model addressed in the lesson	Main learning activities
Lesson 1: What Is Advocacy?	• Define the skill of advocacy • Explain the relevance of advocacy related to personal and community health	Skill introduction (step 1)	Exploring Advocacy (p. 277)
Lesson 2: Becoming an Advocate	• List the skill cues for advocacy • Describe characteristics of effective advocacy	Steps of the skill (step 2) and modeling (step 3)	Analyzing Advocacy (p. 279)
Lesson 3: Data, Data Everywhere!	• Analyze YRBS to identify critical issues in the community • Identify an advocacy topic based on personal interest	Skill practice (step 4)	Examining Health Issues in Our Community (p. 281)
Lesson 4: Finding Evidence	• Research information about a health topic of choice • Use evidence to support a health-enhancing position on a health topic (8.8.1) • Examine the likelihood of injury or illness if engaging in unhealthy behaviors (1.8.8) • Examine the potential seriousness of injury or illness if engaging in unhealthy behaviors (1.8.9) *or* • Analyze the potential severity of injury or illness if engaging in unhealthy behaviors (1.12.9)	Skill practice (step 4)	Finding Evidence to Support a Position (p. 283)
Lesson 5: Advocacy Action	• Take action and advocate for a topic of choice	Skill practice (step 4)	Advocacy Action (p. 285)
Lesson 6: Peer Feedback	• Work collaboratively with peers to provide feedback on advocacy projects (8.8.3 or 8.12.3)	Skill practice (step 4)	Sharing Advocacy (p. 289)
Lesson 7: Collaborating for a Cause	• Work collaboratively with peers to determine advocacy strategies for a topic of interest (8.8.3 or 8.12.3)	Skill practice (step 4)	Collaborating for a Cause (p. 291)
Lesson 8: The Finishing Touches	• Design and create an advocacy project	Skill practice (step 4)	Creating Public Service Announcements (p. 293)
Lesson 9: Assessment—Advocacy in Action	• Advocate for a health-enhancing position • Describe ways to reduce or prevent injuries and other adolescent health problems (1.8.8) *or* • Propose ways to reduce or prevent injuries and health problems (1.12.5) • Describe the benefits of and barriers to practicing healthy behaviors (1.8.7)	Feedback and reinforcement (step 5)	Student Presentations (p. 295)

Performance indicators are from: Joint Committee on National Health Education Standards. (2007). *National Health Education Standards: Achieving Excellence* (2nd ed.). Atlanta, GA: American Cancer Society.

ASSESSMENT

Here is a sample assessment that will provide students with the opportunity to demonstrate their proficiency with the skill of advocacy. Students will create an infographic with a health-enhancing position about a topic of their choosing.

The lessons in the unit provide opportunities for students to acquire the knowledge and skills they need to successfully demonstrate the skill of advocacy in the assessment described here. They will examine data, determine a position, gather evidence, and take action. There is opportunity for students to complete individual and collaborative work and to advocate in a variety of ways. A rubric is provided for the assessment based on the skill cues included in this chapter. It should be modified if you change the skill cues or for any additional criteria that you would like to have included in the evaluation. We included the performance indicators for grades 9 through 12 as the objectives that will be addressed in the assessment; these could easily be interchanged with the middle school performance indicators.

Objectives

Through this assessment, students will demonstrate their ability to

- utilize accurate peer and societal norms to formulate a health-enhancing message (indicator 8.12.1);
- demonstrate how to influence and support others to make positive health choices (indicator 8.12.2);
- work cooperatively as an advocate for improving personal, family, and community health (indicator 8.12.3); and
- adapt health messages and communication techniques to a specific target audience (indicator 8.12.4).

Description

This assessment provides students with an opportunity to advocate for a topic of their choice and that is relevant in their school community. The product for this assessment is an infographic, designed for their peers, advocating for a health-enhancing position on a topic that they choose after examining health data for their community. During the unit there are other assignments that could be used as additional formative or summative assessments.

Modifications

This assessment is based on information and activities contained in this chapter, and, as with the lessons, should be modified to address changes to the objectives or as necessary for your students. Modifications to the assessment may include:

- *Assessing additional objectives:* This assessment is focused on evaluating whether students are able to access and evaluate health information, products, and services; however, the assessment could also include a measure of the health topic knowledge.
- *Assigning topics:* You could assign topics or provide choices for students rather than allowing them to pick their own.
- *Modifying the deliverable:* Instead of an infographic, students could create a video or a public service announcement (or other product of their choosing), or give a presentation.

Implementation Tips

■ Have students complete the assessment in parts so that you can provide feedback as they work on their assessment.

■ Provide students with examples of effective advocacy by adolescents.

Assessment modified from a submission by Andy Milne, high school health teacher in Illinois.

Advocacy Assessment Worksheet

Your task: You are going to be an advocate to help your peers to be healthier! You are going to choose a topic that you care about and create an infographic that will encourage your peers to engage in healthier behaviors.

During the unit you will

- explore local data to determine important issues in your community,
- choose a topic from the data that you care about,
- create a health-enhancing position about the topic,
- find and use evidence to support your position,
- design and create an infographic that advocates for your position, and
- share your infographic with your classmates.

You will be assessed using the following rubric:

	3	2	1
Position	The infographic demonstrates a clear, health-enhancing position.	The infographic's health-enhancing position is somewhat clear.	The position is not clear in the infographic or is not a health-enhancing position.
Evidence	The infographic includes at least four pieces of evidence to support their position and is supported by valid and reliable sources.	The infographic includes two or three pieces of evidence that supports their position and are supported by valid and reliable resources.	The infographic includes zero to one pieces of evidence that supports their position or is not supported by valid and reliable resources.
Passion or conviction	The infographic shows passion or conviction toward the topic.	The infographic shows limited passion or conviction toward the topic.	The infographic does not show passion or conviction.
Appeal	The infographic clearly appeals to the intended audience.	The infographic is somewhat appealing to the audience.	The infographic is not appealing to the audience.

LESSON PLANS

The lesson plans included here are the ones outlined in the unit outline earlier in the chapter and that will advance students toward achieving unit objectives and being able to successfully demonstrate the skill (evaluated in the assessment). The included lessons assume a 50-minute class period. Consider this prior to implementation.

Lesson plans include suggested activities, and those activities follow the lesson plans. Lesson plans and activities can be used together or independently to meet the needs of your classes.

Throughout the lesson plans, you will see the steps of the skill development model in **boldface type** after activities that address each skill development step.

The lessons and activities in this unit are based on a submission by Andy Milne, high school health teacher in Illinois.

LESSON 1: What Is Advocacy?

Purpose

The first steps of the skill development model set the stage for the remainder of the unit in which students will develop the skill. During this lesson, students are introduced to a definition of advocacy, and they discuss the relevance of advocacy for personal and community health.

NHES Performance Indicators

None addressed

Objectives

Students will be able to

- define the skill of advocacy, and
- explain the relevance of advocacy related to personal and community health.

Skill Development Step

Step 1: skill introduction

Materials

- Materials for Exploring Advocacy activity
- Computers

Instant Activity

After students take their seats, they write their responses to the prompt: "What do you think it means to advocate for something?"

Introduction

Tell students that this is the first lesson in their advocacy unit. You may want to explain that advocacy provides an opportunity to use many of the skills that have been covered in previous units. Review the lesson and unit objectives.

Main Activities

1. Have the class do the Exploring Advocacy activity (page 277). **(relevance)**
2. As a large group, ask students to share their ideas from their instant activities. They can share what they wrote, or they can share revised versions after the Exploring Advocacy activity. Decide on a definition that will be used for the rest of the unit. **(definition)**

Closure

Ticket to leave—have students write down two or three reasons why it is important for teens to advocate.

Differentiation

Pair English language learners with fluent English-speaking peers during the Exploring Advocacy activity to support students with social language.

Homework

Ask students to find other examples of advocacy. Have them bring in their examples for the next lesson (optional).

Resources

Parenthetical, https://parenthetical.wisc.edu/supporting-speaking-up-helping-your-teen-self-advocate/

Exploring Advocacy

LESSON 1

NHES Performance Indicators

None addressed

Objective

Students will be able to explain the relevance of advocacy related to personal and community health.

Skill Development Step

Step 1: skill introduction

Duration

20 to 30 minutes

Materials

Examples of advocacy

Description

Preparation

Find examples of advocacy geared toward teens (even better if they are *by* teens as well). Try to include a variety of media (print, commercial, YouTube video) for a variety of topics. You should include as many examples as needed for students to be able to work in small groups.

Activity

1. Place students into small groups. Have them examine the examples of advocacy you provided. Encourage them to think about what the advocacy example is trying to do. Is it trying to get a person (or people) to take action? Change a behavior? Think differently about a topic? Why is this company, person, or group advocating for this topic?

2. Have students rotate to at least two advocacy examples.

3. Have students record their ideas (or at least be prepared to discuss their thoughts).

4. After the allotted amount of time, bring the group together and discuss student reactions to the advocacy campaigns.

Tips and Extensions

Students could have to find their own examples of advocacy as part of class time or for homework.

Modification

Create a worksheet or form for students to fill out during their small group work.

Resources

- Advocates for Youth, www.advocatesforyouth.org
- Youth Activism Project, http://youthactivismproject.org/success-stories/
- Resource Center for Adolescent Pregnancy Prevention, http://recapp.etr.org/recapp/index.cfm?fuseaction=pages.YouthSkillsDetail&PageID=8

Purpose

After providing a definition of advocacy and discussing the relevance, students need to know the steps or critical aspects of the skill. They also need to see examples of the skill and skill cues being applied effectively. This will help them as they work on their own projects and skill development.

NHES Performance Indicators

None addressed

Objectives

Students will be able to

- list the skill cues for advocacy and
- describe characteristics of effective advocacy.

Skill Development Steps

- Step 2: steps of the skill
- Step 3: modeling

Materials

- Materials for the Analyzing Advocacy activity
- Tablets or desktop computers

Instant Activity

After students take their seats, they write their responses to the prompt: "Identify three characteristics of an effective advocate."

Introduction

Review the definition of advocacy from the previous lesson and ask one or two students to share why advocacy is relevant for teens. Review the lesson objectives.

Main Activities

1. As a large group, ask students to share their ideas about what it takes to be an effective advocate (from the instant activity). Write the ideas on the board. Use student ideas to discuss or create the skill cues. **(skill cues)**
2. Have the class do the Analyzing Advocacy activity (page 279). **(modeling)**

Closure

Ask students to consider the advocacy efforts viewed in class and share with a partner how their own efforts to advocate for a cause would mirror or be different from what they viewed today. Tell students that in the next lesson they will choose a topic for their advocacy project based on issues in the community.

Differentiation

You may need to create a worksheet or visual for students for the Analyzing Advocacy activity.

Homework

Students ask parents, guardians, or trusted adults the following question: If you could advocate to improve something, what would it be? Why? Optionally, students report during the next lesson.

Analyzing Advocacy
LESSON 2

NHES Performance Indicators
None addressed

Objective
Students will be able to describe characteristics of effective advocacy.

Skill Development Steps
- Step 2: steps of the skill
- Step 3: modeling

Duration
20 to 30 minutes

Materials
Examples of advocacy

Description

Preparation
You can use the examples of advocacy from lesson 1 or use new examples. Just make sure you have an appropriate number of examples to facilitate small-group work in your class. For this activity (unlike the activity in lesson 1), include examples of effective and ineffective or less effective advocacy.

Activity
1. In small groups, students should evaluate the advocacy examples using the skill cues. Identify which skill cues were addressed and how they were addressed. If they evaluate an example that does not demonstrate all of the skill cues, have students make specific suggestions for how to improve it.
2. Review the examples as a whole group, making sure to review skill cues, and be specific with the ways that the skill cues were or were not demonstrated in the example. Talking through each example will help to reinforce principles of effective advocacy.

Tips and Extensions
Have students work in pairs rather than small groups.

Modification
Create a worksheet for students to use for their evaluation.

Purpose

In lessons 1 and 2, students learned a **definition** of advocacy, discussed the **relevance** of advocacy, were introduced to **skill cues,** and examined examples of effective advocacy. Now students have the chance to start practicing the skill.

NHES Performance Indicators

Utilize accurate peer and societal norms to formulate a health-enhancing message (indicator 8.12.1).

Objectives

Students will be able to

- analyze the YRBS to identify critical issues in the community and
- identify an advocacy topic based on personal interest.

Skill Development Step

Step 4: skill practice

Materials

Materials for the Examining Health Issues in Our Community activity

Instant Activity

After students take their seats, they write their responses to the prompt: "What do you think are the critical health issues in our school? Why?"

Introduction

Review the skill cues from lesson 2 with students. Tell students the objectives for the lesson. Ask students to share their ideas from the instant activity. Write their ideas on the board. You will refer back to these ideas later in the lesson.

Main Activity

Examining Health Issues in Our Community (page 281). **(practice)** *Note:* If you used the Perceptions, Norms, and Behaviors lesson from the Analyzing Influences unit in this text, this would be a good time to refer back to that lesson to remind students about the implications of perceptions and norms, as well as how advocacy can influence both perceptions *and* norms.

Closure

Compare the findings from the YRBS exploration to the students' ideas from the instant activity. How close were students? What does that tell us? Tell students that they will be choosing one of the issues that they identified as an advocacy project. The homework for next class asks students to think about what issue they would like to advocate for and to explain why. Students will be sharing their ideas with the class during the next lesson.

Differentiation

Have students choose whether they want to work in partners or individually to complete the Examining Health Issues in Our Community activity.

Homework

Students complete a two- to three-paragraph explanation of the issue that they will be addressing and why they chose that issue. Students will also include the health-enhancing position they will be advocating for on the issue.

Resources

CDC Youth Risk Behavior Survey, www.cdc.gov/Features/YRBS, or substitute your local or state YRBS for data that are "closer to home"

Examining Health Issues in Our Community

LESSON 3

NHES Performance Indicators

Utilize accurate peer and societal norms to formulate a health-enhancing message (indicator 8.12.1).

Objective

Students will be able to analyze the YRBS to identify critical issues in the community.

Skill Development Step

Step 4: skill practice

Duration

30 to 40 minutes

Materials

Data from data sources

Description

Preparation

Review data sources prior to this activity. Be sure that whichever data sources you use are appropriate for your students. Try to find data that are as close to representing your community as you can; this will make the activity more meaningful for students. Group students by topic area and create a guide for students so that they know which aspects of the data relate to their topic. For example, you have a guide that tells students that their topic is mental health and that questions 5, 7, 11, and 15 from the data source all relate to mental health.

Activity

Put students into small groups and provide each one with a guide. Explain that the students' task is to analyze the data and determine whether or not their topic is a significant issue in their community. They should use their understanding of data and also their understanding of health topics to justify their position on the significance.

Have each group present their findings. Be sure to review any key points about the data and the health topics. This activity should highlight key issues in the community and help students understand how to use data to support a position.

Tips and Extensions

Have students interview peers not in the health course and see if they are surprised by the issues that were identified from the data. Have students share their findings in the next lesson.

Modifications

- Connect with a math teacher and see if there are additional activities you could do with the data.
- Create a worksheet or guide to help students analyze and interpret the data.

Resource

CDC Youth Risk Behavior Survey, www.cdc.gov/Features/YRBS

Purpose

In the previous lesson, students examined data to determine health issues in their school community. For homework, students chose a topic of interest to advocate for. A critical aspect of advocacy is being able to find supporting evidence. This lesson gives students a chance to apply the skill of accessing valid and reliable information in order to gather evidence to support their health-enhancing position on their topic of choice.

NHES Performance Indicators

Grades 6 Through 8

- Examine the likelihood of injury or illness if engaging in unhealthy behaviors (indicator 1.8.8).
- Examine the potential seriousness of injury or illness if engaging in unhealthy behaviors (indicator 1.8.9).
- State a health-enhancing position on a topic and support it with accurate information (indicator 8.8.1).

Grades 9 Through 12

- Analyze the potential severity of injury or illness if engaging in unhealthy behaviors (indicator 1.12.9).
- Utilize accurate peer and societal norms to formulate a health-enhancing message (indicator 8.12.1).

Objectives

Students will be able to

- research information about a health topic of choice and
- use evidence to support a health-enhancing position on a health topic.

Materials

- Materials for the Finding Evidence to Support a Position activity
- Final advocacy project rubric

Instant Activity

After students take their seats, they write their responses to the prompt: "How do we find valid and reliable information?"

Introduction

After reviewing the lesson objectives and telling students that they will be doing research on their health issue, review their answers from the instant activity. This should be a review of the skill cues of accessing valid and reliable information.

Main Activities

1. Have the class do the Finding Evidence to Support a Position activity (page 283). **(practice)**
2. Before closing out the class, share the final assessment project parameters with students (found in lesson 6).

Closure

Tell students that they should now begin working on their advocacy projects (the final assessment). Share the rubric with students so that they know the expectations as they start. They have their issue, a health-enhancing position on the issue, and evidence to support their position. They should begin to create their infographic. Tell students that they will be getting feedback on their infographics in lesson 6.

Differentiation

Implement typical accommodations to meet student needs.

Finding Evidence to Support a Position

LESSON 4

NHES Performance Indicators

Grades 6 Through 8

- Examine the likelihood of injury or illness if engaging in unhealthy behaviors (indicator 1.8.8).
- Examine the potential seriousness of injury or illness if engaging in unhealthy behaviors (indicator 1.8.9).
- State a health-enhancing position on a topic and support it with accurate information (indicator 8.8.1).

Grades 9 Through 12

- Analyze the potential severity of injury or illness if engaging in unhealthy behaviors (indicator 1.12.9).
- Utilize accurate peer and societal norms to formulate a health-enhancing message (indicator 8.12.1).

Objectives

Students will be able to

- research information about a health topic of choice and
- use evidence to support a health-enhancing position on a health topic.

Skill Development Step

Step 4: skill practice

Duration

30 to 40 minutes

Materials

Computers or other electronic devices for conducting the research

Description

In a previous lesson, students examined data to determine health issues in their communities. Students were asked to identify one of those topics as one they would like to explore for their final unit assessment. Students should come to this class with a health-enhancing position related to the topic that they chose.

   During this activity, students should be using valid and reliable online resources to gather evidence to support their position. The goal is that by the end of this activity they have facts and information they can use to support their position and encourage peers to make health-enhancing choices.

Tips and Extensions

- Review the skill cues for accessing valid and reliable information.
- Provide students with some examples of valid and reliable resources to use.

Modification

Have students who chose the same topics work together rather than doing individual work.

Purpose

Students now have evidence to support their position and have some visuals to support their findings. In order to help students begin to take concrete actions to support their cause, they will use this class time to take some advocacy action.

NHES Performance Indicators

- *Grades 6 through 8:* Demonstrate how to influence and support others to make positive health choices (indicator 8.8.2).
- *Grades 9 through 12:* Demonstrate how to influence and support others to make positive health choices (indicator 8.12.2).

Objective

Students will be able to take action and advocate for a topic of choice.

Skill Development Step

Step 4: skill practice

Materials

Materials needed for the Advocacy Action activity

Instant Activity

After students take their seats, they write their responses to the prompt: "What persuades you? Is it colorful ads, catchy music, teens your age? Think of your favorite products and write down what it is about that product that persuades you to buy it."

Introduction

Tell students the lesson objectives and let them know that today they are going to be participating in an advocacy challenge.

Main Activity

Advocacy Action (page 285) **(practice)**

Closure

Ask some students to share how they did in the challenge. Ask students to discuss their experiences with the various advocacy activities. What was harder? What was easier? What do they think will make the most difference? Why? Remind students to bring their drafts of their infographics for the final assessment for the next lesson. They will have opportunities for peer feedback.

Differentiation

Implement typical accommodations to meet student needs.

Homework

Have students try to continue to earn points outside of class. Students come to the next class being prepared to share their additional advocacy efforts (optional).

Resources

You're the Cure campaign by the American Heart Association, www.yourethecure.org/get_ready_to_ take_action_in_2017

Advocacy Action

LESSON 5

NHES Performance Indicators

- *Grades 6 through 8:* Demonstrate how to influence and support others to make positive health choices (indicator 8.8.2).
- *Grades 9 through 12:* Demonstrate how to influence and support others to make positive health choices (indicator 8.12.2).

Objective

Students will be able to take action and advocate for a topic of choice.

Skill Development Step

Step 4: skill practice

Duration

30 to 40 minutes

Materials

Computers or other electronic devices

Description

1. Put students into pairs based on the topics they chose (they should be partners with people with the same topic).
2. Using an advocacy action triangle (see sample figure), have students see how many points they can earn during class.

Tips and Extensions

- Create your own advocacy action triangle for your students.
- Have a challenge that continues outside of class to see how many advocacy points they can earn.
- Have students share the advocacy efforts made after a predetermined amount of time.

10 points
- Make a movie or podcast
- Meet with an administrator
- Get a school club to support your cause

5 points
- Create a pin board and share it
- Create and display posters
- Write a blog post
- Follow five advocacy accounts on Twitter

3 points
- Post on an advocacy website
- Participate in an online discussion

2 points
- Post an advocacy comment online
- Talk with a teacher about your advocacy topic

1 point
- Watch an educational video
- Explore an advocacy website or blog
- Research advocacy ideas online
- Discover advocacy pins on Pinterest
- Discuss your advocacy topic with a friend

Advocacy action triangle.

Modified from a submission by Andy Milne, high school health teacher in Illinois.

Purpose

Students have had time to work on their final assessments. Providing peer feedback at this point can help students improve their projects and is also a way for them to review the skill cues and key points for the assessment. Students will also meet with other students who are working on different issues to debrief about challenges and successes as well as discuss similarities between their efforts, even though they are looking at different issues. This can provide students with some perspective and broader understanding of advocacy.

NHES Performance Indicators

- *Grades 6 through 8:* Work cooperatively to advocate for healthy individuals, families, and schools (indicator 8.8.3).
- *Grades 9 through 12:* Work cooperatively as an advocate for improving personal, family, and community health (indicator 8.12.3).

Objective

Students will be able to work collaboratively with peers to provide feedback on advocacy projects.

Skill Development Step

Step 4: skill practice

Materials

Materials for the Sharing Advocacy activity

Instant Activity

After students take their seats, have them pair up and use the Peer Feedback form to evaluate each other's work and share their feedback with each other based on their project so far.

Introduction

Tell students the lesson objectives. Let students know that providing feedback and discussing their experiences can not only help improve their final products but also help them understand how to be an advocate for a variety of issues.

Main Activities

1. Have the class complete the Sharing Advocacy activity (page 289). **(practice)**
2. Have students find new partners (or have prearranged pairs for both the Sharing Advocacy activity and this step, which is a second feedback opportunity). Have pairs complete the same Peer Feedback form that is used in the Sharing Advocacy activity in the new pairs. They should also share their feedback and discuss project strengths and areas for improvement.

Closure

Ask students to share what they learned from the peer feedback and group discussions. Make connections to the larger concept of advocacy and key takeaways.

Differentiation

Instead of letting students choose partners at the start of the lesson, prearrange partners for the feedback activity.

Peer Feedback

Please provide your classmate with clear feedback on their draft so far. The more specific the feedback you can give, the more helpful it will be. You should complete the rubric and provide comments.

	3	2	1
Position (Ask yourself: Does the message make a clear, healthful statement?)	The infographic demonstrates a clear, health-enhancing position.	The infographic's health-enhancing position is somewhat clear.	The position is not clear in the infographic or is not a health-enhancing position.
Evidence (Ask yourself: Does the supporting information back up the claims being made?)	The infographic includes at least four pieces of evidence to support their position and is supported by valid and reliable sources.	The infographic includes two or three pieces of evidence that supports the position and are supported by valid and reliable resources.	The infographic includes zero to one pieces of evidence that supports the position or is not supported by valid and reliable resources.
Passion or conviction (Ask yourself: Does this message campaign demonstrate excitement and enthusiasm about the topic?)	The infographic shows passion or conviction toward the topic.	The infographic shows limited passion or conviction toward the topic.	The infographic does not show passion or conviction.
Appeal (Ask yourself: Would this message campaign make me more likely to engage in the healthy behavior?)	The infographic clearly appeals to the intended audience.	The infographic is somewhat appealing to the audience.	The infographic is not appealing to the audience.

Strengths of the infographic:

Areas for improvement:

Sharing Advocacy
LESSON 6

NHES Performance Indicators

- *Grades 6 through 8:* Work cooperatively to advocate for healthy individuals, families, and schools (indicator 8.8.3).
- *Grades 9 through 12:* Work cooperatively as an advocate for improving personal, family, and community health (indicator 8.12.3).

Objective

Students will be able to work collaboratively with peers to provide feedback on advocacy projects.

Skill Development Step

Step 4: skill practice

Duration

15 to 20 minutes

Materials

- Computers or other electronic devices for students to do their research and share their resources
- Peer Feedback form

Description

1. Place students into small groups so that they are working with peers who are advocating for different topics.
2. In their small groups, students share their experience working on their own projects (for the final assessment) and also the in-class activities. Students should discuss what they have learned about their topic and about advocacy. They should discuss challenges and successes.
3. Put students into partners in order to facilitate peer-to-peer feedback. Partners will provide feedback on the work that has been done on the advocacy project so far based on the Peer Feedback form. Both partners will need time to share and receive feedback. This activity will allow for multiple members of each group to get feedback on their advocacy project. You might want to encourage groups to share feedback received (or even provide time in class).
4. After students have had time to share in small groups, bring the large group together and discuss some key takeaways about their experience so far. Discuss any main pieces of feedback to benefit the whole group.

Tips and Extensions

Instead of creating a template for students, they could create their own resources to share the information.

Purpose

Having access to valid and reliable resources can be helpful for students when trying to maintain or enhance health. During their work on their advocacy project, students have accessed a variety of resources. In this lesson, they will share their resources, creating an online resource that can be accessed by teens. They will also provide specific examples of and resources for advocacy for this topic (using what they learned in lesson 5). This is also a form of advocacy.

NHES Performance Indicators

- *Grades 6 through 8:* Work cooperatively to advocate for healthy individuals, families, and schools (indicator 8.8.3).
- *Grades 9 through 12:* Work cooperatively as an advocate for improving personal, family, and community health (indicator 8.12.3).

Objective

Students will be able to work collaboratively with peers to determine advocacy strategies for a topic of interest.

Skill Development Step

Step 4: skill practice

Materials

Materials needed for the Collaborating for a Cause activity

Instant Activity

Have students complete a reflection that describes their experience with advocacy so far during the unit. This could be used as a formative assessment.

Introduction

Review the learning objectives with students. Explain that today they will be working together to share resources related to their topics.

Main Activity

Collaborating for a Cause (page 291) **(practice)**

Closure

Remind students that they will have some time to work on their final projects in the next class and that most of the time will be spent making public service announcements for their topic.

Differentiation

Provide students with more options for the public service announcement format.

Resources

- Google Sites, www.sites.google.com
- *Teacher's Guide on Use of Google Sites in the Classroom,* www.educatorstechnology.com/2013/01/teachers-guide-on-use-of-google-sites.html

Collaborating for a Cause

LESSON 7

NHES Performance Indicators

- *Grades 6 through 8:* Work cooperatively to advocate for healthy individuals, families, and schools (indicator 8.8.3).
- *Grades 9 through 12:* Work cooperatively as an advocate for improving personal, family, and community health (indicator 8.12.3).

Objective

Students will be able to work collaboratively with peers to determine advocacy strategies for a topic of interest.

Step Development Step

Step 4: skill practice

Duration

15 to 20 minutes

Materials

- Computers or other electronic devices for students to do their research and share their resources
- Template provided on Google site

Description

One form of advocacy is sharing resources. This can be especially useful for teens who not only spend a lot of time online but also look for health information online. This activity requires students to work collaboratively to find and share valid and reliable sources about the topic they are advocating for. This information will then be used to support the development of advocacy strategies most likely to have an impact on the intended audience. This should connect to the activity students completed where they accessed resources to find evidence to support their topic.

Students will write a short description about the resource and provide links to the resource. Students should enter their resources and descriptions into the template you provide (Google site or other format; see the following example).

- Site name and web address:
- Organization:
- Description of site and organization:
- Reasons this is a valid and reliable source of information:
- Advocacy strategies this organization uses that you will also use:

Purpose

While there are many ways to advocate your position, the final assessment for the unit is to create an infographic. In this lesson, students will have some time to work on their infographics that they will present during the next class, but they will also work together with peers addressing the same issues to create public service announcements that can be used in future units as well as shared with other students and perhaps the community.

NHES Performance Indicators

Grades 6 Through 8

- State a health-enhancing position on a topic and support it with accurate information (indicator 8.8.1).
- Identify ways in which health messages and communication techniques can be altered for different audiences (indicator 8.8.4).

Grades 9 Through 12

- Utilize accurate peer and societal norms to formulate a health-enhancing message (indicator 8.12.1).
- Adapt health messages and communication techniques to a specific target audience (indicator 8.12.4).

Objective

Students will be able to design and create an advocacy project.

Skill Development Step

Step 4: skill practice

Materials

Materials for the Creating Public Service Announcements activity

Instant Activity

There is no instant activity today.

Introduction

Tell students the objectives of the day. Let them know that the first 15 minutes of the lesson will be a chance to work on their infographic projects that they will present in the next lesson. The rest of the time will be spent in small groups creating short public service announcements.

Main Activity

Creating Public Service Announcements (page 293) **(practice)**

Closure

Remind students that the next time they meet, all groups will present their final advocacy infographics.

Differentiation

Allow students to create their presentations using a different form of media such as a slideshow, poster, video public service announcement, or audio commercial.

Resources

ReadWriteThink, www.readwritethink.org/classroom-resources/printouts/podcasts-nuts-bolts-creating -30311.html

Creating Public Service Announcements

LESSON 8

NHES Performance Indicators

Grades 6 Through 8

- State a health-enhancing position on a topic and support it with accurate information (indicator 8.8.1).
- Identify ways in which health messages and communication techniques can be altered for different audiences (indicator 8.8.4).

Grades 9 Through 12

- Utilize accurate peer and societal norms to formulate a health-enhancing message (indicator 8.12.1).
- Adapt health messages and communication techniques to a specific target audience (indicator 8.12.4).

Objective

Students will be able to design and create an advocacy project.

Skill Development Step

Step 4: skill practice

Duration

30 to 40 minutes

Materials

- Electronic devices to record the public service announcements (PSAs)
- Public service announcement criteria and rubric

Description

Students are placed in small groups by their topic of choice. Students begin by discussing what they have learned about their topics. They will then decide which facts are the most compelling or important for their peers to know. Once they have done this, the group decides which type of PSA they would like to complete. Next, students create their PSA, which should meet the following criteria:

- Must be one minute in length
- Must send a health-enhancing message
- Must contain valid and accurate information
- Must be compelling for the intended audience
- Must be presented in an appealing way

Tips and Extensions

- Consider extending the time to include homework or multiple in-class lessons to complete.
- Budget less time in the lesson for students to work on their final project to allow more time for students to work on their PSAs.

Modifications

Provide other options for students than a PSA. Consider allowing students to draft a written commercial, letter to the editor, or postcard campaign.

Resources

- Teaching Matters, Inc., PSA development support and information, www.teachingmatters.org/digidocs/printable/manual/psa_manual.pdf
- Take the Challenge, www.takethechallengenow.net/wp-content/uploads/2014/10/HS-Lesson-13-Creating-PSA-Radio-Ads.pdf

LESSON 9: Assessment—Advocacy in Action

Purpose

In order to truly be an advocate, students must show passion and conviction for their cause. One way to do this is to have students present their final infographics in class. You might wish to add an evaluation of their presentation to their final grade.

NHES Performance Indicators

Grades 6 Through 8

- State a health-enhancing position on a topic and support it with accurate information (indicator 8.8.1).
- Demonstrate how to influence and support others to make positive health choices (indicator 8.8.2).
- Describe ways to reduce or prevent injuries and other adolescent health problems (indicator 1.8.8).
- Describe the benefits of and barriers to practicing healthy behaviors (indicator 1.8.7).

Grades 9 Through 12

- Utilize accurate peer and societal norms to formulate a health-enhancing message (indicator 8.12.1).
- Demonstrate how to influence and support others to make positive health choices (indicator 8.12.2).
- Propose ways to reduce or prevent injuries and health problems (indicator 1.12.5).

Objective

Students will be able to advocate for a health-enhancing position.

Skill Development Step

Step 5: feedback and reinforcement

Materials

None

Instant Activity

There is no instant activity for this lesson.

Introduction

In this lesson, students will present their advocacy message to the rest of the class. Students will formally present their infographic campaigns they have been working on.

Main Activity

Student Presentations (page 295) **(feedback and reinforcement)**

Closure

Have students reflect upon the Advocacy unit. Ask students to write down

- three new things they learned,
- two new strategies they are going to use, and
- one way they can support others in their quest to be healthier.

Differentiation

- The infographics could be on the walls of the classroom, and the presentations could be conducted as a gallery walk where students walk around individually and look at the projects.
- Groups of students could present to small groups. Rotate so that all students get to present.

Student Presentations

LESSON 9

NHES Performance Indicators

Grades 6 Through 8

- State a health-enhancing position on a topic and support it with accurate information (indicator 8.8.1).
- Demonstrate how to influence and support others to make positive health choices (indicator 8.8.2).
- Describe ways to reduce or prevent injuries and other adolescent health problems (indicator 1.8.8).
- Describe the benefits of and barriers to practicing healthy behaviors (indicator 1.8.7).

Grades 9 Through 12

- Utilize accurate peer and societal norms to formulate a health-enhancing message (indicator 8.12.1).
- Demonstrate how to influence and support others to make positive health choices (indicator 8.12.2).
- Propose ways to reduce or prevent injuries and health problems (indicator 1.12.5).

Objective

Students will be able to advocate for a health-enhancing position.

Skill Development Step

Step 5: feedback and reinforcement

Duration

50 minutes

Materials

None

Description

Prepare students to present their infographic with the following parameters:

- Each student will present their infographic and make a case for their healthful behavior.
- Following each presentation, the class will have an opportunity to ask questions or provide feedback.
- If there is extra class time following all of the presentations, discuss how the infographics and public service announcements can be shared with the greater school community.

Tips and Extensions

Students could share their presentations with other students or to another group such as parents or community members.

Modifications

Students could create a different product. Instead of an infographic, students could design another visual product to present.

Resources

Sites for developing infographics such as Piktochart (www.piktochart.com) or Canva (www.canva.com)

About the Authors

Sarah Sparrow Benes, EdD, CHES, is a senior director and lecturer in the School of Health Sciences at Merrimack College. Sarah teaches a variety of undergraduate- and graduate-level courses in health sciences, does service projects in local communities, and conducts research on health education and physical activity in schools. Dr. Benes was the program director for physical and health education programs at Boston University for six years before coming to Merrimack College. She has numerous publications in refereed journals and has written chapters examining health education; she also has made more than a dozen presentations on skills-based health education and related topics at state and regional conferences. Sarah serves on a variety of health education committees, including the health education council for SHAPE America (Society of Health and Physical Educators) and is the former vice president of health education for the Massachusetts Association for Health, Physical Education, Recreation and Dance. Benes is consulted by school districts on health and wellness issues, with a focus on skills-based curriculum development and implementation. She is a certified health education specialist and a member of SHAPE America. Sarah received a bachelor's degree in athletic training from the University of Connecticut, a master's degree in education from Boston University, and a doctorate in curriculum and teaching from Boston University; she is currently working on a master of public health degree. She lives in Natick, Massachusetts, with her husband, two daughters, and yellow Labrador retriever. She enjoys spending time with her family on nature walks and the sights and sounds of the Northeast. Photo courtesy of Merrimack College.

Holly Alperin, EdM, MCHES, is a clinical assistant professor in the department of kinesiology's health and physical education program at the University of New Hampshire. Throughout her career, Holly has worked to improve the health and academic outcomes of young people by leveraging partnerships that strengthen school-level policies and practices, both in the health education classroom and throughout the school. In addition to her teaching of preservice and graduate health and physical education majors, she provides training and technical assistance to preK-12 educators, administrators, and staff and develops and implements trainings to advance the capacity of state and national stakeholders to improve the health and academic outcomes of children. Holly is a sought-after presenter, having been invited to numerous local, state, national, and international events. She is an advocate for ensuring that health educators receive high-quality professional development, and she takes this responsibility to heart. Volunteer roles have included participation on a variety of professional task forces for organizations such as SHAPE America; American School Health Association; and New Hampshire Association for Health, Physical Education, Recreation and Dance. Holly received her bachelor's degree in health education and health promotion from Central Michigan University and her master of education degree in policy, planning, and administration from Boston University. Holly currently lives in New Hampshire with her husband and two daughters. Together they enjoy the best of New England—ocean, mountains, cities, and countless adventures. Photo courtesy of University of New Hampshire.